Shadow Diplomacy

Lev Parnas and his Wild Ride

from Brooklyn to Trump's Inner Circle

By Lev Parnas and Jerry Langton

To my amazing wife, Svetlana, my kids Zarina, Aaron, Daniel, Milana, Andrew, Nathan, Olivia, and my always supportive sister, Lyudmila.

I know my parents in heaven, Zhanna and Aaron, are proud.

Bronxkill Publishing
New York NY
bronxkillpublishing@gmail.com

Special discounts are available on quantity purchases by corporations, associations and others. For details, contact the publisher.

All photos are the property of Lev Parnas unless otherwise credited.

ISBN 979-8-218-25597-8

Bronxkill

Chapter 1
A Trip to Vienna

Vienna was absolutely beautiful. The fragrant leaves on the lindens were just beginning to change color, and the courtly Habsburg-era mansions of the city's exclusive Hietzing district were spectacular in their grandeur and opulence.

But I wasn't paying any attention to what was passing by the windows of the limo I was in. I was on an important diplomatic mission for the United States of America.

I was in Vienna at the beginning of autumn 2019 on orders from Rudy Giuliani, President Donald Trump's personal lawyer and right-hand man.

Giuliani had asked Trump several times to make him Secretary of State, but had been turned down. It was because Trump felt that Giuliani could be far more effective doing essentially the same job if he did not have an official government title.

Giuliani was still eager to prove himself, and caught Trump's ear when he told him that he had begun to investigate rumors of wrongdoing in Ukraine by Joe Biden's son, Hunter, and perhaps even Biden himself. Hunter Biden had been on the board of Burisma Holdings, a Ukrainian natural gas company that had been under investigation for corruption.

With Joe Biden likely to be Trump's opponent for the White House in 2020, any compromising information against either of the Bidens could be of great value for his own campaign. Both would be even better.

None of the other heavy hitters in the administration, certainly not the actual Secretary of State, Mike Pompeo, or National Security Advisor John Bolton, wanted anything to do with such an investigation. They let Trump know that they considered it underhanded and beneath them.

Giuliani was not only willing, but eager. That brought him closer to the President, and his orders were followed by many, including me. Trump and Giuliani had made me America's secret point man for communication with Ukraine. It wasn't because I had any diplomatic experience or even skill. I represented my country's interests simply because I spoke fluent Russian and some Ukrainian, and I had developed important contacts over there.

Giuliani would often take me to Yankees home games.

I also did what I was told and I kept my mouth shut. Those were important abilities I had learned on the rough-and-tumble streets of Brooklyn in the 1980s and 90s. In that time and place, dealing with gangsters was the only way to get by, if you wanted to get ahead. I actually had a lot in common with the settings that Giuliani and Trump grew up in.

As my car approached its destination, I watched as a black — no doubt armored — Mercedes SUV with opaque black windows blocked the one-way street behind me. Closer to the massive iron gates in front of the property, another big black SUV blocked the road ahead.

It didn't unsettle me at all, I'd been through the same routine on the previous trips I had made to this house and others like it. I also knew that the guys protecting Dmytro Firtash seriously outgunned anyone who might want to hurt him. And he was on our side.

As we turned down the only open lane toward the main building, we drove past a legion of security guards in black with dark sunglasses and AK-47s. Nothing out of the ordinary.

When the car stopped, I approached the off-white main building, built in 1908. The villa, as it's been called, sports 14,000 square feet on three floors, 15 bedrooms, seven bathrooms, four terraces, an elevator, an in-house movie theater, a wine cellar, a spa, an English lawn dotted with ancient lindens and an infinity pool with its own pool house.

It was but a pied-à-terre for its resident. A place to stay until some nastiness could be resolved. It was nice, but not that nice — more like a millionaire's house than a billionaire's house. I'd seen a lot of both.

The house was not there to impress me. I knew the resident, Firtash, was immensely wealthy. As a translator between Firtash and his American legal team, I knew that all Giuliani had to do was send a text, through me, and ask for money. Then it would appear, thanks to one of Firtash's companies. The cash was primarily for travel and once covered a $36,000 transfer to pay for the charter of a lavish Gulfstream IV to fly Giuliani from the Dominican Republic to Washington.

Later, both of those guys would say that they had never dealt with the other. That incredible affront to reality still makes me laugh these days, as I look over the dozens of texts between them that I translated.

Giuliani told me it was important to get him to help with the Biden investigation and, back then, I was dogmatically and enthusiastically a part of Team Trump, with Giuliani serving as my manager. As soon as Trump or Giuliani asked me to do something, it got done.

What they needed done in the autumn of 2019 was simple: Get Ukraine to announce criminal investigations into the Biden family. Months of flying to meetings, emailing, texting and calling brought me here. I put in a lot of footwork for Trump and Giuliani.

Firtash was not only wealthy, but he was also powerful and extraordinarily well-connected — and he needed a favor. There are rich people and there are wealthy people. And then there are people like Firtash who have amassed unfathomable fortunes. He is one of a group of people we call oligarchs because they use their incredible wealth to influence political decisions to best benefit themselves and their peers, kind of like a shadow government.

Firtash was at, or at least near, the head of a large class of multibillionaires who made their ridiculous piles of money just before and right after the collapse of the Soviet Union in 1991. It was a brutal, chaotic time and only the tough survived.

In 1991, the second-most powerful nation on Earth suddenly ceased to exist and its authoritarian system was not, as many in the U.S. expected and believed it would be, immediately replaced by a Western-style democratic economy. Instead, Russia and the other former Soviet republics fell into economic chaos characterized by desperate and cynical piracy. That meant that everything that could be taken, even the aluminum from street signs, was sold to get money to buy the Western products that were by then suddenly flooding their markets.

Any American with contacts over there could get rich almost immediately — if they were smart enough and bold enough to try. I was one of them. But once things, inevitably, started to get violent, I left that behind.

The toughest players, mostly the locals, kept going. As millions turned into billions, the violence reached crisis levels. Governments, filled almost entirely with people in the pockets of the extremely wealthy, were powerless to act even if they wanted to.

But the invisible hand of the free market intervened and put a sudden damper on the wild growth. The markets had been flooded. Not only were there too many people importing Western goods, the corporations themselves had moved in. Everyone was fighting for too little money because the people of the former Soviet Union had run out of things to sell. Except for one.

Some of the new countries, particularly Russia, were rich in natural gas. As Senator John McCain once famously said: "Russia is a gas station masquerading as a country." Western Europe is virtually devoid of the stuff but almost all of its constituent states use it to heat the vast majority of their buildings and homes. Suddenly, the tide turned. You couldn't get rich importing to the former USSR anymore, but you could get wealthy exporting from it. As long as the product was natural gas.

That was how I thought I'd make money. I had a plan to ship liquefied natural gas from Texas, where it's dirt cheap, to Eastern Europe, where it's absolutely vital.

Natural gas made Firtash rich. But not at the beginning. His first product was powdered milk, which he traded to other former Soviet republics that were even worse off than Russia and Ukraine, like Uzbekistan and Turkmenistan. If his trading partners did not have sufficient cash, he'd gladly accept alternative commodities, often cotton, in exchange.

Not only did he move up to handle natural gas, he swept his native Ukraine for anything of value — real estate, nitrogen, titanium and then electricity production (powered by natural gas, of course).

Nobody ever became a billionaire in the former Soviet Union by being a nice guy. Firtash had well-documented ties to some of Russia's most notorious gangsters, including "boss of bosses" Semion Mogilevich — a longstanding member of the FBI's 10 Most Wanted list. Mogilevich once acted as Firtash's head of security. Firtash even cabled a message to U.S. Ambassador to Ukraine, William B. Taylor Jr., in 2008 that read:

> "It was impossible to approach a government official for any reason without also meeting with an organized crime member at the same time."

And, of course, like any other Eastern European billionaire still alive, he was close friends with Russia's autocratic President Vladimir Putin. He kept that friendship running smoothly by frequently donating huge sums of cash to pro-Russian groups in Ukraine. It was a setup not unlike those in the Brooklyn I grew up in. You always have to pay the boss.

With all that money comes immense power. With that power comes enemies and hard questions. So, Firtash's DFG Media acquired Inter Media, which owned the nation's most-watched TV stations. And to make absolutely certain he would be shown in a positive light, he also purchased Ukrinform, the Ukrainian National News Agency.

It's also been determined that he owned significant stakes in SCL Group and Cambridge Analytica, two British firms that specialized in influencing elections for conservatives (until they got caught, of course), through a convoluted series of shell companies. Interestingly, that same media empire had launched the career of a provocative comedian named Vladimir Zelenskyy.

Just as political upheaval brought Firtash almost uncountable wealth, a movement threatened to take it, and maybe even his freedom, away. It should be clear that Ukraine is not Russia. Its language, culture and history are different. While Russia seems obsessed by World War II, the event that sticks in Ukrainian minds and colors many of their beliefs happened a few years earlier. The Holodomor of 1932 and 1933 was a human-made famine that killed between 3 million and 5 million Ukrainians. Most historians believe that Soviet Premier Joseph Stalin intentionally starved the historically grain-rich nation to suppress independence movements, while others maintain that it was simply the result of poor Soviet planning and Moscow's general disregard for the fate of Ukrainians. Either way, Russia was to blame.

The result was that Ukrainians are, as a rule, mistrustful of strongman leaders and suspicious of foreign interference, especially from the East. A significant minority of Ukrainians, however, are Russian speakers and most of them would prefer a closer connection to Russia.

So, when voter intimidation and electoral fraud ran rampant during their 2004 Presidential Election, the Ukrainians wouldn't stand for it anymore and protested. They attracted too many people to ignore.

The crisis further exacerbated tensions between the oligarchs and the rest of the country. Ten years later, came what Ukrainians call the Revolution of Dignity or the Euromaidan Uprising. Its main cause was that, under intense pressure from Putin and many oligarchs, the government rebuffed popular offers to bring Ukraine into closer association with the European Union and, instead, promised to forge even stronger ties to Russia.

The government responded to the protests by sending in the Berkut, a federal police force known for racketeering, terrorism, assault, torture, voter intimidation and pro-Russian sentiment. When the dust finally settled, 121 people were dead and 1,811 injured.

The use of force backfired. With the protesters surrounding the parliament building in Kyiv on February 21, 2014, the government stood down and Viktor Yanukovych, the embattled president, fled to Russia, where he was set up in a $52 million estate in Rublyovka, the most expensive community in the metro Moscow area. It's not hard to guess which boss he was working for.

Two days later, Russia invaded Ukraine's gas-rich and strategically critical Crimean Peninsula.

After the protests, the change in government and the Russian encroachment, smart oligarchs knew that Ukraine might be able to end its status as their playground.

Even with all his billions and his stranglehold on the media, Firtash needed help. He used his most important asset — lawyers. And since all business eventually leads to the U.S., he needed help from America.

Paul Manafort had been working in Ukraine for years and had helped Firtash in his aborted 2008 attempt to buy Manhattan's Drake Hotel. But Manafort's best ability was as a strategist, He held positions on the presidential campaigns of Republicans Gerald Ford, Ronald Reagan, George H.W. Bush and Bob Dole.

After representing some African and Asian kleptocrats, he became interested in Ukraine. The gap between African warlord and Eastern European businessman is narrow if it even exists at all.

His first major client in Europe was Russian aluminum baron Oleg Deripaska, who had been denied a visa to enter the U.S. in 2004. He was part of a consortium bidding on the flailing DaimlerChrysler Group.

The reason for the visa denial was never made official, but The Wall Street Journal reported that it was due to his alleged involvement with organized crime, and The New York Times elaborated that the federal government suspected that Deripaska came to the U.S. to launder money. Leaked U.S. diplomatic communications referred to him as "among the 2-3 oligarchs Putin turns to on a regular basis" and "a more-or-less permanent fixture on Putin's trips abroad."

Deripaska hired Manafort to help iron out the visa situation. It paid dividends almost immediately. Lobbying from Manafort's old friend, Bob Dole (through his legal firm), is widely thought to have helped snag Deripaska a multi-entry visa.

But the Orange Revolution of 2004 and 2005, in which Ukrainians had also demonstrated against the power of oligarchs and corrupt politicians, put Deripaska's interests and friends in jeopardy.

One of them was Rinat Akhmetov, the richest man in Ukraine. Exactly how Akhmetov made his fortune is not entirely clear. He says that he began trading coal and invested wisely in commodities that he believed were unpopular at the time but would be in great demand later on. He must have guessed right, since he made a colossal amount of money.

It was widely alleged that he and his brother, Igor, had been involved in organized crime as early as 1986. Notably, he was widely linked to the 1995 assassination of business associate Akhat Bragin, owner of the Shakhtar Donetsk soccer team, and six of his bodyguards. Akhmetov — who claimed that the bomb that killed Bragin almost killed him as well — then inherited the company, the team and a huge amount of wealth from Bragin's estate. He was not a relative or even a close friend. It just went to him. That's how it works over there.

Afterward, he became a major donor to the Party of Regions, a collection of generally pro-Russian politicians supported by oligarchs. It was founded by Manafort.

Manafort took Akhmetov to D.C, meeting with luminaries like Dick Cheney, to gain friends in the U.S. Like most Ukrainian oligarchs, he was decidedly pro-Russian and funneled funds to the Party of Regions. Manafort also operated what was referred to as a "black ops" campaign to discredit Secretary of State Hillary Clinton, who appeared to be the likely Democratic candidate for President after Obama's second term. In Ukraine, she was a symbol of Western influence and criticism of Putin. Manafort's blueprint to defame her included altering the Wikipedia entries of Clinton and her allies, setting up a fake, anti-Clinton think tank, meeting with journalists from Breitbart to implore them to write articles attacking Clinton and a social media blitz "aimed at targeted audiences in Europe and the U.S. that put her in a negative light."

All communication between Manafort and his Ukrainian associates were translated by Konstantin Kilimnik. An intelligence officer for the Soviets, the U.S. intelligence community regarded him as a spy for Russia at the time. He was also responsible for collecting Manafort's fees.

Manafort must've pleased Deripaska, who rewarded him with a $10 million annual salary. He also introduced him to Firtash.

The Revolution of Dignity in February 2014 made the situation desperate for the oligarchs. The new, reform-minded government had them in their sights, especially after Russia invaded Crimea and armed and supported separatists rebels in the east of Ukraine, a region called the Donbas by the Ukrainians and Novorussia (New Russia) by the rebels.

And that's about the time when Firtash needed American help badly. The Department of Justice, during the Obama administration, had labeled him an "upper-echelon [associate] of Russian organized crime." A subsequent investigation found that Firtash's company, Group DF, had allegedly bribed Indian officials $18.5 million for the right to mine titanium there. The titanium was headed for Boeing — whose Dreamliner uses 100,000 pounds of the stuff. Since Boeing is an American company, the case came under the jurisdiction of the Department of Justice, even though Boeing was not accused of any wrongdoing.

In 2015, the feds indicted Firtash in absentia for bribery, racketeering, and money laundering and started the extradition process. It was widely believed that the U.S. was making an example of Firtash to send a message to all of the oligarchs. That indictment meant that he could not go west, because he'd wind up in an American prison. He couldn't go back to Ukraine, I knew, because they saw him as a gangster and a traitor. And he couldn't go to Putin's Russia because — in an ill-fated attempt to change the Ukrainian public's opinion of him — he openly supported the Ukrainian military. Any move east and he'd be a dead man. After being released on $155 million bail, he was safe in Vienna, but the clock was ticking.

In June 2019 — just months before our meeting — the Austrian Supreme Court decided that Firtash had no grounds to fight extradition to the U.S. They said it would probably happen in 2020. That left him believing he had little time to act.

He probably first called Manafort, but he was already out of the picture. By the time Firtash needed him, he was already serving time. So Firtash had instead retained American lawyers Lanny Davis and Dan Webb.

On a trip to Paris, Rudy and I had a meeting with a Ukrainian we knew from one of the bars my business partner Igor Fruman owned in Kyiv. Igor considered him a close friend, but he hadn't seen him in a long time. Unbeknownst to us, he was Firtash's right-hand man.

He introduced us to Firtash. We wanted to talk to Firtash because we knew that he was connected to Mykola Zlochevsky, owner of Burisma Holdings, Ukraine's biggest oil and gas company. He told us that he had heard things about Hunter Biden, Joe Biden's son, bad things. Things we might be interested in. He recommended that we talk to Firtash about it. He wasn't the first person we talked to, but we believed that he had a great deal of pull with the Ukrainian government. We believed that he could get us what we wanted — a Ukrainian investigation of the Bidens.

I could tell that Giuliani was delighted at the prospect. He had been desperately hunting for incriminating information about the Bidens — that would make Trump, who was likely to face Joe Biden in the 2020 Election, very happy. An investigation was all we wanted. Even if it didn't turn up anything, it would always be a huge stain on Biden's credibility.

Giuliani was eager to get Firtash on our team, but there was one problem, Lanny Davis. The only way Giuliani would work with Firtash was if he were to sever ties with Davis, and hire Giuliani or one of his team to represent him. Giuliani told me that he could never work with Davis, a Democrat who had worked for the Clintons (Davis would also later help Michael Cohen with the Stormy Daniels debacle after Trump fired him). He was also actively keeping people, people like Rudy, away from Firtash.

Once we got word to Firtash, he refused a meeting, saying that he didn't want to get involved in any Trump-Biden conflict. In an effort to change his mind, Rudy and conservative commentator John Solomon put together a package — which included confidential information — that could help Firtash with his case in the U.S. I took it to Firtash in Vienna in June 2019 and he seemed impressed. I made it clear to him, if you help us, we'll help you.

He was still reluctant, but much less so. We stayed in close contact, negotiating. The package I had delivered had shown Firtash that we were dealing in good faith.

But Andrew Weissman, who was lead prosecutor for the investigation of Russian collusion in the 2016 Election, had gotten there first. He offered a deal in which Firtash could avoid prison if he testified about the relationship between Trump and Russian President Vladimir Putin. The inclusion of Putin meant that Firtash would never take the deal. Nobody over there wants to make Putin angry.

Nobody else knew about the deal he was offered. Giuliani and Solomon wanted Firtash's legal team to make it public. His Viennese lawyers were against it, so Firtash was reluctant. Soon, in a heated meeting in Vienna, an argument between some of Firtash's legal team led to Victoria Toensing, who was on our team, confronting Dan Webb about it months later. Webb — who was connected with Weissmann, William Barr and other heavy hitters — admitted to the deal.

Still, we convinced Firtash that we — who were representing Trump's interests — could help him with his extradition far more effectively than Weissman.

The real goal for us was to get Firtash to use his contacts to pressure President Zelenskyy to announce an investigation of the Bidens.

Our pitch was successful, Firtash agreed to hire Giuliani for $1 million. And $200,000 for me to be official translator and to be under the attorney-client privilege umbrella.

When Giuliani ran the plan by the Boss, Trump's handlers were astonished. No, they answered unanimously, Giuliani could not represent a foreign billionaire who allegedly had strong ties to organized crime and a long history with Putin. It just wouldn't look good.

Unfazed and determined, he employed a workaround. Giuliani hired Victoria Toensing and Joe diGenova — a husband-and-wife lawyer team who made their fame singing Trump's praises on Fox News — to be the official face of the operation, while he pulled the strings from behind the scenes. Toensing was the boss of the couple and diGenova took even the most mundane directions from her without question. Firtash agreed to give Toensing a $1 million check for a retainer.

Giuliani later told me that Toensing would share the money with him. Firtash got what he wanted, Giuliani and Trump got what they wanted and nobody but Trump's most inner circle was aware of any of it.

***

I was welcomed into a suite and instructed to wait. On the off-white walls were a map of Eastern Europe and a painting of Firtash's hometown (a small community on the Dnipro River, close to the Romanian and Moldovan borders; when he was born, it was called Bohdanivka, but has been Synkiv since the fall of the Soviet Union).

I told Firtash what Giuliani wanted — an investigation into the Bidens. Hunter Biden sat on the board of Burisma Holdings, owned by billionaire and Yanukovych ally Mykola Zlochevsky. Any information that discredited Hunter Biden we felt they could use against Joe.

The Obama administration had supported the pro-Western movements and governments in Ukraine and were diligent in helping them root out corruption. Joe Biden had been the leader of their operation.

Firtash did not want to become one of Biden's targets, and he also knew that if Biden ever became President, there would be renewed pressure from the West to stamp out the influence of people like him, maybe for good.

So, I was quite surprised when Firtash produced a sealed statement of testimony to the Viennese court from Ukraine's corrupt former top prosecutor Viktor Shokin.

In it, Shokin claimed that Joe Biden had forced the Ukrainian government

Me along with some of Firtash's lawyers in Vienna. In front, from the left, are Joe diGenova, Victoria Toensing, Ralph Oswald Isenegger and me.

to fire him from his post to prevent him from investigating Burisma — and Hunter Biden in particular.

It was bullshit. The U.S. was one of many nations and NGOs calling for Shokin's head over widespread reports of his corrupt practices (in fact, the Obama administration was considering its own investigation into accusations against him for money laundering).

There were plenty of reasons to fire Shokin. He refused to prosecute government snipers who had shot and killed civilian protesters, and ignored many businesses well known to be operating outside the law. One of his more laughable scandals occurred when two of his staff were caught with an immense amount of diamonds, cash and other valuables. Shokin decided not to prosecute them and fired any prosecutor who dared to investigate them.

And, as many in Ukraine but few in the U.S. knew, Shokin had an active grudge against Burisma because they wouldn't cut him in on the action. He threatened to investigate Zlochevsky unless he got paid $5 million. That's what started this whole thing.

Even with Shokin's reputation, I knew that Trump supporters would consider any statement from him to be a smoking gun if we could get it to them. It didn't hurt that Joe Biden had threatened to withhold $1 billion in loan guarantees unless Shokin was fired. "I looked at them and said, I'm leaving in six hours. If the prosecutor is not fired, you're not getting the money," Biden described the situation later. "He got fired. And they put in place some-one who was solid at the time."

That replacement, Yuriy Lutsenko, wasn't much cleaner than Shokin.

Since I was one of Trump's most loyal operators, I always knew that the Shokin document in Firtash's and then Trump's hands might be enough to derail a Biden presidential campaign. Trump and Giuliani wanted it badly.

In exchange for the statement, Firtash wanted the Department of Justice to call its dogs off and drop all charges against him. Giuliani had me assured him that the U.S. could provide Firtash with exactly what he wanted. On his behalf, Giuliani had official and unofficial meetings with Attorney General William Barr to discuss Firtash's case.

The belief among Team Trump was that when word got out, even without any other evidence, that Joe Biden had allegedly used his position as Vice-President to keep his son's illegal activities secret, his credibility as a candidate would be shot.

***

After the Firtash meeting, I flew back and forth from the U.S. to Vienna, usually with Toensing there to help negotiate.

While I was in Vienna, news broke about a whistle blower complaint that mentioned me pressuring Ukraine to open investigations against the Bidens.

I immediately called Rudy who said that he had spoken with Trump and that they agreed that, as an involved party, they promised to take care of me and provided one of Trump's lawyers, John M. Dowd, to represent me. I then flew first class to Boston.

A black SUV with security took me to Chatham, Massachusetts, on the "elbow" of Cape Cod. Firtash paid for all of it. There was a conference call set up by Trump's legal team at Dowd's beach house. Dowd told me that the reason we met on Cape Cod was to keep the media away from me.

Dowd had been Trump's legal advisor for the Russia collusion case, but was fired/quit with much public acrimony between him and the President. Still, he worked for Trump for free. That sort of thing happened a lot.

I was tired from my day of flights and meetings. But before I could turn in, Dowd insisted that I see his collections of baseball and military memorabilia, as well as his awards.

Dowd was a noteworthy lawyer. He had defended drug boss Robert Reckmeyer, Iran-Contra scandal heavy Colonel Robert C. Dutton, food giant Archer-Daniels-Midland (in the case that inspired the feature film The Informant!), John McCain, Arizona governor Fife Symington and, of course, Trump. But he was probably best known for flipping off the media when he was losing a case and telling a photographer: "Fuck you, I hate you, I'm not telling you a thing." He later said that he hadn't said the "fuck you" part.

In Dowd's home office, he set up a conference call with Giuliani, Jay Sekulow (another of Trump's attorneys), Toensing and diGenova. There might have been other lawyers, but I didn't hear any. Dowd laid out the plan, and it was simple: stonewall. He instructed us all not to say anything to Congress and not to worry about subpoenas because we'd only get letters requesting our appearance, which we could ignore. Trump, he said, would tell them to go fuck themselves and everybody else was to follow suit.

I was stunned. I thought we were going to have to testify, I didn't think you could tell Congress to go fuck themselves. Dowd explained that we didn't have to say anything to anyone because every conversation any of us had about Russia or Ukraine had been in front of Giuliani or Dowd. Since they were the President's lawyers, all of those exchanges fell under attorney-client privilege. That was a tried-and-true gangster trick I had learned on the streets of Brooklyn.

Dowd also reminded me that I was represented by Kevin Downing, the same lawyer who had represented Manafort during the investigation into Russian interference in 2016.

***

Another private jet was waiting for me later that day to take me to my home in Boca Raton. Another was then chartered to take me, my wife Svetlana, my business partner Igor Fruman, our assistant DeAnna Janse van Rensburg, and some bodyguards to D.C. Of course, Firtash was footing the bill.

When we arrived, another bodyguard guided us to a large black SUV that took us into the city.

We were taken to the Trump International Hotel. Trump fans had labeled it @americaslivingroom on social media — and it served as something of a branch office for Team Trump. I spent two years going to Washington and I didn't see the monuments — all I saw was the Trump hotel.

We made a beeline for David Burke's BLT Prime, one of the hotel's restaurants and a favorite haunt of Trump and his allies. Trump ate there frequently. He enjoyed sitting in the middle of the often-adoring crowds as the center of all attention.

On a typical night, it's been said that he would order a tomahawk steak, insisting that nobody else could have one bigger than his. He'd instruct them to prepare it "very" well done, then smother it in ketchup. It would often be accompanied by Sour Cream and Onion potato chips and a Diet Coke. Every one of BLT Prime's employees had been instructed on how to perform the precise seven-step process that Trump demanded be followed whenever he was offered a Diet Coke.

Our team met in an upstairs room with a usually closed door so that nobody could overhear us. It was reserved for Trump family members and their closest friends — the innermost of circles. Besides, Don Jr. had told me that the room was swept for listening devices every week.

Inside the restaurant was, as usual, a lineup of Trump faithful trying to get a seat and perhaps a glimpse of their hero. I walked right past them. I wasn't just a regular, I was a VIP. I remember hearing the people in line wondering aloud who I was. Some took pictures.

I headed upstairs where Giuliani usually held court, the BLT's VIP room.

Inside, there was a round table and a wall of windows overlooking the rest of the restaurant. Giuliani, Toensing and diGenova, Solomon, Igor and I met there regularly. Since the room was our headquarters, we had begun calling ourselves the BLT Team. Every time you heard Trump say "I've been hearing" or "people are saying," we were the "people" — nobody was closer to him and he didn't really listen to anyone else.

Once inside, I saw exactly who I expected. Dowd had beaten me there, and he had invited Downing. As previously instructed, I handed Dowd a check for $100,000. Giuliani had told me that it would serve as a retainer and allow me to claim attorney-client privilege on anything I said in the company of Downing.

Over a dinner of steak, salad, oysters and BLT's justifiably famous bacon, we discussed keeping ahead of Congress with their annoying investigations. It was only a couple of hours and I didn't really learn anything new, but the main purpose of the meeting was for me to hand over all of my documents. And we over the plan we had discussed over the conference call in Cape Cod was going into action.

After the meeting, all I wanted to do was to go home to Boca Raton and rest. Not only had I been run ragged by Team Trump, but Yom Kippur was coming soon and I knew that it would be a busy time.

Any rest I found was short-lived, A day or two after the BLT Prime meeting, I got a call from one of Firtash's people. He had gotten in touch with Burisma's CFO, Alexander Gorbunenko, who he said was ready and willing to talk about Hunter Biden and potentially hand over a copy of the hard drive from Hunter's laptop.

Even though Trump was already facing impeachment for back-room dealings in Ukraine, Giuliani was happy that one of his own back-door operations was bearing fruit.

We all agreed that Gorbunenko presented too good an opportunity to waste. We would all fly to Vienna to meet him. Giuliani and the whole team were absolutely jubilant that the plan was approaching fruition.

On October 6 (two days before the beginning of Yom Kippur), I flew to Washington to discuss the trip to Vienna with Giuliani and Toensing.

Giuliani told me that he wanted to meet Shokin and that it might also be a great idea to bring Fox News personality and ardent Trump supporter Sean Hannity to interview him.

That was a key part of the plan. Team Trump had not been very successful at getting our message into what Trump called "fake news" and the "lame stream media," so we depended on Fox News and like-minded outlets for any publicity. Not only would millions of Americans see the interview, but it being on Fox News would lend us an air of credibility among many people.

Just before we left for Vienna, I received a phone call from Firtash warning me that Shokin had become anxious about the interview, and was threatening to back out.

I called Shokin. He answered, but he was tense, even panicky. He told me that he was sure "they" were going to kill him. He was absolutely convinced that he would be poisoned, just like Viktor Yushchenko, who had angered Putin while running for the Ukrainian presidency. There was no way, he said, that he would get on a plane no matter what.

Firtash told me not to worry. He'd see to it personally that Shokin was flown to Vienna safely and would be present for a live interview with Fox's Hannity.

Part of the deal was that we'd also get Shokin's sealed testimony to the Viennese court and the hard drive from the laptop Hunter Biden used when he was working in Ukraine. It was supposed to have come from Alexander Gorbunenko, who was CFO of Burisma. If there was any evidence of him doing anything illegal in Ukraine, we were sure we'd find it there.

I met up with Toensing and diGenova, who were to make a live appearance on Laura Ingraham's show, also on Fox News, on October 8. The rest of the team — Giuliani and John Solomon (a conservative writer and steadfast defender of Trump) — were already there and were allowed to meet with Toensing and diGenova in a Fox News conference room.

At the meeting at Fox, we decided to have Hannity interview Shokin over a live feed from New York. In it, he would reveal the existence of Hunter Biden's laptop. Fruman, Giuliani, Toensing, diGenova and I were to fly to Vienna the following day to make it all happen.

Later that night, Toensing called me to say that diGenova had came down with a cold and that they would not be able to make the flight. I instructed my assistant to get tickets just for me, Igor and Giuliani. They were one-way because I had no idea when we were coming back and, because Firtash was taking care of it, money was no object. Still, the only tickets she could get had a stopover in Frankfurt.

Giuliani called for a breakfast meeting for the following morning, One of the things about him that really irked me is that he never seemed to need sleep. Giuliani would stay up late every night, well into the morning hours, and then be ready for a live TV appearance at 6 a.m. the next day. It was remarkable, especially since Giuliani appeared to be drunk or at least drinking all the time. The real problem was that he expected everyone else to keep the same hours as he did.

Giuliani greeted me in the lobby. Like his boss, Giuliani loved any attention he received from the public. He'd court their curiosity any way he could, including openly smoking cigars in the hotel. It was totally illegal, of course, but who was going to stop him?

Once I was in the VIP room, Giuliani informed me that he couldn't go on our flight to Vienna. The President had requested a meeting with him on Friday. I was taken aback because I knew how important it was for Giuliani to attend the meeting. He said not to worry, he'd be

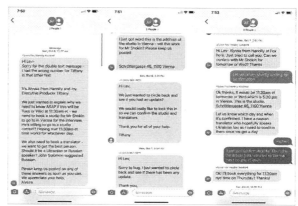

Fox News tried hard to get Shokin on Hannity's show.

there in a day or two and told me to remind Firtash that he had promised Giuliani tickets to an opera in Vienna he really wanted to see on October 11 (Strauss' Ariadne auf Naxos).

He told me to handle everything until he got there.

That reduced the group of five who were supposed to go to Vienna that day down to Igor and me. Hannity was still on board, and said that he was prepared to do the interview remotely. Giuliani arranged for us the same kind of police escort through airport security that he always had.

With some time before our flight, we decided to relax in the Lufthansa first-class lounge. Almost as soon as we got inside, I noticed two big guys watching us intently and pretending as though they weren't. Even though I was on a mission for the President, they made me nervous. I never drank, but I was a dedicated fan of cannabis. In fact, I was told that Trump had once floated the idea of putting me in charge of federal cannabis policy.

When they finally called the first-class passengers for our flight, Igor and I were last in line because I wanted to take a couple of last hits on my vape. I just couldn't resist. In the tunnel to the plane, I noticed a single attendant standing at the end, in front of the entrance to the cabin and another stairway to the tarmac that I assumed was how the employees boarded.

As we approached her, four or five guys jumped out of the stairway behind her and demanded to see our passports. I recognized one as a plain-clothes FBI agent who I'd seen follow me before. Vienna, maybe? I turned around to see 20 or 30 more cops. The plane's door slammed shut.

Finally, the agent right in front of us told us we were under arrest and we were roughly handcuffed. I asked why.

"We'll explain later," replied the officer who was leading me away from the plane. I knew it wasn't about the vape.

Chapter 2
Waiting to be Rescued

The FBI agents brought us down to the tarmac. If I had any hope that this wasn't a big deal, they evaporated immediately. They had shut down the runway, maybe the whole airport, and there were all kinds of vehicles with flashing lights lining our route.

The airport had its own holding facility — its own little jail — and we were taken there. Immediately, Igor and I were separated.

The FBI agent I had recognized told me that he understood my confusion, and that I was allowed to call my lawyer. He also told me that I had to be processed and that I'd go in front of a judge the next day. The agent then handed me my phone, which he had confiscated earlier, and told me I could call my lawyer.

After I got Downing, I told him that I didn't know what was going on, so I gave the phone back to the FBI agent. He explained that we had been arrested, were going to be processed and then arraigned in the Alexandria, Virginia, courthouse. Downing said okay and hung up.

Still stunned, I was in kind of a daze when they processed me and itemized my stuff. I asked if I could make a phone call. I was told I couldn't until after they were finished. It took more than an hour, maybe two.

While the process was still going on, the FBI agent I had been dealing with told me he had some bad news — my house was being raided. "As we speak," he added.

My thoughts immediately went to my family. I worried about my wife and kids, we even had a baby in the house. What could the FBI want with them? Nervous, worried and wondering why I was being raided (or even arrested), I asked for my phone again.

This time, he handed it to me. I pressed Svetlana's number and it immediately went to voicemail. They must have taken her phone, I realized. I didn't know what was going on, but I didn't want to take any unnecessary chances. I locked my phone before handing it back to him.

"What did you do that for?" he asked angrily. "I was doing you a favor." I snapped back that I didn't see how locking my own phone affected that.

They took my gold watch and handcuffed me again. Nobody read me my Miranda rights.

I sat there, doing my best to figure out why all this was happening. I scanned my memory for anything I could have done that was illegal, bad enough to get me thrown into a jail cell. I couldn't think of anything.

For a few months, I had been working on a mission given to me by the President of the United States and the world's favorite mayor, Rudy Giuliani. I smiled to myself thinking about how embarrassed the jailers were going to be when his guys came to get me and Igor released.

Then they led Igor and me into two cars. There were no more big black SUVs for us, we rode to the courthouse in Alexandria in the backseats of beat-up old government-issue Tauruses.

Igor and I were then led into a cell together. It was absolutely, utterly filthy. There was one mattress. I let Igor have it because he was always complaining about his aches and pains. I laid on the floor.

I didn't sleep at all. I just waited for Giuliani to rescue us.

The next morning, three federal agents arrived at our cell door. One, who looked surprised to see us in the same cell, shouted: "You guys can't be together!" Immediately, I was escorted to another cell.

Soon, I was shackled and led outside to a bus with bars on the windows. It was overcrowded, so some of the guys had to stand or sit on the floor. Several of the inmates were screaming for the whole trip.

There were hundreds of members of the media already at the courthouse. Someone shouted: "Look! It's Giuliani's guys!" and suddenly I was mobbed by reporters and looking into the lenses of uncountable cameras.

Led into another holding cell, I was given my first food. It was a nasty sandwich with past-its-date bologna and an orange. I didn't eat either.

Both cases before us were both suspects accused of spying for the Russians.

In the courtroom, I was greeted by Downing and maybe a hundred more reporters.

Downing said to me: "Don't worry, I'll get you out." But Downing was not licensed to practice law in Virginia, so another lawyer nobody — I had ever met — took over.

It was then that I found out that I was facing two serious conspiracy charges, one for the falsification of records and another for lying to the Federal Election Commission.

The lawyer requested that I not be moved again, to make sure my time in custody didn't turn into a show trial. The judge granted the request.

While waiting for my next appearance, I was taken to another holding cell. I'd been taking Oxycontin for knee pain and Lexapro for anxiety and, deprived of both, I was undergoing serious withdrawal. Constantly vomiting, I literally forgot where I was.

I did, however, find out that the feds were trying to add espionage charges, which could mean a life sentence or, in some states, the death penalty.

After an unbearable time I could not even try to estimate, a guard came up to my cell and shouted: "You're moving." So, shackles and all, I was escorted into what the guards called the "Manafort Wing" of the jail because Trump's campaign chief had spent a lot of time there.

There were three or four eight-by-eight foot cells, each with a cement block for a bed and a combination toilet and sink in the middle. I was given two sheets, a towel, a green jumpsuit, a tiny (almost useless) bar of soap and a paper-thin mat that I later learned was my mattress. I asked if I could get some reading material. The guards laughed at me.

I didn't like it, but I was already famous. The other prisoners jeered day and night that Trump had disowned me and had publicly claimed that he didn't even know who I was.

After a few days, my lawyers arrived. The facility was locked down and the other cells were covered in shades so that the prisoners couldn't see me walking by. Shackled, I marched down the aisle, maybe two inches at a time.

Igor had already been bailed out, using his real estate holdings as surety. He had promised to bail me out too, but he didn't. He later mumbled something about me having to have my own real estate holdings to get out.

My case was then turned over to Manhattan's Judge J. Paul Oetken and I, and my co-defendants, were to appear, in Courtroom 318 of the Thurgood Marshall United States Courthouse, on October 17.

I was led into a room where Dowd was sitting behind a table and Downing was standing beside him. Immediately, I started asking questions. I wanted to know why I was still behind bars while Igor was free. I wanted to know what Trump was going to do for me.

Suddenly, Dowd slammed his fist down on the table and shouted at me: "Who do you think you fucking are? Trump is President and he will do whatever he damn well wants to do!"

I'd had enough. I had been stewing, forsaken and behind bars. I thought: Fuck this guy. I really couldn't help it, I lunged at Dowd.

Shocked, Downing pressed the big, red call button on the wall. Immediately, a gang of officers stormed in and dragged me out.

I screamed "you're fired!" several times as I was being dragged away.

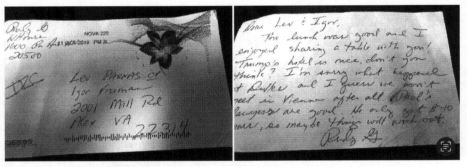

Giuliani's postcard didn't exactly fill me with confidence that he'd come to my rescue.

I was thrown back into my cell. I was deeply in shock. I really thought my life was over. I had no contact with Svetlana and the kids. And I had no attorneys because I'd just fired Dowd and his crew. I couldn't do anything but lay on my cement bed. Sleep was out of the question.

At around 2 or 3 in the morning, I heard a loud commotion. At first, I thought I was hallucinating. I only realized that I wasn't when I saw someone had slipped something under the door of my cell. I leapt upon it.

It was a postcard. I turned it over to see that it was postmarked from the White House. I immediately could feel the hope rise inside me like I'd just had an injection.

It was from Giuliani. It began: "The lunch was good and I enjoyed - sharing a table with you! Trump's hotel is nice, don't you think?" The handwriting was definitely Giuliani's. It continued with him apologizing for not going on the flight with us: "I'm sorry what happened at Dulles and I guess we won't meet in Vienna after all." Then: "Paul's lawyers are good. He only got 8-10 years, so maybe things will work out." It was signed "Rudy G."

I dropped the postcard. I suddenly realized what it really meant to be part of Team Trump.

Chapter 3
Growing Up Gangster

I t's Rome. Leonardo da Vinci airport. 1976. I am confused and impressed by everything. We, the Parnas family, sitting there, waiting for a connecting flight to Israel. We were coming from Odessa, in Ukraine (then part of the Soviet Union). At the time, the USSR was having another one of its periods in which they allowed, actually greatly encouraged, Jewish families to leave the country. Like most of them, we took a chance and made plans to emigrate to Israel. Dad was kind of in trouble anyway because he

The new-to-America Parnases: (from left) Lyudmila, me, my mother and my grandmother.

had openly protested for better working conditions at the factory he managed. There were me, 3, my sister Lyudmila, 13, my parents, Aron and Zhanna and my grandmother, Zina.

As we all waited, I saw an important-looking man in a suit, followed by a small, happy group. As he approached, he gave us all pieces of paper. I didn't know it at the time, but the man was John Volpe,

U.S. ambassador to Italy. As part of his country's bicentennial celebrations, he was handing out lottery tickets for Green Cards. My sister won. The Parnases made a life decision. We changed our destination from the Land of Milk and Honey to the Land of Opportunity.

A Jewish organization helping us led us to Detroit. My dad had been something of a big shot back in Ukraine, but — without great English skills, he had to start at the bottom. He worked as a mechanic.

Once, I went to visit him. A customer, not looking the right way ran me over. In his panic, he stopped the car on top of me. My dad literally lifted the car enough for me to be pulled out from underneath the tire. It cost him, though. He had a heart attack he never really recovered from. I wound up in a body cast.

We didn't want to stay in Detroit after that. Too many bad memories. After considering Florida, we moved to Brooklyn. In fact, we moved to Little Odessa — and enclave of people, mostly Jews, who had emigrated from Odessa. It was surrounded by largely Russian-speaking Brighton Beach. Our street signs, newspapers and radio stations were all in Russian.

My dad died when I was 13, and I thought it was my duty to bring in money for the family. Since everybody knew everyone else in the community, my dad with greatly respected and I was a good kid, getting a job was no problem. My friends and I hung out at a shop called Neptune Video and I started working there. The next year, I was managing the place. You have to understand that we were not like other 14 year olds in our neighborhood. We talked like adults, acted like adults, dressed liked adults, smoked, drove cars and had girlfriends.

Later, a customer of my mom's beauty business suggested I work for her. She was a realtor and also an alcoholic. She wanted me to mind the shop when she took afternoons off to drink. I jumped at the chance. It paid more than Neptune and gave me more of a future. Besides, I was already 15.

King's Highway Real Estate was always very busy in no small part due to the fact that we handled Trump properties in the south side of Brooklyn. At the time, in the late 80s, Fred Trump (Donald's father) was managing a small empire of buildings over a large swath of Queens and Brooklyn. I was familiar with the name Trump because I knew they owned the buildings I was showing, but didn't really have a good idea who any of them were individually. I also knew that the Trump buildings were going from rental units to co-ops and my job was to help convince renters to buy their units. The rich get richer, I thought. These people, the Trumps, were bosses.

One afternoon, Lisa was out drinking and I was minding the shop. An older gentleman with a huge mustache, piercing blue eyes, bizarrely colored hair and an old-school suit walked in. He asked to see an apartment in a specific building. Okay, that was weird, I thought. Everyone we rented to was Russian speaking — King's Highway only advertised in Russian-language newspapers — and this guy was definitely not Russian. It was even stranger that he would ask to see a unit in a particular building. That had never happened to me before. Clients normally just said the number of bedrooms they wanted, assuming that all the buildings in the neighborhood were more or less equal, and that they had to take whatever was available — they still hadn't shaken off their old Soviet habits.

Still, I knew better than to let a live one get away, so I agreed to take him to the building.

We spoke pleasantly as we walked to the building, a Trump building, and took the elevator up to the unit together. When we got inside, I began my

pitch. I described all of the minor details of the unit and told the man everything he would need to know about the neighborhood. I even made sure to include a couple of not-so-enviable facts about the area, just to make the whole thing sound more sincere.

I was still talking when the man told me to stop my spiel, he was already sold. "Do you know who I am?" the old man asked me.

I had to admit I didn't.

Fred Trump (Library of Congress)

"My name is Fred Trump," he told me. "I own this building and dozens more in Queens and Brooklyn." He told me that I really knew my stuff, that I was a great salesman and was sure to have a brilliant career. Trump often went under-cover, usually under the name Fred Green, to see for himself if his emp-loyees were working hard enough.

It blew me away. I didn't know about Fred specifically, but I knew that the Trumps owned half of Queens and Brooklyn. And this guy looked like he could be a patriarch, the guy in charge. It felt like I was meeting the President, you know? I was awed. So much so that I felt guilty about the cup of coffee I had spilled on his shirt.

I didn't know it at the time, but years later I realized that I had gotten something both rare and precious — praise from Fred Trump.

Fred was a strangely authoritarian father who treated his children like employees from a time before labor had any rights. He was so hard on his oldest son, Fred Trump Jr., that his daughter, Mary L. Trump, blamed Fred Jr.'s alcoholism and early death on his own father's constant berating and undermining. Even Fred's favorite son, Donald, had to put up with almost inhuman criticism and attacks on his self-esteem. The few sincere kind words I had received from Fred Trump were more praise than Donald had gotten from him in his whole life. I got something Donald would spend his days hoping for and searching for and never found — Fred Trump's respect.

When the owners of Kings Highway found out that I was 16, they had to let me go, and told me to come back when I was 18. I was old enough to drive, so, I bought a black Lincoln Town Car and a radio and started driving what we in Brooklyn call a black car and what other people call a gypsy cab. The money started to get good once I gave some Rangers tickets to a dispatcher who liked hockey.

That's how we did it back then. It was always something for something. Quid pro quo. Even if you stood to gain by helping someone out, you'd still expect something from him. It was hard-wired into our community.

It was the 1980s, it was Brooklyn, of course I got involved in organized crime. Back then, they were a significant part of our community. In a neighborhood where it was not uncommon to see a lady get out of a Mercedes and buy her groceries with food stamps, gangsters were not seen as criminals because everybody was in on one scam or another. Instead, we saw them as celebrities. You know the old trope: Nice cars, nice clothes, all the women and money they could want and they could do anything to anybody and they just had to shut up and take it. They were our heroes, kind of.

The girl that I was dating (who I would later marry and have a daughter, Zarina, with) had an uncle named Arkady Seifer. He was a very important man in our community. Seifer had been in prison four times and was connected to the Franchese, the Colombo and the Genovese families — among others. And everybody knew exactly how he made his money — the gas tax.

Seifer and I became quite close very quickly and I found myself referring to the old gangster as my uncle. After I gained his confidence and trust, Seifer let me in on his gas scam.

The trick was easy. Seifer's men would calibrate gas station pumps so that they gave a teeny tiny bit less fuel than they said they did. The amount was so small — never exceeding 2.25 cents per gallon — that drivers couldn't notice it. But because it was applied to every pump at just about every filling station in Brooklyn and Queens, the revenue was immense. The station owners received a small cut to keep their mouths shut and Seifer's people took the rest. In the time before everything was computerized, most consumers relied on trust to get a fair deal. In Brooklyn, we called those people suckers.

My primary task was to collect Seifer's taxes on local businesses, but I also found myself with side gigs, like chauffeuring important people around Brooklyn in a limo. My main job was to drive from station to station collecting the profits, filling my trunk with millions in fives, tens and twenties.

The money was flowing and the gangsters were loving it. I would help count the day's take, usually $9 million to $10 million, the connected guys would grab their shares and head to Atlantic City to play cards. These were guys who thought nothing of betting $100,000 on a single hand of blackjack. Seifer also started a Brighton Beach restaurant that served as a mafia hangout. To nobody's surprise, he named it Rasputin.

I was pretty well liked by the crew. I did my job and kept my mouth shut. My dad's reputation as a solid, stand-up guy didn't hurt, either. I believed that I had a bright future.

But, as often happens with illegal operations that employ many people, word got out and then to the authorities.

While on my way to the office one day, I was driving down the Gowanus Parkway. Finished with a cigarette, I flicked it carelessly out my window. The driver beside me — who also had his windows open — was incensed. He flipped me the bird and then cut me off. I instinctively jerked the steering wheel away from the other car, hit a guardrail and thought my life was finished as my car flipped over three or four times.

I woke up lying in a gurney in the hallway of a nearby hospital, there was a breaking news report on TV about FBI raids all over New York, Long Island and New Jersey. It was about the gas scam. I watched as my friends were arrested and paraded in front of the media. Had I been there — or if anyone had bothered to search my trunk after the accident — I knew I would have been with them and going to jail. My anxiety went through the roof.

It was at that moment I gave up any ambition of being a gangster or working at all with organized crime. I was already in the hospital, I just watched everyone I worked with get marched off to jail and some of the guys I knew were dead. It might be cool and a way to get rich, but it wasn't for me.

Chapter 4
To Russia with Lev

The people of Little Odessa knew something before the rest of America did — the Soviet Union was falling apart. The signs were obvious to us. First, the Soviets stopped controlling the affairs of their satellite nations, then they held minor elections that the Communist Party could actually lose. By the summer of 1990, the Baltic Republics were edging toward independence and the emboldened states in the Caucasus were fighting for their own freedom.

It was time to make money off the situation, everyone in the neighborhood knew, but they weren't sure how to get their products over there. Of course, I wanted to get in on it, but I didn't really know anyone in Ukraine or Russia, except my cousins, certainly not anyone important.

Still, I knew I'd find a way. I rented a 500-square-foot office at the corner of Avenue J and Coney Island Avenue, named my firm Progressive Consulting and appointed myself president. It was nothing more than a simple desk with one chair behind it and two more in front, along with a small couch. To keep the mood international, I put a world map up on the wall. I was still just 18. But I was fortunate to have a sister like Lyudmila, who has always helped me with my business projects. Still does.

I kicked off my new enterprise by putting an ad in a Russian-language newspaper looking for people who might have connections in the soon-to-be-former Soviet Union. I also put the word out in Little Odessa through friends and family.

Immediately, my little office started to get visitors. They were older people — mostly in their 40s and 50s — and all of them said they knew who I was, even if I didn't know them, and they all knew and respected my dad. All of them had people they wanted me to see after I made it past the rapidly rusting Iron Curtain.

It didn't take long for me to find out why they all needed me to go. They had never bothered to file the required paperwork to stay in the U.S. when they arrived, so they couldn't get passports and couldn't fly overseas. No citizenship, or at least a Green Card, then the borders are closed. Mom and dad had done everything they had to for us by the book, and I had been a U.S. citizen for most of my life. Besides, many of them fled the Soviet Union for reasons that might catch up to them if they ever returned.

All of the clients were over-the-top excited that I could actually go back to whichever old Soviet republic they had come from. Not only could I import products and perhaps make them rich, but I could also get in touch with friends and relatives they hadn't heard from in decades.

All of them had gifts for me to give to their loved ones overseas. I limited the haul to two suitcases, not only because I couldn't carry any more, I didn't want to arouse too much suspicion. They rapidly filled up with things like jeans, watches and other Western items that would be status symbols over there.

One man was swimming against the current. His family had done quite well as members of the Communist Party and feared what would happen to their wealth after the communists were inevitably kicked out. So, they wanted to send $10,000 back to America for safekeeping. I was leery. How was I going to get $10,000 out of the USSR without getting into trouble? After all, possession of U.S. dollars was illegal for Soviet citizens. The man looked at me as though I was crazy and told me just to say I had it on me when I came in. I agreed to do it.

Some of the people ultimately became my partners because we saw that it was obvious that our individual skills and contacts could benefit all of us.

The people who had entrusted me to visit their contacts came from a variety of places, and an itinerary for me was quickly put together. First, I'd go to Moscow and St. Petersburg (officially Petrograd, but nobody ever called it that). Then it was on to Ukraine, where I'd stop at Odessa (now Odesa) and Kiev (now Kyiv). Finally, I would go to Kazakhstan and Uzbekistan. Since I was fluent in Russian, so I was confident that I'd be understood in all of those places.

Not surprisingly, mom was extremely worried. Her boy was going to the Soviet Union all by himself. She knew that I didn't know anyone over there and she didn't even know if I could call home. Still, she did her best to prepare me; she even tried to teach me the basics of the Russian alphabet, but she didn't have much time — or all that willing of a student.

Before I left, I decided not to bring any money with me, because of the $10,000 I had agreed to collect. Besides, I had been told that all of my expenses would be taken care of while I was over there.

The guy who was expecting the $10,000 reminded me that all I had to do was claim that I had it with me when I came in and then truthfully tell them that I hadn't spent a penny of it in the Soviet Union on my way out. That way, I'd only be taking out what I brought in with me. Still, I never felt confident without some cash in my pocket, so — against all advice — I secretly kept a $20 bill with me.

I received one other piece of essential advice — never, ever speak Russian to any authorities, including customs agents. I was told that, as a foreigner who could speak Russian, I'd be identified as someone who had managed to get out and live a better life. I'd be labeled a traitor, and subject to any torment they could think of. But if I spoke only English, I'd be identified as American. At that time, in that place, Americans were always respected and treated like a big deal.

I flew on Delta at the end of winter 1990, and all the way to my stopover in Helsinki, nothing seemed out of the ordinary. But as I came out of the clouds approaching Moscow, everything changed. Strange and unfamiliar, it looked far worse than I had ever imagined. It was not at all like flying into the Bahamas.

Even though it was just 3 or 4 in the afternoon, it was dark. Everything looked cold and gloomy. I was chilled as the plane landed at Sheremetyevo International Airport.

The airport was depressing and full of defeated-looking people going from one Soviet place to another. At customs, the lineups went on for what seemed like miles. The entire place smelled like people who hadn't taken a shower in far too long. There were also military-style guards with AK-47s and angry-looking German Shepherds everywhere. Reinforcing the stereotypes of Soviet Russia, I had to wait more than two hours before getting to the front of the line.

When I finally arrived at the desk, I was greeted brusquely by what I considered to be a very attractive woman in her late 20s or early 30s. She took a glance at my declaration form, then took a long look at me, as though she was assessing something about me.

"How long will you be here?" she asked in English.

I told her I'd be staying two or three weeks. And when she asked where I would be staying, I told her that my friends had arranged my hotel, but they hadn't told me which one it would be.

She went back to my declaration form, and calmly said: "Oh, you have $10,000." I nodded uneasily. "Count it for me," she said coldly.

Unfortunately, the last movie I had seen before getting on the plane was Midnight Express, in which an American is caught smuggling in Turkey and suffers almost indescribable misery in prison. I really should not have watched that movie, I thought to myself with a sad chuckle. It kept invading my mind all the way there, but after I arrived, it was playing non-stop. I felt myself droop physically.

I could tell by her face that she had seen me turn suddenly pale, so I tried to regain my composure and use the old street smarts. I started looking for the money in my clothes and then in my suitcases as she watched. It was almost like a scene from a Peter Sellers movie.

"What's wrong?" she asked, clearly amused by my predicament. I told her that my wife must've packed it because I certainly couldn't find it. "Keep looking," she told me. "I've got time."

With the help of some of the armed guards who turned up out of nowhere, I emptied both of my suitcases full of gifts, so that they could search everything I had on me.

Since the search was dragging on for at least a half hour, people behind me in line were yelling things in Russian like "let's go!" and "What's your problem?"

"No more games," the customs officer said in Russian. "I know you speak Russian, that you are Russian — you were born in Odessa."

I answered in English, saying that I couldn't understand her.

She was clearly losing her patience. "We can do this one of two ways," she instructed me in English. "You can go ahead or I can tear up your form and send you to the back of the line to fill out another one."

That was the moment when I finally realized that she was angling for a bribe. I thought to myself that as an American, I had never bribed anyone, it just wasn't done there. We don't bribe, we tip after the job is done, and not for services like this. Then it dawned on me that I didn't even know how.

For what seemed like ages, I squeezed the $20 in my pocket. My hand, like the rest of me, was covered in sweat. So much so, that the bill was soaked. Finally, I hid it in my palm under my thumb and handed it to her as sur-reptitiously as possible.

There were guards everywhere and who knows what kind of intelligence-gathering devices were there.

"Finally!" she said, and took the bill from me. Then, she openly unwrinkled it on her desk, laid it flat and smoothed it with the side of her hand. Then she grabbed it by both ends and held it up to the light to determine if it was real. To my utter surprise, nobody cared.

"See?" she said, looking at me as though I was a small child who'd just learned my ABCs. "That wasn't so hard." Then she stamped my passport with her ring and waved me through. "Welcome to Moscow," she added.

Outside the terminal in Moscow, I was smacked by a huge culture shock. Nothing looked like what I was used to back in the U.S. I was reeling when I realized I had no idea who I was meeting, where or when.

Everybody looked almost exactly alike, somber and bundled up in bargain-basement clothes. That is, except for a group of five or six men, all of whom were wearing expensive-looking leather jackets and Cartier sunglasses. They were surrounded by 50 or 60 other guys, who were obviously with them, but dressed in cheap Soviet clothing.

Finally, the leader of the slick guys asked if I was Lev. I said I was, and they guided me to a shiny and illegally parked Mercedes-Benz S 600, one of the most luxurious and expensive cars in the world. I put together that these guys were emissaries for my contacts and the other, larger group were their bodyguards. I had heard that Moscow was a tough place, and the size and number of bodyguards made me believe it.

As we got on the road, I noticed that our small convoy of shimmering Mercedes and BMWs stood out like $1,000 bills among a pile of dirty pennies. All the other cars were beat-up old Russian things. Tiny, slow and ugly, they all looked like they were on the verge of falling apart or bursting into flames.

The bodyguards took me to the Hotel Moscow (now the Four Seasons Moscow) in Red Square near the State Historical Museum and the notorious GUM store, known for its day-long lineups of shoppers.

I had to present my passport, which the hotel staff informed me that I must do every time I wanted to go out or come back in again. I also noticed that there was a woman on every floor whose job was described as "taking care of things," but I quickly realized was actually there to keep an eye on everyone's comings and goings and to look out for any suspicious behavior.

Inside, I was surprised the Moscow's most well-known and centrally located hotel was a Motel 6 kind of situation. It was spartan to the point of being bare, just a step above camping, really, but comfortable enough to sleep in.

In the hallway, I was introduced to two guys who would be my bodyguards in Moscow. Hamsa was a huge former boxing champion and an Uzbek, while Dimitri was short and stocky like the wrestler he was, and looked to me like a Russian from St. Petersburg. They were assigned to be at my side 24/7 and go with me everywhere. Hamsa told me to relax in my room and that they would pick me up (actually knock on my door, as they were stationed in the hallway) for dinner.

I really wanted to call home, but I was told that could only happen at certain times, then I had too take my turn. I mentioned it to the bodyguards when they came to fetch me for dinner, and they assured me that they could arrange for me to call my mom back in Brooklyn.

They took me to a Russian restaurant because, at that time, that's all they had in Russia. Western restaurants were illegal. Our sleek BMW 7-series was parked out front with similarly expensive cars. Off to the side, about 50 little Russian vehicles, all in poor states of repair, sat. All of the bodyguards had walkie-talkies (cellphones were not widespread yet, certainly not in the Soviet Union) and stayed outside the building.

Inside, I met Bahte. Instantly, I could tell he was important. Although he was only about 5-foot-5 and a skinny little dude, everybody listened to him It was obvious he was in charge. With a sweeping mustache and a booming voice, he was brimming with confidence and good cheer. His dark complexion led me to guess he was an Uzbek (I was right), but what I was seized by were Bahte's eyes. He could intimidate you with his look. There was no guessing about this guy, he was an old school gangster.

In our conversation, I found out that Bahte was working for a boss named Salim Abduvaliev. I would later learn that Salim, along with his partner, Gafur Rahimov, really ran things in Uzbekistan, no matter who was officially in charge. Salim is still there, as President of the Wrestling Association of Uzbekistan and a sometime movie producer. Gafur, President of the International Boxing Association in Uzbekistan, fled to Dubai in 2019 after the

U.S. sanctioned him and named him as an active member of the mafia.

I'm pretty sure that Salim is still very powerful, if not all-powerful, in Uzbekistan.

I realized that all of these guys seemed to be Uzbek. Talking to them, I learned that they were all ex-wrestlers or boxers and they'd all served in the Red Army.

While the bodyguards waited outside, me, Bahte and the others in the meeting ate and drank all night. Well, I didn't drink. I never got into alcohol, mostly because I had seen people who drank too much — and they always did stupid, embarrassing things. I didn't want that to be me. But, with the drinks flowing, everybody else got very friendly and talkative. They actually made me feel like I was welcome.

After we ate and drank all we could, we began to head for home. As we were splitting up, I was asked by some guy if I was doing okay. I assured him that I was. Then the guy asked me if I wanted any girls that night. I laughed and said no; I really just wanted to go back to my hotel room and sleep.

The next day, I was set up in a Moscow office. As I entered, I could see that there was a lineup waiting for me already. The place was about 3,000 square feet and came with conference rooms and a kitchen. From behind a desk, I handed out the gifts to gangsters, politicians and businessmen from all over the Soviet world. I made sure to tell them all to use my business for anything they needed from America. They all left satisfied.

When I was finished, one of the men told me that I was going to Uzbekistan to see Salim. I didn't argue, packed my things and let them take me back to the airport.

Once I landed in Tashkent and got off the plane, I couldn't believe what I saw. Moscow had seemed like it was in the Stone Age to me, but Uzbekistan was way behind that — there were donkeys in the streets and people were selling their homemade bread everywhere. I looked down the street and saw an immaculate Mercedes-Benz S 600, no doubt bulletproof, and knew it had to be my ride.

I was taken to a 3-star hotel downtown (the best they had at the time) that followed the same procedures I had experienced at the Hotel Moscow. After a long lunch of plov, Uzbekistan's national dish of simmered rice and mutton, we talked business before I headed back to the hotel to fight off my jet lag. I'd barely put my head on my pillow, when there was a knock at my door. One of the men who had met me at the airport told me that Salim was holding a party in my honor and it was time to go.

We drove through the rocky countryside when an immense, almost unbelievable, estate appeared out of nowhere. It had to be worth at least $100 million, even over there. There were guest houses and guard houses, tennis courts, rivers and forests of palm trees and Christmas trees. It was some wild and crazy stuff.

As I was being led in, I noticed that there was not a single woman inside. All the cooks, all the servants and, not surprisingly, all the bodyguards were men.

Salim, his old wrestling days still obvious in his solid frame, greeted me warmly, as if we had known each other for years.

I was quickly brought into a room in which there were mountains of plov and walls full of liquor.

Salim and 19-year-old me partying in Tashkent.

I was given a seat and the feast began. As the eating and drinking began to slow, I started to do business, to spread the word of my company. Salim held my arm and told me that I didn't have to look for business, everybody at the party had already signed contracts to work with me. Then, Bahte handed me the $10,000 — a stack of crisp, new hundreds about half an inch thick — and told me that I was going back to New York the next day. Relieved, I finished my plov.

Things were significantly different for me on my second trip to the Soviet Union in 1991. Not only was I much richer since my imports became more frequent and of much higher value, but the USSR itself had changed.

That was underlined for me when I was sitting in my room at Hotel Moscow, waiting for my contacts to take me to who knows where. I was shocked by the most threatening noise I had ever heard. Instinctively, I looked out my window. What I saw floored me. There were tanks rolling down the streets of

Red Square. This was no parade, the tanks were on roads and sidewalks, smashing anything in their way. And they were surrounded by soldiers arm-ed with assault rifles and other lethal weapons.

I knew that I was witnessing history, but I had no idea what was going on. Some old school Communist hardliners had been appalled by the changes in the Soviet Union, originating from Gorbachev. They were sure he was leading them to the end. They'd lose their power, their livelihoods and all of their possessions — if not their freedom.

The old guard had taken a bold chance — they kidnapped Gorbachev and placed him under house arrest at his vacation home on the Black Sea coast of Ukraine's Crimean Peninsula. They announced that Gorbachev was "indisposed" and did not have the ability to govern.

Four days later, the coup collapsed, its plotters were arrested and Gor-bachev was back in power. Days later, the Soviet Union ceased to exist, re-placed by new versions of its constituent states. Of course, the most powerful of them was Russia.

But I didn't know any of that, I just knew that what I saw out the win-dow was serious and potentially very violent.

I was still numbly staring at the standoff when I was interrupted by one of my contacts storming into the room without knocking. "C'mon, get into the car," he ordered. "You're going home."

I didn't begin to relax until my plane had been in the air for hours.

The third time I came to Moscow, I wasn't even in the Soviet Union, I was in Russia.

Changes were everywhere. There would be dollar stores, in which they took Western currency, right next to ruble stores, where they only took rubles. The dollar stores had pretty much everything most people would want, but their prices were about ten times what they'd ask for in New York or a Western European capital. The ruble stores, on the other hand, had vir-tually nothing. Since Russians still weren't allowed to use dollars, I could see the East-West disparity right in front of me.

My handlers took me to a seafood restaurant, one of the first Western restaurants in Moscow (after McDonald's, of course). I could tell it was a huge deal for the guys and that they were showing off, so I acted impressed. Then, when I saw the staff carrying a wet bag of frozen oysters through the dining room, I knew that the food wasn't going to be as good as what I was used to back home. I ordered a grilled steak, fries and a salad. It'd be hard to screw that up.

After the meal, the handlers put me in the back seat of a luxury car and took me to a loud and gaudily lit place just outside Red Square. It was Night Flight, Moscow's first Gentlemen's Club. Started by two Swedish investors just before the coup attempt, Night Flight was stuffed with young Russian girls who spoke English and Western visitors who were eager to meet them. I was even more surprised to see people from Brighton Beach (including some from Little Odessa). Moscow had really opened up since my last trip.

I was not taken there to do business. The gangsters just thought I'd like being around other Westerners and the seemingly unlimited supply of women looking to meet them. And my business was running smoothly anyway. I found myself importing pretty much anything, mostly shoes and jackets. But I wasn't limited to clothes and accessories. Sometimes, I'd go to an unfortunate store's close-out sale and just buy everything. Once it made its way to Russia, it sold immediately and for much more than it would have in America. I made an oil deal once and a few more for aluminum, but I quickly found my niche — cars. Russians, who had grown used to waiting decades for the chance to buy some piece-of-shit Lada, jumped at the idea of owning cars from the West. There were, of course, markets for BMW and Mercedes-Benz, as there are in every country, but the real money was to be made in more affordable luxury cars. By talking with loads of Russians, I found out that the Ford Taurus and its clone, the Mercury Sable, were important status symbols there. It was big, it was distinctive and it was American. So, I found a guy in Russia who'd buy every one he could get his hands on, no matter what condition they were in. I found an almost unlimited supply of them in New York and the Russian dealer paid me $1,500 on top of the original purchase price for every one.

After a while, my trips to Russia became more stressful and dangerous as the big boys were making themselves known, often by getting rid of their competition.

One evening, it was all getting to me. I couldn't sleep on my flight there. Once landed, I was taken from the airport to Bahte's house. Out in the tree-lined streets of a posh Moscow suburb, the gigantic marble-and-granite mansion looked almost like a castle. It was on about thirty acres, had a huge fence with a tall iron gate. It did not surprise me to see about 50 armed guards surrounding the place. Inside, it looked to be about 20,000 square feet and, although it was filled with high-end Western furniture and art, it was decorated with a distinctly Middle Eastern motif. But the opulence of Bahte's place didn't interest me long. After all, I'd been in Salim's house, and he was Bahte's boss.

The boredom was getting to me and I couldn't sleep due to jet lag. Finally, I built up the confidence to tell my bodyguard that I wanted to go for a schvitz. From the Yiddish word for sweat, to schvitz is to sit in a steam bath or sauna, and has long been a beloved and almost sacred activity among many Jewish men.

The bodyguard initially said no because it was the middle of the night and Bahte had given orders not to let me out of the house until the next day. But after some discussion, reluctantly gave in. He said that he knew a private place we could go, where the only other people there would be friends.

So, we drove to the bath house and I began to enjoy my long-awaited schvitz. You don't look that close at the other men because everyone is nude or wrapped in a towel, but I did notice that everyone except for me was covered in prison tattoos. I quickly realized these were all potentially bad dudes, but I didn't worry too much. I knew gangsters back in New York. I knew how to act.

It was working, and the warmth and the steam were slowly taking the knots out of my muscles, when I was shocked by what sounded like a bolt of lightning. It was followed by a stream of heavily armed cops.

We were led out of the bath house, still nude, and made to lay face down in the snow at gunpoint. "I'm an American," I yelled in Russian, hoping it would get me out of trouble.

"We don't care," yelled one of the AK-47-toting officers. "You're all going to jail." Then he told the men that he was looking for counterfeit currency. None of the guys said anything.

Still laying on the ground, I turned my head to the side and I could see what was going on inside the building. The cops were clearly frustrated that they couldn't crack the wall safe. Suddenly, one had an idea. He spoke with his superior officer and, a few minutes later, I saw a crew trying to take down the wall around the safe with battering rams. As soon as they broke through, millions of fake dollars came flowing out.

The cops rounded us up and they took us back to the police station. Bahte showed up a couple of anxious hours later to bail me out.

The biggest difference I found between me and the Soviets was their near-obsession with alcohol. They saw every single night as an occasion to get smashed.

My preference was cannabis. I got so used to having it with me that I'd just throw it in my luggage like a pair of socks. I didn't know anything back then, certainly not how the Russians felt about it. To this day, I have no idea how I was never caught at customs.

Once, I arrived at a Moscow hotel, and my handlers told me to unpack and get ready for dinner. In an effort to relax and unwind, I thought I'd light up a joint.

I went into the bathroom for some privacy and out of habit. But it was a very old school hotel and the bathroom didn't have a window. Thinking that wasn't a huge deal, I just lit up the joint anyway.

After a few minutes, I heard some kind of a commotion in the hotel, but I didn't associate it with me. What I didn't know was that the smoke from my joint was rapidly spreading throughout the whole hotel. Another thing I did not know was that cannabis was considered a dangerous drug by most Russians. Once they smelled it, they were on high alert and frantically searching for the culprit.

I was totally unaware of what was going on until I heard an urgent knocking on my door. I opened it and one of my bodyguards flew in. He told me that the cops were in the hotel looking to see who was smoking. Once I realized what was going on, we started trying to open a window to let some smoke out and air in. But this was Russia. Since it was a high-end hotel, there were expensive paintings hanging on the walls. They were so valuable that the windows had been sealed shut to deter would-be thieves.

The smoke was thick now, I could see it as well as smell it.

Luckily, the bodyguard had been around and he got past the security measures and opened a window. But that set off an alarm that rang throughout the entire building.

Immediately, we closed the window and ran out of the room into the mayhem of the hotel. The bodyguard found the manager, paid him off and that was the end of the excitement. It all disappeared. That's just how things worked in Russia.

The next day, Shurek, Bahte's right-hand man, told me that if I wanted to smoke weed — something he couldn't understand because cannabis was seen as a poor-man's pleasure in Russia — that he would assign me a body-guard to carry it. I was, he said, too valuable to take chances with. In fact, he told me that when he found out what had happened at the hotel, he nearly had a heart attack.

So, the next time I went out, with Shurek and his crew, I made sure my favorite of the bodyguards, Oleg, had some decent cannabis on him. We were eating dinner at Thaihana, an Uzbek shish kebab house in Moscow, and at 2 a.m., the food was done, all eight of the bosses were black-out drunk while I was stone-cold sober.

I told Oleg I wanted to go smoke, so he made a beeline for our car to get everything ready. I joined him in the backseat and another bodyguard sat in the driver's seat, just in case.

Just as we were lighting the joint, a police car drove by and stopped. In Russia, any three guys in a stopped car looked suspicious. The cops were go-ing to check our papers and maybe shake us down for a bribe. We were in a big Mercedes after all.

Oleg saw them first, so he flicked what was left of the joint out the win-dow toward the rapidly approaching cops, then threw me out the other side. As the cops approached with their AK-47s drawn, I thought I'd play dumb and speak English into my cellphone. One officer screamed at me to drop the phone while pointing his gun at my head, but I foolishly continued to pretend that I could not understand them. When it was clear that wasn't working, I finally did run and high-tailed it into the restaurant, risking getting shot the whole way.

I didn't know it, but it was actually a smart move. At the time, rank-and-file Russian cops could not enter restaurants or certain other places. I was at least temporarily safe. Oleg was not so lucky; the police found guns, a knife and my cannabis on him. I saw him be thrown roughly into the back of a police car.

Still only 19 and shivering in fear, I watched out the window as one of the senior bodyguards went up to the police captain and tried to pay him off. There was a problem. Of all the cops in Russia, I'd found myself in the sights of the one police captain who wouldn't take a bribe. It was personal. He wanted me.

Shurek took matters into his own hands and went outside to talk with the stubborn cop. He offered him $1,500 — an almost incomprehensible sum for a Russian in those days — but the obstinate captain still would not budge.

Shurek came in to talk to me. I was hot with fear and a bit of shame. He tried to calm me down. He told me that the guy was being a total hard ass and that he wouldn't take a bribe. The good news, Shurek said, was that all he wanted was to see my papers. That was a problem. The Russians would stamp a visitor's passport for the hotel they were staying in. If I wanted to stay anywhere else, I'd have had to go back to a government office, wait hours in line and get another stamp. I had been staying at Shurek's place and hadn't gotten a new stamp. The penalty for being caught, we all knew, was one year in prison and being prohibited from visiting Russia for five years.

Shurek assured me that he'd take care of it. I could tell that everyone was eager to find out what I had done to make the police captain so determined to take me in. I explained to them that I was smoking cannabis because I didn't like to drink. The guests were relieved. One of the bodyguards asked: "Who do these cops think they are?" Everyone in the restaurant told me not to worry. Something so minor would be easy to fix. They encouraged me to go outside and talk to the cop with Shurek.

I walked out of the restaurant and toward the captain, who had started arguing with Shurek. Just before I got there, two big cops snatched me. They threw me in the backseat of a car. The two of them got in the little Lada and sat on either side of me, pressing on me so hard in the narrow bench seat that I could hardly breathe. As soon as they and the driver were inside, they sped off. Quickly, another Lada drove in behind it to try to block the guys' cars.

As we were careening through the icy streets of Moscow at top speed, I turned my head as much as I could to see behind me. What I saw was a fleet of Mercedes and BMWs rapidly gaining ground. I was in a cops-and-robbers chase, but I was with the police — and we were being chased.

We made it to the station and they dragged me inside. Still handcuffed, I was thrown into a cell and jabbed with a syringe, taking my blood. The hard-nosed captain seemed delighted to have me in his hands. "If we find cannabis in your blood," he beamed, "You'll get five to 10 years in prison." I had the 45 minutes or so for the results to come back to ponder that future. I wondered if they still had hard labor camps in Russia.

As I was contemplating my fate, I heard someone come in, shouting. In a booming voice that commanded authority but also betrayed a distinct and deep level of intoxication, the man bellowed: "Where's the American?"

I then heard some heated words between the man who walked in and the captain who was determined to get me. I couldn't make much of it out, but I heard the guy in charge tell someone to "unlock him."

Seconds later, a guard opened my cell door and told me I was free to go. I later found out that Shurek had paid the boss $4,000 — mere pocket change to him, but a year's salary to most Russians — to set me free. The tough-guy captain got nothing for all his efforts.

Chapter 5
Home Sweet Home

The lure of the West, particularly America, was very strong with all the Soviets I knew, and Bahte became fascinated with the idea of seeing it for himself. So, I got his papers in order to apply for an L visa, claiming that he worked for my company. Bahte was pleased and suggested that we fly into Montréal, because he had a good friend there.

The friend, who I knew only as Sliva, was Vyacheslav Sliva, who would be called a "Russian kingpin" and a "mob boss" by both the CBC and the RCMP years later. The Canadian government would accuse him of founding and participating in organized crime groups, contract killings, racketeering and money laundering.

Several noted crime experts have since opined that Sliva and his crew set up in Canada because of its lenient judicial system and the fact that its banks are comparatively easy to launder money through.

I did Bahte's paperwork in Sliva's Montréal mansion. When I was finished, I rented a car to drive to New York because I didn't want to deal with airlines. We drove south on Autoroute 15 until we reached Blackpool, Quebec, (now called Saint-Bernard-de-Lacolle) on the U.S. border facing Champlain, New York.

When we arrived, I was told to get out of the car and step inside to talk to Immigration. We were assigned a red-haired officer who seemed to be a bit of a hard ass. When he was presented with the papers, he looked at his computer screen, then shook his head and chuckled a bit. "Are you crazy?" he asked me, then looked at Bahte and said: "You're never getting in; we know who you are. Go back to Moscow."

Back in the car, I came up with an idea. I'd go to another border crossing and just smuggle Bahte over, hiding in the trunk like it was a drive-in movie.

When I told my assistant in Brooklyn, she saw what a potential disaster it would be. Showing some initiative, she booked us airplane tickets. I drove back to Montréal-Dorval International Airport and got on the plane.

When we reached Immigration at LaGuardia, I explained that I was the president of a company and that Bahte was there to work for me in Brooklyn temporarily. The officer didn't bother to look at her computer, issued Bahte an L1 visa and said "Welcome to New York." We walked away confused but relieved.

Almost as soon as he got to Brooklyn, Bahte started throwing his weight around. Once, he bankrolled my Uncle Robert, who had a plan to put a restaurant in the pool area of the popular resort, El Caribe. Robert was my mother's brother. Several notches above most tough guys, he had spent time in a Soviet prison for conducting a business without state permission. After he moved to New York, he was a taxi driver until he was shot in the neck during a robbery. That left him paralyzed on his left side and he started walking with a cane. But he still didn't take shit from anybody.

Everybody knew that the compound — which was owned and operated by Morty Levine, Michael Cohen's uncle — was a playground for Old Mill Basin's Italian mafia. Morty was a doctor and has never been charged with any type of crime.

The pool there saw plenty of action in the summer (Cohen wrote about the time he saw a guy get "shot in the ass" there, while he watched), so it should have been easy to turn a quick and substantial profit.

But there was a problem. The Genoveses found out that someone was setting up a business at a place where they, their friends and families frequented. The Cosa Nostra is not used to paying other people for something that they consider to be rightfully theirs. Orders were issued.

Soon, Uncle Robert and some of his guys found themselves in the basement of El Caribe's main building, surrounded by armed men. They were told that they were not going to leave the basement alive. Desperate, Uncle Robert called me. Concerned, I called Bahte, who promised to sort everything out, but only if I would come with him.

When we arrived at El Caribe, we were led down to the basement. I started to talk, but soon Bahte took over, while I translated what he said into English for a neighborhood boss, Ernest "Butch" Montevecchi. At the time, everybody knew Butch. He was strikingly handsome with dark hair and green eyes. He ran Brooklyn's Sheepshead Bay, and Little Odessa, for the Italians. Later, he'd become so close to me and my family that he served as something of a surrogate father for me, and I started to call him my uncle.

After a brief discussion, Butch told Bahte that the Italians wanted to go to war because the restaurant plan was an unforgivable insult. Bahte shrugged and said that he'd blow up the building with everyone but him and me inside. It seemed as simple to him as getting a cup of coffee.

Somehow, Butch and I managed to sort things out and the two sides negotiated a peace. In fact, we worked out a friendly working arrangement between the Italians and the Russians on several fronts that would last for years. Nobody was hurt, everybody would make money and we all left as friends.

Still just 20, I was not only getting rich, I was making a name for myself in Moscow and in Brooklyn. I began to believe I had the magic. You know, that ability to charm everyone around you and get them to do things for you.

Just like Trump.

Chapter 6
Making My Way the Only Way I Know How

G oing back to Russia was not what I wanted to do. People were getting killed left and right over there. People I knew. I began to understand the constant need for bodyguards in a new context. And, I saw first hand, that no number of bodyguards can prevent anyone's death if the other side is determined enough. It was no life, I thought, to be constantly looking over my shoulder and wondering who would betray me.

It was time to leave Russia and Uzbekistan and all those other places behind. It was just too dangerous for me and, besides, I had already made enough money to start something new. I was using some of it to build a beauty salon called Paradise of Youth for mom on Sheepshead Bay Road, but knew I needed something more to call a career.

While I was wondering what to do next, I got a phone call from my cousin, Oleg Ferdman. We had grown up together and were about the same age, but hadn't seen each other in quite a while. I wanted to impress him with my Russia money, so when Oleg suggested a sushi place that I knew was expensive, it was all the better to show off in.

I was sitting in the restaurant, waiting for Oleg, when I saw a bright red brand new Ferrari 360 Modena pull up and park in the lot. I had never seen a Ferrari in real life before, not even among the richest guys in Russia or Uzbekistan. When the door opened, out popped Oleg. He was dressed in a tailored pinstripe suit and looked like something out of the movie Wall Street."

I was too stunned to say anything as I watched Oleg saunter in and slip into the seat across from me. Oleg pushed it further. He pulled a check out of his pocket. It was made out to him and it was for more than $56,000.

I asked him what it was.

"My paycheck," Oleg replied with a proud grin. "That's what I made this month."

I was silent for a moment. Finally, I asked: Who did you kill?

Oleg laughed and told me: "And I owe it all to you." I looked confused and intrigued, so Oleg continued: "Do you remember that old guy, the one from the newspapers?"

How could I forget? When we were younger, Oleg and I worked together calling people to try to sell them subscriptions to The New York Post or its rival, The Daily News (nobody took both).

We did okay, but I had this one guy, clearly an older man, that I called every day. He'd make me recite my entire spiel, compliment me on my salesmanship abilities and then not buy anything. At first it was frustrating, but it got so that I enjoyed it and looked forward to calling him. I'd change my speech every time, just to keep us both on our toes. I eventually left the job without selling the guy a single paper.

Of course I do, I answered.

"After you left, I kept calling him every day," Oleg said, "you know, just to keep it going — he thought I was you." He left a moment for me to process what he was saying. "So, one day he finally gives in."

I asked if he bought a subscription.

"No, he told me that I had done enough to sell him and that it was time for me to get a real job and asked me to come to his office," Oleg told me. "Turns out the guy was Ace Greenberg," he said, rather dramatically.

I did not need Oleg to explain to me who Greenberg was. Alan C. "Ace" Greenberg was a guy from the Midwest who was hired by Bear Stearns — at the time, an immensely successful global investment bank, securities trading and brokerage firm — as a clerk in 1949 and, in 1978, became its CEO. Even among Wall Street big shots, he was a celebrity.

"I've made a lot of money at Bear," he said, pointing out that the Ferrari was just one of four cars he parked at his $5 million home on Long Island. "But I'm starting my own firm — and I want you to work there, for me."

I had never dreamed of working on Wall Street. Those kinds of things didn't happen to guys like me from Brooklyn. I was under the belief that the only guys who could get jobs on Wall Street had fathers who worked there.

Oleg wasn't kidding. On September 15, 1993, he and his partner, Steve Jaloza, founded Joseph Dillon & Company, a brokerage firm named after both of their sons.

I started with menial jobs and since Oleg wouldn't promote me, I left. I went to Barrett Securities on the Upper East Side.

I knew it was a chop shop, run by some guys we knew from Brooklyn.

If you've seen the 2000 film, The Boiler Room, in which a young outer boroughs street guy becomes a stock broker among greedy, unethical scammers who love to quote Gordon Gekko from Wall Street, I can tell you that it was exactly like the days my friends and I put in at companies like Barrett. Roger Ebert described the movie as having "the high-octane feel of real life, closely observed." I know. I lived it.

I realized that I didn't have to work for anyone else. I'm a top broker, I should be able to write my own check. My friend and partner, Gary, and I agreed that we were a hot commodity, so we opened up our own franchise of Security Planners.

For an office, I knew who to ask. "Of course I have a place," Uncle Butch told me. "No problem." The place was big enough, and it was on top of an Italian steakhouse in Staten Island. We liked it.

We hired 50 guys we knew from boiler rooms around the city, and went to work. It was doing quite well until the older Italian guy who owned the steakhouse and was of friend of Butch's, told me that some feds had been poking around and asking questions.

At about midnight, Gary collected all 50 traders and told them to take everything, and he meant every-thing, out. Gary even instructed them to wipe down anything, anywhere that might have their fingerprints. They finished at 3 a.m. Afterward, everyone went home.

Except for me and Gary.

We installed ourselves in a 24-hour Dunkin' Donuts across the street and sat next to the window, sipping coffees. At 6 a.m., we watched as the feds arrived to raid the place.

That scared me. Just as I didn't want to operate in brutal Russia, I did not want to tangle with the SEC. Let someone else take that responsibility, I'd rather just make money as a broker. So I called Oleg. It was good timing, Oleg had opened an office of Joseph Dillon in Boca Raton, Florida, and was not satisfied with the guy running it. He just wasn't an aggressive salesman like we were, he said. Oleg would appreciate it, he added, if I could go down there and straighten things out.

My old assistant from Barrett, Barbara Bella Ison, moved down to Florida and we were married. Together, we had two sons, Aaron and Daniel.

I approached one of my clients — Dr. Neal Tolar of Apopka, Florida —

who fronted me $5 million to start my own company. I bought an Orlando firm called Program Trading and renamed it Aaron Securities, after my son.

But the market was changing. Small trading houses were being edged out by the big, corporate ones. In Boca, the house that was dominating the trading was Knight/Trimark — now known as Knight Capital Group, the Jersey City-based giant is the largest-volume trader in the U.S.

Finding it difficult to compete with the big guys, I was considering closing Aaron Securities. That's when a guy — maybe 24 or 25, heavyset, unshaven and definitely an Orthodox Jew — walked into my office with a proposal. The guy, Eliyahu "Eli" Weinstein, said he was determined to buy into the firm, that he wanted to be a partner in Aaron Securities. I instinctively did not trust the former Lakewood, New Jersey, used-car salesman. But I did want his money, so I let him buy in, which would make getting out of the company much easier for me.

Later, Weinstein would be sentenced to 24 years in prison for operating a Ponzi scheme targeting other Orthodox Jews with fake real estate promises as well as for tricking investors into thinking he could fast-track them to get shares from the Facebook IPO.

Ironically, in January 2021, Weinstein was one of the 140 people pardoned by Donald Trump — including strategist Steve Bannon and Trump's son-in-law's father Charles Kushner — as he was leaving office.

But Weinstein, along with four other guys, were indicted in June 2023 for conspiring to defraud investors of more than $35 million, and with conspiracy to obstruct justice with a real estate Ponzi scheme. It's alleged that Weinstein used the fake name "Mike Konig" when he is said to have masterminded the scheme.

I was not easily starstruck, but I did like being around celebrities. In Florida's Atlantic Coast at the time, there was always excitement in the air, and everybody wanted to get close to the action.

After building my firm, I was hanging out with local celebrities, mostly athletes like Jaguars halfback Fred Taylor, star Ravens linebacker Ray Lewis and University of Miami cornerback Duane Starks. Among them was Jamie Foxx, who I met while he was filming the Miami Vice movie. He was a talented guy, really fun to hang out with. I was in awe of how quickly he could change from funny guy to serious actor.

By that time, I needed a right-hand man, and found him in David Correia. I had met him when he was a caddie at a Florida golf course, and he taught me how to golf. We became friendly and Correia called me with a real estate deal. We worked on it together and I was impressed enough to hire him. We stayed together for years, with him filling various helpful roles.

Facing another boring year in Boca, in 2010, I was in the process of divorcing Barbara and moved to Beverly Hills. It was finally time for me, I thought, to actually do some living.

Making money in L.A. was not hard for me at all. I found a place, again above an Italian restaurant, and started an underground poker game.

After the divorce, I had a few relationships. One of them brought me my wonderful daughter, Milana.

While at an L.A. party I was throwing, I laid eyes on what was the most beautiful woman I had ever seen. A nursing student 16 years my junior, Svetlana Melandovich was also born in Ukraine. We quickly began a relationship and I knew I wanted her to be my wife. So, I visited her at 4 a.m. with a jar of pickles as a gift, part of an inside joke between us, and proposed. She accepted and became my third wife.

After marrying Svetlana, we decided to move back to Florida to be close to my kids. I set up Parnas Holdings with Correia in Boca Raton.

Correia turned me onto a wealthy real estate investor named Dale Wood, who said he knew me from Wall Street, although I could not remember anyone with that name. Still, I was excited to meet this guy.

Wood tried to sell me on a real estate exchange-traded fund and then laid down the actual pitch. He wanted to be a partner in my company and was offering $50,000 a month as well as paying for my expenses, a driver and a cut of my dealings. I felt like I couldn't refuse.

But when I found out he was crooked, I ended our relationship immediately (and not at all amicably). In 2018, Wood pleaded guilty to conspiracy to commit wire fraud for deceiving investors and keeping their money. He was then sentenced to 151 months in prison and ordered to pay $7,130,410 in restitution.

Dealing with fraudsters like him made me come up with an idea — insurance for investors, I even had a perfect name: Fraud Guarantee. But getting it off the ground proved difficult, so that led to me working with Hudson Holdings, an investment firm that specialized in buying historic buildings cheap, renovating them, then selling them at top dollar. A perfect project had become available. The Railway Exchange Building in St. Louis had been the site of retailer Famous-Barr's flagship store and its headquarters. Macy's had bought the chain in 2008 and closed it in 2013. After that, the building fell into disrepair. Designed by Mauran, Russell & Crowell in the Chicago style and built in 1914, it certainly was a historical site. Its location, within a few blocks from the Gateway Arch, the baseball stadium and the Mississippi River, gave it strong potential as a luxury hotel or condominium building.

But they needed money.

I knew someone who might want to become an investor. It was Ukrainian politician Roman Nasirov, who I knew from Igor's nightclubs. He was then Chairman of the State Fiscal Service of Ukraine (something like Secretary of the Treasury), and was considered the third-most powerful man in the Ukrainian government.

And Nasirov was a very rich man in his own right. He got his start in grain exports, but in March 2017, while he was being treated by emergency personnel for a heart attack, Nasirov would be arrested for suspected embezzlement of $70 million. Either way, he had a lot of money to invest back then. And he, as a Ukrainian government official, wanted to build closer ties to the U.S.

I thought I could interest him in the St. Louis property through Hudson Holdings.

I was right. Nasirov decided to invest $10 million into the Railway Exchange Building through a Hungarian-based shell corporation called GEOS Project Development KFT.

We were promised jobs, the lease of Cadillac Escalades, health insurance and a 50 percent equity in the general partnership we would form. But it turned out to be a rouse, so we filed suit.

Chapter 7
The Unbelievable Happens

T hat sent me back to Fraud Guarantee. Still deeply bitter about the guys I believed put me in my dismal financial situation and had given me a bad name in Boca and L.A. They had scammed me. If they could do that to a sharp Wall Streeter like me, I could only imagine what they'd do to less experienced people.

If there was no reasonable way to prevent investors from getting scammed, I thought, there should at least be a way for them to recover their losses if it happens to them. After much deliberation, I came up with a plan to offer insurance on investments. That way, investors would be protected against fraud, and they could feel safe investing. It just needed a name that would immediately let people know that they had a guarantee against investment fraud.

Many people have since insisted that the name I chose was a clever way for me to circumvent Google searches that associated my name with fraud. It's not true and, if you Google my name and "fraud" you'll get precious little aside from Fraud Guarantee itself and news regarding my 2019 arrest.

At the time, I was a regular on the Florida party circuit, and so were the Trumps. I'd see them all over town. It was clear to me that we were in the same social circle and shared many of the same friends.

Some of the events were for Ivanka's first brand (Ivanka Trump Fine Jewelry, which now sells only costume jewelry), and Donald always came out to support his daughter.

I was in awe, not so much with the man himself as I was with his incredible drawing power. He was everything I wanted to be. He had the magic.

A year later, I was relaxing at home when my son Aaron, who was watching TV, said to me: "Hey, your friend is running for President."

At the time, I had barely even met Donald Trump. He probably wouldn't remember some guy who he posed with for a few of his countless public photos. But Aaron, like everyone else in the family, knew that I had worked for Fred Trump a long time ago, and ran in the same circles and shared some friends with the Trumps.

Trump was the friend of a friend. We weren't exactly best buddies, but I had grown up in the same neighborhood as Felix Sater and it was hard not to know him, even though he was a few years older.

I had also done business with Felix's father, Mikhail Sheferovsky, in the USSR. Our partnership ended when Sheferovsky found out that I had been pursuing a Soviet scientist who had isolated a useful chemical I could sell. Sheferovsky then held the scientist in his house against his will, preventing him from meeting me until after they had finalized their own deal. I remember Sheferovsky as being connected to the Italian mob, in the garbage industry, while others would accuse him of selling nuclear secrets to the Soviets. The FBI would later arrest Sheferovsky for extorting money from restaurants, grocery stores and medical clinics and reporting directly to Russian "boss of bosses" Semion Mogilevich. His partner was said to be Uncle Butch — Ernest Montevecchi. After Sheferovsky was convicted, the word on the street was that he became a rat. I know he got sick, cancer I think it was.

Later, I read that Sheferovsky did turn informant. In exchange for three years' probation instead of prison time, he wore a wire to bring down a group of Polish immigrants in Greenpoint who were doing what people all over Brooklyn had done for decades — Medicaid fraud.

Sheferovsky wasn't the only one in the family who received the help of organized crime. In 1991, Sater got into an argument with commodities trader Stephen Friedman at El Rio Grande restaurant at East 38th Street and Third Avenue.

Sater later said he didn't remember what the fight was over, but described it as: "Two guys full of piss and vinegar and drunk got into a bar fight" (although he testified, and others also claimed, that he was not drunk at the time). As things escalated, Sater said that Friedman hit him with a beer bottle, so he responded by striking him with a margarita glass. Despite a number of media reports that the glass was broken and Sater sliced Friedman's face up with the stem, Sater maintained the glass was whole. Either way, it was Uncle Butch who came to his rescue, making sure it was the police who ended up with him. Sater spent a year behind bars over it.

Now that Trump was running for President, I knew that Sater would become more insufferable than he already was.

He was already mentioning his relationship with Trump every time he could and showing off his Trump Organization business card with the title "Senior Advisor to Donald Trump" to anyone who would look at it. He would have felt at home in the competition scenes from American Psycho.

However, in a 2013 deposition for the Trump SoHo fraud dispute (a related suit included Sater's company, Bayrock, and how they received large sums of money from Kazakhstan and Russia), Trump said, under oath, of Sater: "If he were sitting in the room right now, I really wouldn't know what he looked like." Sater would beg to differ, as would the pile of photographs of them together, often with arms around each other. That was Trump's M.O. No matter how close someone was to him, he'd pretend not to know them as soon as there was a whiff of trouble.

Here I am with Jared Kushner and Ivanka Trump. I found her to be a lot like her father.

According to The New York Times, Sater was even better connected than he let on to the guys in Lower Manhattan. They published emails that they said Sater made to Trump's then-trusted fixer, Michael Cohen. "Michael I arranged for Ivanka to sit in Putins private chair at his desk and office in the Kremlin," began one dated November 3, 2015. It continued:

> "I will get Putin on this program and we will get Donald elected. We both know
> no one else knows how to pull this off without stupidity or greed getting in the

way. I know how to play it and we will get this done. Buddy our boy can become President of the USA and we can engineer it. I will get all of Putins team to buy in on this, I will manage this process."

Trump's announcement that he was running for President was greeted with positive reactions, even relief, from many people in South Florida. Among the rank-and-file voters, he represented a break from politics as usual, a chance to make meaningful change. He was even more popular among the super-rich who had clustered there because of his plans to reduce taxes for the wealthy and to claw back many government regulations that they felt held back their opportunities for even more revenue. People were talking about his candidacy, almost to the exclusion of all else, everywhere. Even though nobody thought he was going to win, it was still great to see someone like us taking on the usual politicians.

There's a reason for that. For generations, politicians have been born and nurtured into polite people who try to hide their lies behind elaborate language. But not Trump. Despite the obvious differences, he grew up a lot like me. For him to succeed in Brooklyn and Queens, he absolutely had to deal with organized crime. The magnitude of Trump's deals and the businesses he was involved in — construction, gambling and high-buck real estate — made him a magnet for connected guys. The feeling was mutual. As his unauthorized biographer, Wayne Barrett, once wrote, "he went out of his way not to avoid" associations with organized-crime figures "but to increase them."

Instead of using steel to make his buildings, Trump used quick-set concrete, a commodity handled by the mafia back then. And when there was a construction worker's strike, the union looked the other way while Trump hired Polish immigrants for less than minimum wage and without even the most basic safety equipment.

Yeah, just like me and every other kid in the New York City area, he liked the gangsters, even admired them. So he began to talk like them, do business like them. Other politicians will smile and tell you what they think you want to hear, but Trump will shout it at you while calling you a childish nickname. It was more familiar and reassuring to plenty of Americans, not just us Outer Boroughs guys. There's a reason gangster movies are so incredibly popular. We're rooting for the bad guy. That's who Trump was to us, the flawed anti-hero we all thought we needed.

Just like Trump, something about me always stands out in any crowd. I just have one of those faces. As I started attending rallies and other events, Trump would send me acknowledgments — nods, winks, waves — during and after his speeches. That evolved into hellos and how-are-yas and then into handshakes and brief conversations. It was like being on vacation in another country and running into an old high school friend.

I viewed the Trump phenomenon as another piece of history that I could be involved with, and wanted Aaron to be part of it. He was quite interested in politics and had emerged as a Republican. So, I asked myself: How many politically minded kids get to meet an actual presidential candidate?

So, I took Aaron to a Florida rally. We had VIP invitations and were taken backstage for a meet-and-greet with Trump before he went onstage.

Me, Trump and my son Aaron. Trump was very friendly when he was a candidate looking for donations

When Trump arrived, everybody was excited to see him. When it was our turn to meet him, I mentioned that I used to work for his father and told him about my interaction with Fred years ago.

Trump was visibly impressed, and when I told him that Aaron was studying law at George Washington University, Trump said that, since I worked for his father, maybe Aaron could work for him some day after he finished school.

Not only did that impress young Aaron, it sparked a friendship between Trump and me.

Later on that week, I was talking with my friend, Alex Podolnyy, on his boat. It was moored behind his restaurant, Lique. It was nighttime and I was smoking a joint on deck. Before long, I was approached by two excited-looking, well-dressed men who were Alex's friends. They introduced themselves as Ted and Robert and joined me on the boat. They seemed friendly and they knew Alex, so I didn't mind sharing a joint with them.

They told me that they had just come back from a congratulatory dinner with Trump and they were amped up. That piqued my interest. The pair were still celebrating the fact the Trump had announced his candidacy for President as a Republican. They were very excited that Trump could actually become President, which they said would make things a lot easier for guys like them. I wanted to stay in touch with them, so we exchanged numbers.

After a couple of hours of conversation, Robert floated the idea of having a Trump fundraiser at his house. It would be great to have him there, even though we all agreed he had no chance of actually winning office. I wondered what kind of connections a world-famous tycoon would have, especially now that he can add a line about the election to his résumé. Robert asked me whether I'd come if he threw the fundraiser.

I told him of course I would.

Robert turned out to be billionaire Robert Pereira. In 1972, he founded Middlesex Corporation in his native Massachusetts. It started out as a small paving company, but grew exponentially and made tons of money building roads, and bridges as well as the construction of railway stations and ports.

And his house wasn't just any house. Very loosely based on France's Palace of Versailles, the property sat on 4.4 acres on an Atlantic Coast strip called "Millionaire's Mile" in Hillsboro Beach, Florida. The compound, Le Palais Royale, featured an on-site nightclub, an ice skating rink, a bowling alley, a go-kart track, a private Imax cinema, a $2 million marble staircase and $3 million in gold leaf, which was everywhere, even the front gates. This guy's 40-car garage had marble floors.

It was exactly the kind of house Trump would love, over-the-top gaudy. It was all gold, just like his own places.

The property also came with 450 feet of beachfront on the Atlantic and another 500 feet on the Intercoastal Waterway, which allowed Pereira to park his 700-ton yacht a handful of steps away from his house. His private jet, a Bombardier Challenger 605, was kept at nearby Orlando airport.

Pereira listed Le Palais Royale for sale at $159 million because, it was speculated, that he wanted a bigger place.

Attendance for the Trump fundraiser Pereira was holding was much lower than he'd originally expected. It was a month before the 2016 Presidential election, and Trump was in big trouble.

A few days earlier, The Washington Post published a video and an article that it described as "an extremely lewd conversation about women" between Trump and TV host Billy Bush (a cousin of George W. and Jeb) while they were in a bus waiting to appear on NBCUniversal's Access Hollywood in 2005. In it, a voice that could be nobody's but Trump's described how he had attempted and failed to seduce a married woman and then warns the person he's talking to that he might kiss any woman they might meet. He pointed out that married Arianne Zucker could be a target. Then he told Bush, who acknowledged the tape to be authentic, how he expressed interest in a woman. "I don't even wait. And when you're a star, they let you do it," he said. You can do anything. ... Grab 'em by the pussy. You can do anything." Lawyers interviewed by The Washington Post described Trump's boasting to be descriptions of criminal sexual assault.

Media companies combed their files for other comments by Trump that could be described as sexist, finding many in which he commented his opinion of several women, including having an attractiveness rating system. CNN ran several instances of similar comments by Trump on the Howard Stern Show, including his commenting positively on Ivanka's body and giving Stern his permission to refer to his daughter as "a piece of ass."

Trump immediately issued an apology, calling it mere "locker room talk," and tried to excuse, or at least deflect, it by pointing a finger at the Clintons, saying: "Bill Clinton has actually abused women, and Hillary has bullied, attacked, shamed and intimidated his victims."

Most Republicans condemned the tape, but the only big name who revoked support for Trump was John McCain. Democrats said that it indicated sexist and entitled, even psychopathic, behavior. Even Billy Bush said: "I'm in a lot of locker rooms, I am an athlete, and no, that is not the type of conversation that goes on or that I've participated in." NBC still fired him.

The timing of the Pereira fundraiser could hardly have been worse. Lurid stories of Trump's misbehavior were coming out daily and his responses were sounding increasingly defensive, often blaming the alleged victims.

But on that nice day at the beginning of October 2016, me and about 20-some well-heeled Trump supporters came to Le Palais Royale for a very expensive meet-and-greet with the nominee. Tickets were $50,000. The mood was intensely anxious until Trump arrived. I couldn't get there until after sundown because it was Yom Kippur.

Everyone there, including me, was in awe of Trump. It was just something about him. I was caught up in Trump's charisma and the magnitude of his following and the events. I was drinking the Kool-Aid — but I also knew that by getting close to Trump's handlers or even maybe Trump himself, I would have important connections and credibility for life.

Even if Trump didn't win, his name would still be even more famous than it already was and, if he did, I knew I'd have access to all kinds of business opportunities just because I'd been seen with him so often.

The meal had been prepared by Alex's restaurant.

After some mild conversation made up mostly of compliments to and from Trump and picture taking, it was time for dinner. Because I was friends with Pereira, I was given an enviable seat at a long, rectangular table with the host, Trump, Rudy Giuliani, lobbyist Brian Ballard and several others.

Trump spoke. As part of his "I'm not a politician" shtick, he said: "I don't want to give up golf and do all of this stuff, but I feel like I have to do this

This was my view of Trump speaking at the dinner at Pereira's mansion. Pereira is to the right of Trump.

to save our country." It got a laugh, but the funny part of that is that Trump did not "give up golf" after he was elected, taking more than 275 taxpayer-funded golf trips during his presidency (nearly one every five days).

At any event, Trump tends to pick one person he feels comfortable with to talk to, and, over dinner, he chose me. We spoke about the controversy and his plans for his upcoming debate. I could tell that the other people were impressed and envious. We really seemed to make a connection.

Afterward, guests divided for conversation. I spoke with, and took pictures with, everyone. I didn't think much of Giuliani at first, but that was probably because Trump filled up the room.

In fact, I spent much more time speaking with Ballard and a partner at his firm, Syl Lukis, than I did with Giuliani. As lobbyists, both Ballard and Lukis were very interested in my experiences in Eastern Europe.

Before he left, Trump invited Pereira and I to be his special guests at the third debate in Las Vegas and at the Hilton for his election night party.

While I knew I wasn't getting any investors right away, I did have some fruitful conversations with well-connected people.

And I also got very close to Trump. Ballard mentioned his desire to deal with important people in Eastern Europe and to bring out the Russian expat vote for Trump. With my connections and my personality, I knew I could do both.

***

I knew Igor Fruman through common friends. Born in Belarus, his family emigrated to Detroit when the USSR was shedding even more Jews, Igor was six years older than me and had moved to South Florida, where the Russian, Ukrainian and Belorussian communities were tight. Still, he spent most of his time in Ukraine where he made his money.

I knew about Igor from various Jewish charities we were both involved in and mutual friends, but we weren't really friends at the time.

Igor became interested in me because of the pictures I was posting of myself with Trump on social media and because I was hosting events for Russians for Trump. Igor wanted to get deals done in the petroleum industry and thought I could help.

He owned two popular nightclubs in Kyiv, Mafia Rave and the more up-scale Buddha Bar. Both places were very popular with well-heeled men from both the West and East. They mingled at Buddha Bar, got to know each other and made deals, often huge deals.

That final month of campaigning for the election was particularly ugly. Much of the fighting was done on Twitter, and often by proxy.

Early in his campaign, Trump fans had begun chanting "Lock her up!" after any mention of Hillary Clinton. There was never any definitive reason why Clinton should be behind bars, just some vague rhetoric about deleted emails and the growing sentiment that the Clintons were just not trustworthy. Of course, at the time, Trump allies, including many overseas, were running covert online campaigns to discredit Hillary.

At first, Trump appeared to take the high road. When the chant broke out at a July 29 Colorado Springs rally, he said: "Let's just beat her in November." But at the October 9 debate, he promised:

> "And I'll tell you what. I didn't think I'd say this, but I'm going to say it, and I hate to say it. But if I win, I am going to instruct my attorney general to get a special

prosecutor to look into your situation, because there has never been so many lies, so much deception. There has never been anything like it, and we're going to have a special prosecutor."

Although WikiLeaks, a site that purports to reveal government secrets, claims to be neutral, its Twitter account sent direct messages to Don Jr., asking that he "push" its claim that Hillary asked: "Cant we just drone the guy?" — which they said was an attempt to kill its founder, Julian Assange (Clinton denied that she ever said that). Don Jr. was ahead of them, answering: "Already did that."

On July 4, WikiLeaks announced that it planned to release a million documents related to the election, implicating the Democrats. Trump adviser Roger Stone then pushed that concept on Twitter over the next few days.

At the same time, the Department of Homeland Security and the Director of National Intelligence announced that they believed that the Russian government broke into U.S. political computer systems and was releasing the information they retrieved through WikiLeaks and the very similar DCLeaks. A later indictment by the Department of Homeland Security and Office of the Director of National Intelligence alleges that DCLeaks was run by 12 GRU officers through Russian hacking group Happy Bear.

In 2016, many online investigators said that the data came primarily from a self-described hacker called Guccifer 2.0. The person who claimed to be Guccifer 2.0 said in an interview with Vice that he was from Romania. His account and four more accused of hacking Democrat computers were investigated by a Republican activist group, two of them were later identified as coming from Russia.

The man behind the group, Republican donor Peter W. Smith, would commit suicide in 2017 after he had given his information to the Wall Street Journal, but before they had made it public.

In the Vice interview, the self-identified Guccifer 2.0 said that his account was leaking hacked information to WikiLeaks. There was much communication between the Guccifer 2.0 Twitter account and Stone's throughout the latter part of the campaign.

On July 5, Don Jr. retweeted a WikiLeaks post that said that it had an "860Mb archive of various Clinton campaign documents from Guccifer 2.0" On the following day Stone tweeted: "Julian Assange will deliver a devastating expose on Hillary at a time of his choosing. I stand by my prediction."

the day after that, WikiLeaks began publishing thousands of emails between Hillary and her campaign chief, John Podesta.

They didn't say much that was incriminating and the news was largely drowned out by the furor surrounding the Trump and Billy Bush tape, which was released the same day. Still, much of the hacked information was used to promote the idea that Hillary's emails on private servers instead of government ones and their subsequent deletion indicated a cover up on her part. Many people on the right were adamant that the scandal should be invest-gated (it had been and an official report was issued in May 2016) and that Hillary was already deemed to be guilty in their eyes and deserved jail time.

At the same time, many supporters of the Democratic Party believed that the Russian government was actively helping the Trump campaign, in part through WikiLeaks. They had a point. In the summer of 2016, Secretary of State John Kerry, a Democrat, told his Russian counterpart that the U.S. knew about Russia's interference in the election and warned him that it could adversely affect relations between the two countries.

Once the allegations of Russian interference became part of the national consciousness, Trump began to repeatedly and falsely claim that he had nev-er done business in Russia, despite his many tweets to the contrary and the fact that his 2013 Miss Universe Pageant in Russia had been broadcast worldwide by NBC, Telemundo and Channel One, showing Trump sitting right beside Azerbaijani oligarch Aras Agalarov in the front row of the audi-ence. Trump even told CBS News: "I have nothing to do with Russia. No-thing to do. I never met Putin. I have nothing to do with Russia whatsoever." His lawyer, Michael Cohen, said that Trump called him right after that claim to check up on the status of Trump Tower Moscow.

Days later, the FBI would begin its own investigation into links between Russia and the Trump campaign.

Trump addressed the accusations again the same day at a news confer-ence, saying: "Russia, if you're listening, I hope you're able to find the 30,000 emails that are missing." Not only did that indicate that he was indeed looking for dirt on Hillary, but he was widely accused of "urging a foreign adversary to conduct cyberespionage" on another American, which is a seri-ous crime.

Trump would laugh off those allegations by saying that he was merely being "sarcastic."

At the beginning of August, according to the Mueller Report, Trump campaign chief Manafort met with Konstantin Kilimnik, his translator who is widely believed to have been a Russian spy, at the Grand Havana Room, which was frequented by Trump's closest allies and was in the 666 Fifth Avenue building (then owned by Jared Kushner, Trump's son-in-law) in Manhattan. It was also where I would later spend a lot of time with Giuliani.

At the meeting, Manafort is said to have given Kilimnik up-to-date polling data and a briefing on Trump's campaign strategy with the intention that Kilimnik hand over the data to oligarchs Serhiy Lyovochkin, Rinat Akhmetov and Manafort's previous employer, Oleg Deripaska. They are also alleged to have discussed the status of the Republican campaigns in the battleground states of Michigan, Minnesota, Pennsylvania and Wisconsin in detail.

In exchange, Kilimnik is alleged to have told Manafort that Ukrainian President Viktor Yanukovych had a peace plan for Ukraine that would allow for tacit Russian control of the country. The plan, he is reported to have said, would not work unless it had the support of the U.S. President, which they correctly believed would be Trump, despite essentially every poll saying the contrary.

Manafort and Kilimnik are also said to have left the restaurant at separate times to make it look like they had no connection to one another.

Trump and Clinton faced off in their second debate at the start of October. When talking about her deleted emails, Trump threatened to put her in jail if he was elected. Although some in the crowd cheered that remark, many in media reported it showed a decidedly anti-democratic, even authoritarian, streak in Trump.

In the few days after the release of the WikiLeaks information and the Trump-Billy Bush tape, there was a flurry of communication between WikiLeaks and the Trump team. "Hey Donald, great to see you and your dad talking about our publications," WikiLeaks' account wrote in a personal message to Don Jr.'s on the 12th. "Strongly suggest your dad tweets this link if he mentions us wlsearch.tk."

About fifteen minutes later, the older Donald tweeted: "Very little pickup by the dishonest media of incredible information provided by WikiLeaks. So dishonest! Rigged system!"

On the following day, Stone publicly denied that he had ever communicated with WikiLeaks.

But when The Atlantic later published Twitter direct message exchanges between the two, he said that he had only spoken with WikiLeaks via an intermediary — a "journalist" he declined to name — despite the magazine's evidence to the contrary. When asked if the Trump campaign was working with WikiLeaks, his running mate, Mike Pence, said that "nothing could be further from the truth."

At the same time, a Saint Petersburg organization called the Internet Research Agency (IRA), better known as the "Russian Troll Farm," was flooding U.S. social media with anti-Democrat, anti-Clinton messages.

On October 20, Trump and Clinton met for their third debate. The two previous ones had certainly been acrimonious, but this close to the election, both sides pulled out their last-ditch weapons.

Very quickly, the subject of Trump's alleged sexism and sexual harassment came up. Trump denied the allegations by nine women who all claimed he used unwanted groping and sexual advances on them, maintaining that the accusations had been "debunked." They hadn't been. When Clinton asked him to apologize for the contents of the Billy Bush tape, Trump said: "I didn't even apologize to my wife, because I didn't do anything." That was despite the fact that Melania, a few days earlier, told interviewers that he had indeed apologized to her. Trump ended his rebuttal by saying: "Nobody has more respect for women than I do."

When the subject turned to Russia, Clinton asked if Trump "rejects Russian espionage against Americans." He wouldn't do it, instead saying that he wasn't even sure Russia was behind any interference.

When she accused Putin, in particular, of being responsible for the meddling in the election, Trump once again asserted that he didn't know Putin, but he did somehow know that Putin had "no respect" for Clinton or the sitting President, Obama. Trump then pivoted to the idea of the U.S. and Russia joining forces to fight Islamic fundamentalist terrorism (the question had been about immigration) and said of Clinton: "She doesn't like Putin because Putin has outsmarted her at every step of the way."

Later, he claimed that Clinton "shouldn't be allowed to run" for President because of unspecified crimes and then, once again, claimed that the election was "rigged," but only if he lost. That was a concept Manafort had used in elections before, but never before the voting had occurred.

With Trump still way behind in virtually every poll, his staff started amping up their dirty tricks. Just after the third debate, Manafort emailed Kushner to propose that the Trump campaign portray Clinton "as the failed and corrupt champion of the establishment" with Wikileaks as a source of Clinton quotes (some of which were debatable as to their veracity) that could be used against her.

By the time Trump spoke at a rally in Sanford, Florida (the site of the 2012 killing of Trayvon Martin, which bitterly divided much of the nation) on October 25, the rhetoric had gotten even more adversarial. When the "Lock Her Up" chant broke out, he said of Clinton (who he had already called "crooked"): "She shouldn't be allowed to run for president. She shouldn't be allowed, I'm telling you. She should not be allowed to run for president based on her crimes. She should not be allowed to run for president." He also alluded to her emails and called Bill Clinton "Wild Bill." He went on: "This corruption and collusion is just one more reason why I will ask my attorney general to appoint a special prosecutor." A few seconds later, he added: "She has to go to jail." No trial, no nothing, straight to jail. He also incorrectly stated that the word "God" had twice been omitted from the Pledge of Allegiance at the recent Democratic National Convention.

Of course, I was at the rally (which was mostly remembered for the ridiculous image of a white woman holding up a "Blacks for Trump" sign). I don't recall many details from that one event, but the crowd was wildly in favor of Trump, and everyone seemed very excited to be there.

One Trump rally that I definitely remember was the one thrown in Miami on November 2, just days before the election. It was held in front of a smaller-than-usual crowd at Bayfront Park.

I really saw what money and pull could do when I watched Pereira negotiate a six-figure sum to allow his daughter, Seanna (maybe 12 or so), to sing the national anthem. She really wanted to be an entertainer, and he was doing whatever he could to make her dream a reality.

Later that day, I set up a meeting for Ballard and Nasirov.

The Ukrainians were eager. When Ukrainian President Petro Poroshenko found out that Nasirov had an opening into Trump's future administration with Ballard through me, he pressed Nasirov to make it happen. At the time, Ukraine had almost no relationship with the U.S. and even that was in danger of being erased as the Ukrainians were seen as being pro-Hillary.

I explained the situation to Ballard. I told him that it wasn't the president who was in favor of Hillary, just some loud members of his administration. Besides, Ukraine was a sovereign nation and they needed to have some relationship with the U.S. If they hire you, I told Ballard, they could get it done.

The last days before the election were chaotic for all of us. On October 29, Trump loaned his own campaign $10 million. The loan was never repaid and investigators linked it to a state-owned bank in Egypt. The next day, Senate Minority Leader Harry Reid, a Democrat, officially asked FBI director James Comey to investigate Russian influence in the election. The day after that, Obama called Putin on the Red Phone (officially the Washington-Moscow Direct Communications Link) to warn him to stop interfering in the election or face serious consequences. It was only the 11th time the link, which was installed in the 1960s by President Kennedy, had ever been used.

On November 1, a Russian espionage group called Happy Bear operating under the name Anonymous Poland, posted a falsified letter that was supposedly from the Bradley Foundation that said it had donated $150 million to Clinton. That's odd, since the Bradley Foundation has a long history of contributing to conservatives and has been the subject of rumors related to money laundering among the hyperwealthy.

When Election Day came, Trump headquarters was at the midtown Manhattan Hilton at the corner of West 54th Street and Sixth Avenue. In stark contrast to Trump's typically gaudy, bigger-is-better events, it took place in a modestly sized ballroom with a minimum of decoration. Hanging from the ceiling was a Trump-for-President banner with the subtitle "Make America Great Again," but it was blue, instead of his usual bright red.

I was there, of course, with Svetlana, Pereira and his girlfriend. We were escorted into the VIP section upstairs, where there was food, drinks and many televisions.

For everyone involved, election night was surreal.

There was lots of excitement there, but few had much faith that Trump was going to win. Instead, I was there to network. After all, these guys were still going to be very powerful, even if their boss was not in office.

I also noticed that this crowd was almost the opposite of what I'd seen at Trump rallies. When I traveled throughout the country with him, I noticed that almost all of his fans were blue-collar whites. But these people were older and well-dressed — they looked wealthy. Instead of being raucous and intense, they were calm and quiet.

That mood probably came from the polls. Trump was way down, like seriously down — The New York Times gave him 15 percent, 8 percent, 2 percent and finally less than 1 percent chance of winning. The media source who gave him the best odds was FiveThirtyEight, with 29 percent. Sure of a loss, Trump's supporters were not there to celebrate, but to commiserate.

But the media was wrong.

Although the mood brightened as Trump won state after state, the crowd was incredibly anxious even as things were falling in their favor. Even after Clinton lost Wisconsin, which effectively took her out of the race, the mood was, at best, quiet optimism. Only a very small group of supporters had actually thought he'd win even then.

But once Fox News called it, the crowd erupted.

Although many of them were at of over retirement age, the ballroom at the Hilton was alive with exhilaration. Even as dignitaries were speaking, the celebration was deafening

Me, Svetlana, Pereira and his girlfriend, Steffanie, just after Trump won the 2016 election.

(they all turned quiet once Trump took to the mike, though). When he was declared the winner, everyone was screaming and yelling with excitement. It was like a dream. Trump had actually pulled it off.

It was interesting that their cheerfulness — at least judging by their comments and behavior that night — was not based on how good things would be for them, but on how bad it would be for others. Their rage was mainly taken out on the media, who were jeered and otherwise abused — except for those from Fox News, of course.

I was shocked and overjoyed. My ambition of knowing a world-famous tycoon had been upgraded into the reality of befriending that same man, who was soon going to be sworn in as the President. My dreams of making money hand over fist seemed to be coming true.

After the exhausting victory party, I needed to get back to my own hotel. Although the streets of Manhattan were loaded with election night observers — some celebrating, some inconsolable — I noticed that everyone was

I still have the T-shirt.

looking at me as though I was crazy. It was only after I had gotten on the elevator that I realized that the hotel was the site of Democrat Vice-Presidential candidate Tim Kaine's own party. And, I remembered, that I was wearing a "Crookd Hillary" T-shirt.

To some Republicans, it was more important that Hillary lost than Trump won. They had handed them out to everyone at Trump's party, and — in the excitement — I had put one on and forgotten about it.

The elevator ride and walk to my room were deafeningly silent.

Chapter 8
Moscow on the Potomac

"Putin has won."

That was the contents of a text received by Kirill Dmitriev on November 9, 2016, moments after Clinton conceded the 2016 Presidential Election to Trump. The sender has yet to be identified by the U.S., but Dmitriev is an interesting guy.

Born in Kyiv when it was still Kiev to a Russian family in 1975, as a teenager, he watched as the Iron Curtain fell. Then he traveled to the U.S. as an exchange student and stayed. He attended Foothill College (in Los Altos Hills, California), Stanford and then Harvard. After working for Goldman Sachs, he made the uncommon move back to Russia. By 2011, he became CEO of the Russian Direct Investment Fund, which hands out trillions of rubles to help grow Russian businesses and attract foreign companies to Russia. He is also said to be a good friend of Putin's.

In January 2017, about a week before Trump took office, Dmitriev was in the Seychelles meeting with Erik Prince, founder and former CEO of the private military company Blackwater, and George Nader (a Lebanese-American consultant, lobbyist, political adviser and repeat sex offender), who served as Prince's consultant. It's also worth noting that Prince's sister is Betsy DeVos, who was named Trump's Secretary of Education, despite not possessing any pertinent qualifications. Many reports have agreed that the purpose of the meeting was to help establish a back channel between the Kremlin and the White House.

At the same time that Republicans were either playing down or outright lying about Russian involvement in the election, the Russians themselves appeared jubilant at its outcome. Deputy Foreign Minister Sergei Ryabkov told Russian media that "there were contacts" with Team Trump during the race, adding: "I don't say that all of them, but a whole array of them supported contacts with Russian representatives." Maria Zakharova, spokeswoman for the Russian Foreign Ministry, told Bloomberg that it was "normal practice" for Russian representatives to meet with Americans working on the Trump campaign, but that the Clinton campaign had turned them down. She later told a Russian TV audience that: "Our people in Brighton Beach won the election for Donald Trump."

It might be hard to believe in retrospect, but I didn't know anything about Russian involvement in the election. Despite all of my contacts and friends in the former USSR, I was under the belief that Trump was elected simply because the American people wanted change and because of hard-working supporters like myself. I was just so excited that we pulled it off.

The relief of the race being over made me ready for a long rest. But I just couldn't sleep. I was friends with the President of the United States of America. It was a lot to comprehend, but I knew I liked it.

What struck me most about the incoming administration was how unprepared its members were and how little knowledge they had, especially outside of their own borders and interests. Half of them couldn't spot Ukraine on a map (maybe not even Russia). Their expertise appeared to be in getting elected, not in what to do afterward. It was only after they were in office that they worried about how to do their job. And, even with the greatest minds in the world at their disposal, they usually relied on someone they already knew who might have had a passing knowledge on any subject.

Of course the 2016 crop, who suddenly had significant responsibilities, was even more unprepared than most. Aping the populist Trump plan, many of them were elected by proclaiming themselves outsiders, not part of the ruling elite. That resulted in the majority of new electees being part of the oft-sainted "self-made." But what comes with that are people who are unaware of anything outside their little fiefdoms and have no idea about reaching consensus or even simple agreements because they have become accustomed to their orders being carried out without question.

That's where I came in. As a veteran broker during the tumultuous end of the Soviet Union and on Wall Street, I had made lots of friends and contacts — many of whom had become very powerful, politically important and fabulously wealthy — and I knew how to negotiate. My knowledge and contacts were invaluable. I just had to get someone to realize it.

Of course, I was no dyed-in-the-wool Republican. I was where I was because a guy I knew had become President. That could, I firmly believed, only be good for me. Especially financially.

The first person in the new power structure I sought out was prominent lobbyist Brian Ballard. Right after the win, I set up a meeting with Ballard — and his right-hand-man, Lukis. Although we talked on the phone, I preferred face-to-face meetings and would always see Ballard when he was in Florida. Ballard was no dummy, he wanted to talk with me about what I knew and where I had contacts.

Ballard wanted what I had, so it didn't take much to make a deal. I would put Ballard in touch with the right people for 20 percent of any deals he made with them. Although there was some thrill associated with making such high-level deals, I was really in it for the money. I had just had my big fallout with Hudson Holdings and had filed the lawsuit, so I needed to get paid.

I knew just where to go. Nasirov was a major player in the Ukrainian government and eager to talk with Ballard in order to improve Ukraine's relationship with Washington. Because Ukraine's support of Obama and Clinton had greatly offended the new crop of Republicans, he was almost desperate to get on Trump's good side.

So I arranged to meet Nasirov at one of Igor's Kyiv nightclubs, Buddha Bar. I flew there on December 1, 2016 to spend a week in Ukraine. When I arrived at Buddha Bar, Igor told me that the first floor was closed for a private party, so I'd have to meet Nasirov upstairs.

So, with the lights flashing and the music blaring, I walked past the giant golden Buddha that overlooked the dance floor to the VIP room. As I went by, I noticed a group of fit-looking young men, all of them drinking hard. Since the whole first floor of the bar had been closed for them, I knew they must have been important.

The second floor was empty except for me and a few of my friends from Ukraine. I greeted Nasirov and we immediately began to talk about business.

Because he was a nightclub owner, Igor was always surrounded by beautiful women. He told the ones who were already in the club to go upstairs and called a few more — and instructed them all to make sure the men in the bar saw them.

Soon, every one of the men was upstairs. Their leader introduced himself to me. He was Mübariz Mansimov, an Azerbaijani billionaire. who lived and held citizenship in Turkey. He made his money shipping oil through his Turkish company Palmali. That immediately caught my attention. I knew that there was huge money to be had in petroleum and that the U.S. was not taking advantage of all the sources it could. Mansimov was definitely someone I

Me with Mansimov at Igor's nightclub in Kyiv.
Mansimov was very friendly when he was drinking.

wanted to know. The other guys there were the players on a soccer team he owned, Khazar Lankaran FK.

I considered Nasirov a to be friend by then and I introduced him to Mansimov, who had been drinking with his team and was already pretty sloppy. He joined me at my table and we started to talk. I could tell that Mansimov liked me right away. It was obvious that he was in the familiar jolly, everyone-is-my-friend level of inebriation. We talked about all kinds of subjects, and he was impressed at how much, and who, I knew when it came to politics and power on both sides of the Atlantic.

Of course, I was also well aware that guys like Mansimov enjoyed nothing more than talking about their wealth, so I asked him questions about his possessions so that Mansimov would have to top everyone else. That made the billionaire feel good.

The team was in Ukraine to play Kyiv Dynamo. Since we were getting along so well, he invited me to see the game from his private box.

Like any Eastern European meeting, this one was awash in alcohol and beautiful women. Since he was part of the government and Buddha Bar had a reputation as being something of a mafia hangout, so Nasirov didn't want to hang around.

Mansimov wanted American contracts so that his shiping company could move more oil, and that fit in with what I wanted. I knew that the way to accomplish our mutual interest would be to get him in touch with Ballard. So we discussed the idea of having Ballard represent Palmali in D.C.

I didn't have to ask him about his own contacts. The oligarch bragged about how close he was to Turkish dictator Recep Erdoğan. He told me that Erdoğan and some of his people used his private planes to travel. He also told me about his gift of a $25 million oil tanker to Erdoğan's family.

Mansimov was still sober enough to assure me that he wanted contacts in Washington. Who doesn't? And I had come to him at a great time. Relations between Turkey and the U.S. were rocky at best and Erdoğan had big plans, both inside and outside of his country's borders.

I hastened to explain my position in D.C. and my clo- seness to Trump through Bal- lard. I told him that talking to Ballard was like talking dir- ectly to Trump.

I was already dreaming about my huge payday.

There is a much-circulated photo of us in Buddha Bar's VIP room that night, including Mansimov, me, Igor and Tur- kish businessman Fikret Or- man (who had his own soccer

Mansimov liked to show off his wealth, and was proud of Khazar Lankaran FK, his soccer team.

team in Turkey, Beşiktaş J.K.). We are arm-in-arm, and I am pointing at Mansimov.

In the picture, Mansimov, who looks intoxicated, is throwing the hand sign for the Grey Wolves. They are a violent Turkish paramilitary organiza- tion that targets ethnic minorities, the LGBT community and leftists.

When we took the picture, I didn't see the hand sign. I had no idea what it meant or even who the Grey Wolves were. Definitely not my thing.

In 2008, a mass trial of the secularist Ergenekon organization revealed to the public that the Turkish intelligence organization (Millî İstihbarat Teşkil- atı or MIT) provided weapons for the Grey Wolves, employed them to as- sassinate political rivals and offered amnesty for crimes against Kurds in their conflict, which has been officially going on at least since 1921.

By far Mansimov's proudest possession was Khazar Lankaran FK, the most popular soccer team in Azerbaijan. For their game against FC Dynamo Kyiv, Mansimov invited me into his luxury box to watch.

Dynamo was (and is) owned by Ukrainian businessman, sometime politician and billionaire Ihor Surkis, who made much of his wealth with an investment opportunity called Ometa 21st Century. Later identified as a Ponzi scheme, its shares peaked at 1,350 kopeks in 1993 and ended being worth 2.4 in 1997. By the time I went to see the game, Surkis (like many other prominent Ukrainian and Russian billionaires) was dealing mainly in natural gas.

In the private owner's box at the game, Mansimov became blasted drunk and said that he liked his new American pal very much. He vowed to do business with me — and, by extension, Ballard — in the future.

After I mentioned that both Nasirov and Mansimov were looking for contacts in the U.S., Ballard and Lukis were visibly pleased. There had been hopes in Ankara that the new administration in Washington would be more open to Turkey — especially since Trump clearly admired Erdoğan — but what I was offering was priceless. Still, we discussed payment.

Ballard worked with Ukraine's top politicians.

We decided that getting Ballard to lobby on Turkey's behalf was in both of our best interests.

Nasirov wanted his own access to Ballard. Since he was in an important position in the Ukrainian government, I knew he would have a great interest in my suddenly far-more-powerful contacts in Washington.

Nasirov told me that Poroshenko had been complaining about how minute a relationship Ukraine had with the United States and that he hoped that would change if the Americans could see how well the country had turned to capitalism and other clearly pro-Western values. Surely, how much Putin hated Poroshenko must have been noticed by Washington.

I laughed and told him that Trump would never pay attention to Ukraine just because they were playing ball. And, from what I'd heard in the inner circles of MAGA, being an enemy of Putin's was no longer that much of an asset. The country needed a direct path to Trump. I told Nasirov what Ballard wanted — big-time lobbying contracts in exchange for Trump's ear.

Nasirov was interested and we started talking about a deal for Ballard to represent Ukraine.

We spoke back and forth and, eventually, Ballard sent a contract for his lobbying services to Poroshenko. The Ukrainian President invited Ballard to Kyiv to sign the document. But Ballard got cold feet because of the animosity toward Ukraine among Trump's people. When Ballard explained his concerns, Nasirov offered to hire Ballard on behalf of Ukraine, but in a private capacity through one of his companies. Still, Ballard's agenda would be to improve Ukraine's relationship with the United States.

I didn't know it at the time, but Nasirov was in big trouble back home. Along with a fellow Ukrainian politician from Manafort's Party of Regions, Oleksandr Onyshchenko, he was facing charges of diverting the equivalent of $75 million from state-owned gas company UkrGasVydobuvannya. That made Nasirov even more eager to have friends in Washington.

Everything appeared to be going according to plan, but there was a catch. Both Nasirov and Mansimov wanted to attend the inauguration. Ballard told me that it shouldn't be a problem.

Even with my financial situation in flux, I was living pretty high on the hog in those days. I was invited to everything and often had a jet waiting to sweep me off to wherever the rich Republicans or Eastern Europeans wanted me to be. I was invited to Mar-a-Lago more than a few times because of my relationship with Trump, sometimes taking the opportunity to meet with important people to further my business plans.

Even though I was not a member there, I had VIP access to Mar-a-Lago. For an event on December 16, I asked if I could bring along a plus one. Assured I could, I invited Nasirov. I knew he would be thrilled.

When I brought him there, he seemed impressed by everything. When Trump walked in, every eye followed him.

After everyone calmed down a little, I asked Nasirov if he wanted me to introduce him to Trump.

The look on his face literally made me wonder if he'd just shit his pants. He couldn't say yes fast enough.

There's a video that shows me bringing Nasirov over to Trump, introducing them, them shaking hands and them exchanging a few words. Nasirov's mind was blown.

It was exactly what I wanted. By just casually strolling up to Trump and introducing a stranger to him, it was obvious that Trump knew me well and valued me enough to pay some attention to the person I had brought (even though he represented Ukraine, a country Trump, at the time, wanted abso-

lutely nothing to do with).

I was confident that Nasirov — who was still reeling from the moment hours later — would take word of my status as a member of Trump's inner circle back to Kyiv with him.

With the meal and the speeches behind us, people began to mingle. And by mingle, I really mean throwing ourselves

Nasirov was more than a little surprised that I could just walk up to Trump and introduce them.

into a scrum to get a moment with Trump. All of the media who surrounded the resort, but were not allowed inside, saw me with Nasirov, but nobody thought much of it at the time. It wouldn't be for years that either he or I would be well known among the American public.

As the inauguration drew nearer, many Democrats were still smarting over the loss and more than a few pointed accusatory fingers at Russia as the reason. Among them was Obama. He amended his Executive Order 13964 (which applied sanctions to certain foreign nationals) to include those who interfered with U.S. elections. With the weight of overwhelming evidence on his side, sanctions were applied to the GRU (the Russian foreign intelligence unit), the FSB (the security service, an extension of the notorious KGB), three spy software companies, the top five men at the GRU and two hackers.

Although Foreign Minister Sergey Lavrov called for immediate action, even revenge, Putin issued a December 29, 2016 statement that said:

"Although we have the right to retaliate, we will not resort to irresponsible 'kitchen' diplomacy but will plan our further steps to restore Russian-US relations based on the policies of the Trump Administration."

Trump answered him the following day with a Twitter post that read: "Great move on delay (by V. Putin) - I always knew he was very smart!" It's notable that he suggested that Russia was merely delaying their retaliation and not calling it off.

A few days later, agents from Mossad, the Israeli intelligence service, held a conference with their CIA counterparts in Langley, Virginia. Just as the meeting was adjourning, Israeli journalist Ronen Ban wrote, an unnamed CIA bigwig told the guys from Mossad that Putin had "leverages of pressure" on Trump and that any secrets shared with him would make their way to the Kremlin and, from there, Iran, a bitter enemy of Israel. "Be careful," he told them, after the inauguration on January 20.

By that time, many important people in the U.S. considered the Russian meddling and possible collusion with the Republicans to be an open secret. But the incoming administration did their best to dissuade the public of those fears. On January 15, 2017, Vice-President-elect Mike Pence appeared on CBS' Face the Nation and Fox News Sunday to say that Team Trump had no connection to any Russians. Similarly, outgoing RNC chair Reince Priebus appeared on NBC's Meet the Press that very morning and said that it was actually the Clinton campaign who had colluded with the Ukrainians to help sway the election. He offered no evidence to back up his claims. That had become business as usual for Republicans.

Just before the inauguration, many Republicans were still lying about their involvement with Russia. For example, incoming Attorney General, Jeff Sessions, swore that he had not had any dealings with Russians during the Trump campaign — when he was a senior member of the Armed Services Committee and one of Trump's primary foreign policy advisers — despite concrete evidence of him having at least two meetings with Sergei Kislyak, the longtime Russian ambassador to the U.S. Similarly, Kushner — soon to become a major player in the regime — did not mention his trips to Russia, including going into Putin's office with Ivanka, when he applied for White House clearance.

In mid-January, I got an urgent call from Ballard about the inauguration. He told me that getting Nasirov in was no problem, but Mansimov had failed his clearance check. He was just too controversial to deal with, Ballard told me (and would later be imprisoned in Turkey on terrorism charges).

I reminded Ballard that his next big payday depended on keeping Mansimov happy and showing him how much access and control Ballard really had in Washington.

Ballard said he'd see what he could do.

And he pulled it off. About ten days before the inauguration, I got a call from Ballard. He told me had worked his "magic" and managed to get Mansimov into the inauguration.

Mansimov was impressed. So much so that he bragged to an important friend in the Turkish government, Foreign Minister Mevlüt Çavuşoğlu, about being invited to the inauguration as a special guest. The foreign minister said

he'd be there too and wanted to meet Ballard. Not only was he aware that the inauguration was a hot ticket — hard for anyone to get — but also that Mansimov wasn't likely to be at the top of any guest list in D.C. Clearly, this fellow, Ballard, must have moved heaven and Earth to accommodate Mansimov. Ballard was obviously a guy, they agreed, who could get things done. He told

Mansimov, left, was not only at the inauguration, he was just a few inches from the new President.

Mansimov that he wanted to meet this Ballard and discuss the Turkish-American relationship.

I called Ballard and let him know Çavuşoğlu wanted to meet with him and that we could see him at the inauguration.

At 1:33 p.m. the day before the inauguration's final speech, Ballard texted me to join him at 2:30 for lunch at the Watergate Hotel (of all places).

Mansimov and I met Ballard in the lobby and we walked into the restaurant together. There were a lot of bodyguards, Turkish bodyguards. They were there for Manimov's friend, Çavuşoğlu. Ballard had wanted foreign contacts, and I had delivered two heavyweights from unquestionably important countries. I was proud to have done my part of our agreements so quickly and effectively. I handed him Ukraine and Turkey on a silver platter.

All that was left for us to do, then, was to celebrate. The last party of the inauguration was a candlelight dinner for friends and big-money contributors at Washington's Union Station.

Ballard, clearly grateful for my work on his behalf, managed to get me some extra tickets. I wanted the kids to be on hand to witness a historic moment from the reserved seats. Mansimov even flew them up from Florida in his private jet.

Although there were some audio troubles at the beginning of his speech, anyone who knew Trump had a good idea of what he said. He praised himself for his perseverance while overcoming overwhelming odds "I outworked anybody who ever ran for office," praised himself again by how big a win it was with "there were a lot of red states that weren't supposed to be red, that was some big victory … records were set that haven't been beaten since Ronald Reagan," he waxed hyperbolic about the product he was going to deliver, saying his cabinet would be "the likes of which has never been appointed" adding his suddenly less cheap seal of approval with "there's not a pick that I don't love, and if there was, I'd tell you right now" and he couldn't resist a chance to hate on his enemies, adding "the other side is going absolutely crazy."

The inauguration had been planned by two entities: the Joint Congressional Committee on Inaugural Ceremonies, as is always the case, and the 2017 Presidential Inaugural Committee, a tax-exempt nonprofit purpose-made organization.

The Inauguration Committee involved a who's who of Republican donors, including shale oil billionaire Harold Hamm, Las Vegas casino operators Sheldon and Miriam Adelson and Steve Wynn, film producer Diane Hendricks, coal tycoon Joe Craft and Woody Johnson, heir to the Johnson & Johnson fortune and owner of the New York Jets.

Many of them would hold positions in the Trump Administration, including Craft as ambassador to Canada and Johnson to the U.K.

The Committee would later get in trouble for providing inaccurate information on donors and for paying well over market norms for rooms at Trump hotels — a deal negotiated by Ivanka.

It also came under fire for allegedly spending $26 million of its $57 million budget paying WIS Media Partners, owned by Stephanie Winston

Wolkoff, a close friend of and advisor to Melania Trump. The Trumps wriggled out of it like they always seemed to and even tried to heap much of the blame on Wolkoff. In her book, Melania and Me: The Rise and Fall of My Friendship with the First Lady, Wolkoff gives her detailed and well-documented account of the spending, essentially clearing her name.

But, before all of that would come to light, it was time to party — Republican style.

Although Trump himself had predicted "an unbelievable, perhaps record-setting turnout," Dr. G. Keith Still, an expert on crowd safety and crowd-risk analysis, estimated the attendance to be no more than one-third that of the 1.8 million at President Obama's first inauguration in 2009. Trump's new press secretary Sean Spicer announced that it was "the largest audience ever to witness an inauguration, period, both in person and around the globe." Neither claim is true. To back it up, they released poorly altered photos with extra people added, allegedly at Trump's personal demand.

Chapter 9
The Big Show

At the inauguration, Nasirov, Mansimov and I were nothing short of ecstatic to watch our guy become President. For me, it was because I was friends with Trump. I'm sure that Nasirov and Mansimov had their own reasons.

It was a time of immense celebration for Trump fans everywhere, but nowhere more than Washington, Ground Zero. And, at every event, there I was. As VIPs, Svetlana and I lived in a penthouse at the Ritz-Carlton and were invited to all of the events. Still in awe of the dizzying heights at which I was now a denizen, I took pictures or videos of absolutely everything. There were ceremonies to witness, parties to attend and dinners to go to.

Each one of those events meant more people — important people, people with money. I knew that I could use my magic to sell these people on my ideas. Finding investors had never been a real problem for me.

And, if you believe a whistle blower who sent a letter to Democratic Congressman Elijah Cummings, there was plenty more happening on Inauguration Day.

At about the time Trump was declaring the day of his inauguration to be known as the incredibly Soviet-sounding National Day of Patriotic Devotion, a young businessman showed his phone to another he had met that day. It said that their project was "good to go." Alex Copson, identified by the whistle blower as the one who celebrated the text, was clearly excited. So much so that he called it the "happiest day of his life."

The project involved a joint American-Russian team that was set to build dozens of nuclear powerplants in several Middle Eastern nations. The nuclear waste from them — which can be used to make nuclear weapons — was, according to the plan, to be securely transferred to the U.S. The plan had seemed doomed because it broke laws regarding sanctions against Russia and it almost guaranteed that the nuclear waste would be compromised, but — with Trump in charge — its constituents remained hopeful.

The text was from retired Lieutenant General Michael Flynn, who served as advisor to defense-related companies and had worked with Copson. Even though Flynn had been hired by Obama to be director of the Defense Intelligence Agency, he was a Trump man all the way. In fact, during the campaign, he was alleged to have promoted fictional anti-Clinton "news" stories. At the 2016 Republican Convention, he led the chants of "Lock her up!" while he was on stage to deliver a speech.

Turkey's Recep Erdoğan (Wikimedia Commons)

Flynn had formed, with his son, the Flynn Intel Group, whose business was to find intelligence for companies and countries. Two of his first clients were Russian — Volga-Dnepr Airlines, which primarily carries government officials, petroleum industry executives and important employees of Kaspersky Lab, a Russian cyberintelligence firm.

Flynn knew Russia quite well, and not the way you'd expect an American general to. He had been paid $55,000 to deliver a speech on behalf of the Russian state-owned broadcaster, RT. He even sat next to Putin — an enviable spot for many — when dinner was served. Flynn was even the first American ever allowed inside GRU headquarters for any reason.

He had cheered on the coup attempt in Turkey in the summer of 2016, two months later, he was speaking on the government's behalf. In between, he was paid $530,000 by BV Inovo, a Netherlands-based petroleum exploration company owned by Turk Kamil Ekim Alptekin, to lobby in D.C. Ekim Alptekin had close ties to Erdoğan, the target of the coup plotters. Flynn also wrote an editorial published by The Hill that called Turkey a "vital" ally and said that the media had unfairly characterized the country's "crackdown on dissidents." At the same time, Erdoğan was preparing to dissolve Turkey's parliamentary government and assume full, unquestioned power. He called it "the most important governmental reform of our history"

At the time of the inauguration, Flynn was candidate Trump's choice for National Security Advisor (NSA), although Obama warned him that it was a bad idea. It was only then that Flynn registered as a foreign agent, about three months after he had started his job for Turkey.

Flynn had worked with Copson previously and, according to the whistle blower, assured him that sanctions against Russia would be "ripped up" — allowing his project to move forward.

Even if the whistle blower's recollection of the day was not completely accurate, it illustrates the prevailing feeling that day. Executives were sure that regulations (even sanctions) would be lifted with Trump in office, allowing them to make money with fewer limitations.

One of those businessmen was me. I realized what an opportunity the new administration would be for me. After all, I knew people on both sides of the Atlantic who — just like the people in Igor's bars — were dying to meet one another. I would be the catalyst.

Still enthralled by the whole Trump phenomenon, I didn't know who Flynn even was and flat-out refused to believe that the Russians had anything to do with Trump's upset win. I believed that talk of cheating on the part of the Trump campaign was sour grapes from the Democrats, who were surprised by and angry at their loss. Millions agreed with me and Putin would state the same opinion not much later.

Besides, I knew Trump considered me a friend, at least an ally, by the time he was in office. He wouldn't do something like cheat on the election, I thought. I was also aware of the fact that Trump and Putin didn't know each other, so how could they collaborate on such a colossal project while keeping it secret from the entire world? Where would they even find the time? Back then, I didn't think the Russians had anything to do with the 2016 Election. I thought we'd won on our own, that the country supported us.

I took some time out to call Ballard, who was becoming a celebrated name around Washington already. For years, he had been a big-time lobbyist down in Tallahassee and he had finally broken through to Washington with Trump. But it wasn't because he was good at predicting election outcomes. When the 2016 Presidential Election loomed, he threw his support (and money) behind former Florida Governor Jeb Bush. When Bush's campaign started sputtering, Ballard defected to Rubio. It was only after Rubio started to nose dive that Ballard began to back Trump.

Still, it was paying major dividends and the arrow beside his name was definitely pointing up. I knew he'd be able to help me put our connections together.

After the inauguration, I returned to Florida. Immediately, my contacts led me to another major player. Mansimov put me in touch with Farkhad

Akhmedov, a well-connected Azerbaijani-Russian oligarch. Like many wealthy people over there, he got that way while being a friend of Putin's.

Akhmedov had helped with some diplomatic communications between Turkey and Russia. To me, that meant access to all kinds of valuable contacts in both countries. And, just as Ballard had Trump's ear, so Akhmedov is said to have had Putin's as well as Erdoğan's.

Two days after the inauguration, Akhmedov parked his yacht in Miami. He was vacationing with his pregnant girlfriend and she went into labor. I'm not sure if they had planned to stop there, I never asked.

When knowledge of Akhmedov's arrival in Florida came to him, Mansimov assigned me with the duty of entertaining the oligarch. Not very long after, I was on Akhmedov's yacht. Wealthy guys love nothing more than to boast about their boats, but this guy had them all beat. The Luna was a 377-foot monster with three tenders. I had heard that the Luna was armed with surface-to-air missiles, but I never saw anything like that. It wasn't a bad gig for me to be on the boat. I mean, there were 70 people on staff, four chefs, every toy in the book.

On Mansimov's dime, of course, I made Akhmedov's trip to the U.S. a memorable one. He liked to gamble and live the high life, so I took him to the Seminole Hard Rock Hotel & Casino in Hollywood, Florida. He loved it.

On nights when we weren't there, and sometimes even when we were, Akhmedov and I could be found at E11EVEN Miami, which bills itself as a "high-energy social playground and landmark destination with world-class service and entertainment." Akhmedov seemed to really enjoy himself there, especially when he could evoke reactions to throwing around money, sometimes literally.

On one particularly adventurous weekend, I took Akhmedov to a friend's hunting lodge in northwest Florida in search of wild boars and alligators to shoot. Akhmedov managed to bag a couple of gators and was so delighted, he had them made into cowboy boots.

And, in quieter times, we'd just hang out on the Luna, play backgammon and talk.

Akhmedov had been upset on his arrival — his wife, Tatiana, was threatening divorce. But he cheered up when he was with me.

And I looked forward to seeing him. I liked the way I was being treated by this mega-billionaire, who appeared to consider me to be a big deal, truly important. The Americans I dealt with were polite enough, but I could tell that they thought I was just some fast-talker from Brooklyn.

More important, I had found what might have been my calling in life. Through my many experiences in Brooklyn, Russia, Wall Street, L.A. and Florida, I had developed the expertise to deal with people like Akhmedov. I knew I had to be able to use that for a major financial gain somehow.

With another, perhaps even more powerful, oligarch in my fold, I invited Ballard to come meet him.

When Ballard showed up at the yacht, he had — as he usually did — Lukis with him. I noticed that Ballard was somewhat timid when he first met Akhmedov, and that Lukis did most of the talking. But as time went on, I began to see Ballard acting much more natural and relaxed with our wealthy, powerful friend.

After Akhmedov left, I spoke with Ballard about him many times. On a trip to Florida, Ballard took me out for dinner at the Miami Ritz-Carlton. Ballard seemed to me to be thrilled about my efforts.

My commission could not come soon enough. My separation from Hudson Holdings had become acrimonious and led to a lawsuit, and my legal bills were stacking up. At about the same time, doctors found a tumor on Svetlana's hip. It would need to be removed, but my surprise departure from Hudson Holdings had terminated our health insurance.

It was funny, to be scratching for every dime, but also living a life of utter luxury at the same time because of my wealthy connections. My bills were piling up, I was even getting eviction notices, but I always put on a smile and a brave face with these wealthy people. Like my Uncle Butch told me: "If you're broke you're a joke." His advice was to never let anyone know about your financial problems.

I didn't know it at the time, but I didn't really have a choice in the matter. These guys, through their sophisticated security, knew everything about me and my situation. They knew I wasn't rich. But they wanted me for my skills and my contacts, not my money.

Chapter 10
Bosom Buddies

O ne of the first events that I was invited to after the election was
lunch at Mar-a-Lago. I had already begun to be familiar with the
Palm Beach resort and this lunch didn't seem like it was going to
be much more than a free meal and some photo ops.

It was then that I noticed that Rudy Giuliani was a fixture at Trump events; not just attending but also contributing, even claiming to speak on
Trump's behalf. I first saw him at Pereira's fundraiser and again a few times
in the Trump International in D.C. We had been introduced, but had never
actually exchanged anything more in-depth than a hello or a nod. I made a
mental note to try to get to know him better.

Like everyone else, I remembered Giuliani as the tough-talking mayor
who guided New York City adeptly after the 9/11 attacks. But I didn't know
Giuliani's back story. From East Flatbush in Brooklyn, he moved to Garden
City South, a quiet Long Island community, when he was 7. He earned his
Bachelor's degree in Political Science from Manhattan College and his JD
from NYU. His attendance allowed him to take an education deferment for
the draft, preventing him from going to Vietnam. For much of that time,
Giuliani considered becoming a priest.

In his youth, Giuliani was an outspoken Democrat who worked for Long
Island candidates, then 1968 Presidential candidate Robert F. Kennedy and
he had voted for very liberal George McGovern in 1972. He changed to an
Independent in 1975 and, a month after Ronald Reagan was elected in 1980,
he registered as a Republican.

Quickly, he went from a private-practice law firm to become Associate
Attorney General in the Reagan administration. After that, he became U.S.
Attorney for the Southern District of New York, which includes New York
City. He made his name prosecuting Wall Streeters, government officers and,
especially, the Mafia. But he only targeted the Italians. He let everyone else
do whatever they wanted.

Many believe he invented the "perp walk," in which the accused must walk past a crowd of media. He was developing a reputation, and not an entirely positive one. The same Spy magazine that referred to Trump as a "short-fingered vulgarian" called Giuliani the "toughest weenie in America."

His mayoral career — particularly after 9/11 — is well documented and earned him not only Time's Person of the Year but an Honorary Knighthood from Queen Elizabeth II. He would later also run for Senate and President, not achieving either.

As soon as the Trump train began rolling, Giuliani was aboard. Trump reportedly made their relationship clear early. New York Times reporter Maggie Haberman wrote that, while aboard one of Trump's private jets, Trump made it a point to "loudly complain" about "the odor after Giuliani had used one of the plane's bathrooms. When the other passengers laughed, Trump added: "Rudy! That's fucking disgusting!"

Still, Giuliani always spoke flatteringly on behalf of Trump at every campaign stop, extolling his virtues and defending him from the many, often quite serious, accusations thrown his way.

Stumping for Trump meant criticizing Obama, which Giuliani did with visible gusto. At an August 2016 Trump speech on foreign policy, Giuliani, who spoke before him, told the partisan crowd: "Before Obama came along, we didn't have any successful radical Islamic terrorist attack in the United States." That, of course, ignored 9/11 — the event that made him world famous — which happened under the George W. Bush Administration, as were other successful attacks in the U.S. by Islamic fundamentalists.

Trump might not have treated Giuliani with the utmost respect, but they went back a long time.

The relationship between politicians and media in New York is contentious. Not "can be contentious" is it is in other cities, it always is. And it has been for a long, long time.

To help relieve some of the tension, at the beginning of the 20th Century, reporters on the City Hall beat banded together to form a group called the Amen Corner, which would put on an annual charity dinner show. In it, they would poke fun at local politicians. Its success and the desire to include national politicians, morphed the group into The Inner Circle in 1922. The tradition continued, and in 1997, it was a boisterous affair at the Hilton. Giuliani was mayor.

He'd lost to David Dinkins in 1989, when his campaign theme was a dire threat that the city would be "dragged down" by unnamed unsavory elements if he wasn't elected. He ran again in 1993 and echoed Trump at the time, calling for the city to get tougher on crime (the crime rate had actually been falling already, but some violent events, usually exaggerated by Trump's hyperbolic rhetoric, that made headlines gave the impression to many that the opposite was happening).

He made a not-quite-tacit accusation that Dinkins supporters might cheat when Giuliani's team hired off-duty cops and jail guards to "monitor polling places" in Democratic areas. Giuliani claimed the move was to defend against voter fraud.

He won a second term in 1997 (something that hadn't happened in New York City since 1941) by emphasizing his toughness on crime. Many believed he was exactly the macho man the city needed to keep gangsters, muggers and "squeegee men" off the streets.

So, a perhaps unprecedented number of jaws dropped when the crowd first saw Rudina. At the 1997 Inner Circle roast, Rudy walked on stage, according to The New York Times, "in high heels, a full-figured spangled pink gown, a platinum-blond wig and several pounds of makeup." To some, it made sense. Rudy (or, more likely, his handlers) was just lampooning his tough-guy image and helping to promote Victor/Victoria, a musical comedy that lampoons with gender stereotypes that was playing on Broadway.

Drag performances were hardly rare or frowned upon in New York at the time, but it just seemed incongruent with Rudy's persona. After he sang a falsetto version of Marilyn Monroe's Happy Birthday, Mr. President, many attendees were visibly uncomfortable. "I'm supposed to have a meeting with him in a few days," an anonymous City Council official told The New York Times. "I don't know if I can go through with it."

Giuliani later appeared in drag on NBC's Saturday Night Live, but without sexual overtones.

When it came time for the 2000 Inner Circle show, most people regarded Rudina to be a one-off and part of the past. She wasn't.

Giuliani performed as Rudina on video with his celebrity friend, Donald Trump. In it, Rudina is in a run-of-the-mill department store, trying on different perfumes. Trump shows up and compliments her on her looks. He suggests a different scent and sprays it on her without asking. Overcome with passion, Trump then stuffs his face in between Rudina's prosthetic breasts, effectively motorboating the mayor. Rudia then slaps the 54-year-old real estate developer, calls him a "dirty boy" and walks off in a huff. At the end, a seemingly distraught Trump shrugs and says: "You can't say I didn't try."

Although the video did make some in the live audience (including the Clintons, who were the butt of many other jokes) appear nervous, it didn't get even the slightest mention in major media at the time.

Since, it's been trotted out frequently, usually to highlight Trump's many accusations of sexual impropriety, including rape.

But it might actually say more about Giuliani. Rudina appears to be in awe of the presidency and Trump clearly did his close friend a potentially embarrassing favor by appearing in the video with Giuliani's alter ego. They actually were that close. When Giuliani's son, Andrew, was hired as an Associate Director of the White House Office of Public Liaison, Giuliani described Trump as being like his uncle (which was a term all of us in Brooklyn used to describe important mobsters who were close to us).

The fact that Trump and Giuliani seem to find involuntary sexual touching to be fodder for laughs says something about them both.

In the late 1980s, Trump was an outspoken activist against crime in New York City, often using his own money to buy advertising space to make his draconian opinions public. The most well known of his crusades occurred after five young black and Hispanic men were arrested in the 1989 "Central Park Jogger" case in which runner Trisha Meili, who is white, was beaten, raped and left for dead.

Trump bought a full-page ad in The Daily News with a huge, all-cap headline that read: "BRING BACK THE DEATH PENALTY." In the body text, he fumed: "I want to hate these murderers and I always will. I am not looking to psychoanalyze or understand them, I am looking to punish them."

One of the young men arrested, Yusuf Salaam, said his family received several death threats after the ad ran.

The youths were found guilty and sent to prison. In 2001, another man admitted to the crime and the Central Park 5 were exonerated, after they had already completed their sentences. Well after that, President Trump was asked about the ad and responded that he hadn't changed his mind, indicating that he still believed them to be guilty. Salaam, incidentally, has since been elected to city council.

While Trump's decision to publish the ad might well have come from a sincere reaction to what he perceived as an injustice, there is no doubt that it helped Giuliani's 1989 campaign, which was based on getting tougher against crime. In an election decided by just 47,080 votes, many in local media believed that Trump delivered the win.

So, when Trump could use a boost in 2016, Giuliani was there to deliver. Not only was he probably returning the favor, he was also helping an old friend attain the post he was most in awe of, the presidency. Besides, as I also believed, knowing the President was good for business.

One of the things that surprised me about Giuliani was that after serving as a prosecutor, Mayor of New York and in private practice for decades, he always needed money. Not a few bucks till payday, but he needed real money. He'd constantly be hitting people up for money-making ideas.

It just didn't make any sense to me. I'd been through money troubles of my own. I thought that Giuliani must be loaded. He was world famous, after all.

Giuliani's financial troubles first appeared in public consciousness back in 2000, before he was world famous. The missteps that affected his assets often had to do with his romantic relationships. He was running for a senate seat in 2000 against heavily favored Hillary Clinton. When he called a media conference to be held on May 10 in Bryant Park, many thought it would be about something inconsequential. It wasn't.

Before a crowd of media, supporters and the curious, Giuliani announced that he was leaving his wife of 16 years, Donna Hanover. Nobody was more surprised by the news than Hanover. Giuliani went on to announce his diagnosis with prostate cancer.

Fortunately, he said, he had his "very good friend" Judith Nathan, who he would turn to "more now than maybe I did before."

After the conference Hanover talked to the media at Gracie Mansion, the mayor's residence. "Today's turn of events brings me great sadness. I had hoped to keep this marriage together," she said. "For several years, it was difficult to participate in Rudy's public life because of his relationship with one staff member."

Less than two weeks later, Giuliani ended his senate campaign. In 2003, he married Nathan.

But as the divorce proceedings went on, Hanover's lawyer, Raoul Felder, revealed to the media that Giuliani had just $7,000 to his name, despite his $195,000 salary and the couple's two Upper East Side co-ops.

Giuliani's fortunes changed after 9/11. He was to receive a $3 million book advance. He formed Giuliani Partners, a consultancy firm, and one of his first assignments was a $4.3 million deal to help teach Mexico City officials how to reduce their nearly intolerable crime rate. He booked speaking engagements at $100,000 to $200,000 an event.

In September 2004, Russia was reeling from the Beslan school siege. In it, a terrorist group believed to be Chechen separatists took over a school, taking more than 1,000 hostages. An overwhelming Russian military response that included tanks and attack helicopters ended the crisis. But it appeared by many to be driven more by the idea of slaughtering the terrorists than freeing the hostages, regardless of collateral damage. In the end, 333 hostages (most killed by their would-be rescuers, more than half of the victims children) and 32 terrorists were dead.

With the deaths of so many hostages, Russians were angry, but not at their government. Many Russians sought even tougher measures, laws not just against terrorists, but against all Chechens, including banning them from Russian cities. "We showed ourselves to be weak," Putin said. "And the weak get beaten."

It was natural then to invite Giuliani — hero of 9/11 and scourge of all criminals — for a visit.

Along with him were two armed security guards and Ken Kurson, Deputy Director of Communications for Giuliani Partners. Kurson, who later became editor of Kushner's New York Observer, recounted the trip in 2017. He said that Giuliani "was conscious of the threat of espionage," instructing Kurson to act as though he was always being listened to.

But that was hardly Giuliani's first brush with the former USSR. One of the most generous donors to his campaigns was Semyon "Sam" Kislin, a Ukrainian émigré, who had become wealthy in import/export. But, the FBI said he was a "member/associate" of Vyacheslav Ivankov's gang, which ran the Russian Mafia in Brooklyn. He was assassinated in Moscow in 2009. And in 1999, the Center for Public Integrity accused Kislin of laundering money for Uzbekistan-born Mikhail "Michael" Chernoy, who shares ownership of a Moscow house with Igor Putin, Vladimir's cousin. Chernoy has never been convicted of any crime. Kislin was also described as "Trump's old friend" by Leonid Nor, the vice president of the Odessan diaspora office in Brooklyn. Kislin served on Giuliani's Council of Economic Advisors.

After Trump won, many in media believed that Giuliani would be made Secretary of State, since he had been working in so many countries. He definitely wanted the job, but he never got it. Rudy asked to be made Secretary of State three times, and Trump always said no. He thought Rudy didn't have enough experience overseas.

Instead, just before the inauguration, Trump said that Giuliani was his cybersecurity adviser. It was an informal, nebulous title and probably not a very good one. In one of his many demonstrations of a lack of a grasp on technology and related security, Rudy famously asked employees at a San Francisco Apple Store to help him because he forgot his phone's password "and entered the wrong one at least 10 times," one of the store's employees told NBC News. That exposed official files to unvetted Apple Store employees who could have shared any of his data with anyone.

Giuliani was also known to butt-dial people and, on at least two occasions, the calls were to reporters. In the fall of 2019, an NBC News reporter let a call go to voice mail, and inadvertently recorded a three-minute rant by Giuliani about Ukraine and the Bidens. Another voice can be heard on it. The recording ends with Giuliani asking about someone named Robert, is told he's in Turkey, then complains that he needs more money. NBC News speculated that Robert was Robert Mangas, who worked with Giuliani at a law firm and has ties to the Turkish government, but it wasn't. It was Robert Stryk, a lobbyist with ties to Trump.

Although nobody ever mentioned it to me, Giuliani told The Washington Post that he had clients in Brazil and Colombia, among other countries. That potential conflict-of-interest problem would make it even more difficult for him to ever serve as Secretary of State.

But that wouldn't stop him from carrying out his shadow diplomacy.

Chapter 11
In Like Flynn

E ven before I had become very close with Giuliani, I could tell that I was something of a hot commodity at the RNC party. While we were there, Svetlana and I spoke with many important people, including RNC chief Ronna McDaniel Romney, who was there with her mother, Ronna Romney. I had clearly entrenched myself in the political big time.

Ballard was eager to impress Akhmedov. I told Ballard to invite him to the RNC spring retreat in March. Adding to the lure, I mentioned that it was being held at the five-star Four Seasons Resort Palm Beach, just a ten-minute drive down Ocean Boulevard from Mar-a-Lago. In fact, Trump would be hosting a dinner and speech with VIPs at his resort. The media would not be allowed in. And it wouldn't be difficult to reserve a place for him.

Akhmedov agreed that he would like to go. Of course, Ballard said he'd make it happen.

As a megadonor, I was already on pretty much every guest list and Ballard easily could get me on any I wasn't. Never one to back away from a camera, I appeared in thousands of pictures. Later, Giuliani would say I was like Zelig — the guy from the Woody Allen movie who shows up in photos of every important historical event. He was right. No matter who the photo was of, if it was important, I'd be there, often somewhere in the background.

I met several people at the Florida lunch, but none I considered more important than Steve Wynn. A massive donor to the Republican Party and its individual candidates, he had been named vice-chairman of Trump's Inaugural Committee. Wynn had made his sizable fortune with casinos in Macao, Las Vegas and Massachusetts (he came by it honestly, his parents operated bingo parlors on the East Coast).

Wynn, with his leathery perma-tan and dyed hair, certainly looked the way I had come to associate with the modern class of rich Republicans. Still, he was a very pleasant guy who I got along with well. Wynn liked to hear about my early days — he had grown up in relative luxury in Connecticut and Upstate New York — and never bored of my stories about the streets of Brooklyn or the bizarre settings of the former Soviet Union.

His side of the conversation was mostly about his wealth, which he would constantly compare to other swells I knew or at least had heard of. It reminded me of Mansimov and all the other oligarchs. If I would mention a name, Wynn would half-joke that his yacht — the 302-foot, seven-cabin

Aquarius, which featured a helicopter landing pad, a gym, a beauty salon, a bar with an adjacent dance floor and a glass-bottomed pool — was bigger and much better than the other guy's. I silently congratulated myself for knowing exactly how to talk to these personalities, the wealthy.

Wynn and I became close friends very quickly.

I have a picture of Wynn standing with his arms around both me and Akhmedov. We were clearly having a good time.

After he had been appointed as the RNC finance chairman, Wynn and I had dinner at The Forge in Miami, a restaurant that was said to be popular with organized crime figures and was the site of the 1977 murder of gangster Craig Teriaca by Richard Schwartz, Meyer Lansky's stepson, over who would pay a $10 bar bill.

At the Republican get-together, Trump gave a speech to donors at Mar-a-Lago. In it, he complimented himself, made it clear that he would stump for Republican candidates in the 2018 mid-term elections and, of course, he asked for more money.

Trump tried to keep the mood light. "I'm going to entertain you," he announced. In the opposite of a roast, the host made jokes at the expense of the guests. He saved one zinger for Wynn, saying that he "arrived late." That was a clear reference to the fact that he had supported Marco Rubio for the Republican nomination, but had switched to Trump at the last minute.

Meanwhile, the investigation into Russian involvement in the election heated up. At the end of the first week of the administration, acting Attorney General Sally Yates met with White House Counsel Donald McGahn about

Russia, Flynn and Pence. First, she told McGahn about a post-investigation report she had received from the FBI stating that Flynn had been "untruthful" in his statements about his interactions with Kislyak and other Russians and that fact could make him vulnerable to blackmail. "We believed that General Flynn was compromised," she would later testify at a Senate hearing. "To state the obvious, you don't want your national security adviser compromised with the Russians."

Yates also told him that the report said that Pence and other White House representatives had lied to the public by saying that Flynn's meetings with Russians were not about easing U.S. sanctions. "We began our meeting telling him that there had been press accounts of statements from the Vice-President and others that related to conduct that General Flynn had been involved in that we knew not to be the truth," she said. "The vice president was unknowingly making false statements to the American public, and General Flynn was compromised by the Russians."

On the following day, Yates brought up the subject of their meeting to McGahn. According to White House officials, McGahn told her that he had talked about her concerns with the President, but that they had decided that it was not a pressing issue.

There's a reason for that — Trump didn't do it. I'm not denying that the Russians meddled in the 2016 election, nor that they favored the Republicans, especially after Trump won their candidacy. But it is my sincere belief that Trump had no part of it, the Russians did it because he would be willing to help them with their own plans (which he did). Trump was probably unaware that it was even going on at the time. His ego wouldn't allow him to believe that anyone helped him win — he was sure he'd won it by himself. Remember, he actually believes all those things he says about himself. He'd always get so angry whenever the subject came up because he was being blamed for something he didn't do, usually he did do it.

On the same day that Yates spoke with McGahn about the issue — January 28, 2017 — Trump, surrounded by new White House heavyweights, took calls from foreign leaders, including Putin. It was the first time the two men actually spoke to one another, after years of flirting.

According to the White House, the call lasted about an hour, they spoke about several subjects, including Ukraine, before Putin congratulated Trump and wished him luck. Much of the call, according to several accounts, had been about repairing the Russia-U.S. relationship, which both leaders agreed had been damaged by the Obama administration.

Afterward, Trump also announced that the two countries would "work together" to fight terrorism. Secretary of Defense Jim Mattis disagreed, saying that the U.S. military had no plans to collaborate with the Russians.

Yates was fired on January 30, officially for insubordination related to Trump's Executive Order widely known as the "Muslim Ban."

I wasn't surprised that she went down. Like the rest of the Trump faithful, I believed that the Muslim Ban was blown way out of proportion by the other side. It was a complicated idea that many opponents had simplified to match their own opinions and goals, we all agreed. Executive Order 13769 wasn't a ban on Muslims entering the country, it just suspended the U.S. Refugee Admissions Program for 120 days, suspended the entry of Syrian refugees indefinitely and suspended entry to anyone from Iran, Libya, Somalia, Sudan, Syria, Yemen or Iraq (Iraq was later dropped), unless the applicant had a pressing reason. At the time, it seemed fair to many Americans who feared attacks by Islamic fundamentalists that Trump kept bringing up but, in reality, had actually happened very infrequently.

After Flynn left, Trump took a briefing on counter-terrorism from FBI Director James Comey and others, much of it relating to Russian interference in the election. Comey later said that the President took him aside as the meeting was adjourning and said, about the Flynn investigation: "I hope you can let this go."

That might not have been as sinister as it sounds. I spent a lot of time with the man. Trump had much more of his agenda he wanted to push as President. He resented spending precious time fighting against something he hadn't done. Although I didn't see it as an excuse, I had very quickly come to the conclusion that Trump was not aware of how things worked for Presidents. He was still acting the same way he did in New York, making deals, pushing people around and always expecting lawyers to take care of anything that came up against him. He had billed himself as an outsider and he really was. Maybe too outside.

White House Chief of Staff Reince Priebus then asked Andrew G. McCabe, Deputy Director of the FBI, to officially deny reports that associates of Trump's — clearly, he meant Flynn — had been in regular communication with Russian agents. He said no.

In no surprise to me, someone did deny that members of the government met with the Russians regarding sanctions. At his first press conference regarding the subject, Trump did it himself. Many of the questions in the 74-minute event focused on Trump's staff and their contacts with Russians.

When asked specifically if any of his campaign staff had any dealings with Russia, he angrily answered: "Nobody that I know of. How many times do I have to answer this question? Russia is a ruse. I have nothing to do with Russia. Haven't made a phone call to Russia in years." Then, when asked about his own communications with Russia, said: "I own nothing in Russia, I have no loans in Russia, I don't have any deals in Russia. Russia is fake news."

In fact, the President — looking excited and angry — spent much of the press conference undermining faith in the press, pointedly after he was asked about Flynn or Russia. "I have never seen more dishonest media, frankly than the political media. ... The news is fake because so much of the news is fake," he yammered. He later added:

> "Tomorrow, they will say: 'Donald Trump rants and raves at the press. I'm not ranting and raving. I'm just telling you. You know, you're dishonest people. But — but I'm not ranting and raving. I love this. I'm having a good time doing it."

He had been used to pushing around the society columnists at New York's tabloids, sometimes even under a fake persona, but seemed surprised that he didn't have that same power with political reporters. Trump truly seemed surprised that there were any limits to what a President could do.

Operating under the belief that the media had been treating Trump unfairly on behalf of the Deep State that had been running the world in secret, I was in his cheering section. Many people, including me, believed that the Clintons were in cahoots with the clandestine network that Trump was trying to unmask and put a stop to.

Some who ascribed to the idea were from the political fringes. Dennis Kucinich — a former Mayor of Cleveland and a congressman who ran for President twice as a Democrat, but who was an unabashed fan of Trump's — was interviewed on Sean Hannity's Fox News show when the President was under fire in 2017 and shared his views as to why it was happening.

> "This isn't about one President, this is about the political process of the United States of America being under attack by intelligence agencies and individuals in those agencies, yes, as you said there might be good people in there, but there

are certain individuals who are lifers who want to be able to direct the policy of the country. And if the President stands in their way, whether it's a Democrat or Republican, they'll just try to run that person out."

"Let me just repeat what you said," Hannity responded. "You're saying President Trump is under attack by the Deep State intelligence community. Fair statement?"

"I believe that," Kucinich answered, adding:

"Not only that, Sean, it has to be pointed out in October of 2016, that same Deep State overrode the decision of President Obama and Secretary Kerry to come to an agreement with Russia to a ceasefire in Syria. They overrode it and launched an attack against a Syrian military base. So, this is a problem in our country. We've got to protect our nation here. People have to be aware of what's going on. We've got to stand up for America, this isn't about Democrat, Republican. This is about getting what's going on in the moment and understanding that our country itself is under attack from within."

When I entered the Trump universe, I began to believe in the Deep State. I had seen with my own eyes how the oligarchs had used their wealth and power to make veritable marionettes out of their politicians and keep law enforcement at arm's length. What, I thought, made America so different? I began to believe. With that, came the concept that the Clintons were the face of the Deep State and that Trump had taken it upon himself to expose and bring it all down. He'd show Americans who their real bosses were and lead the charge to put them in their place.

I also found that their was no escaping the philosophy in D.C. They all seemed to believe it, at least the Republicans. It was all they ever talked about unless something big happened — you couldn't avoid it.

Many Americans agreed with the idea of the Deep State or ascribed to even more severe versions of it. That helped form Trump's base.

On March 2, the House Intelligence Committee began an inquiry into allegations of Russian interference in the election because of Flynn's actions. The White House was scrambling when the Justice Department acknowledged that Attorney General-designate Jeff Sessions had also met with Russian Ambassador Kislyak twice, despite having no responsibilities or business interests with the country.

As that news spread, Trump claimed that he had "total" confidence in Sessions. A few hours later, however, Sessions recused himself from any investigations into allegations of Russian interference in the 2016 election.

Trump was furious at that. Sessions would further anger the President after he was confirmed in a narrow vote. He resigned as Attorney General, at Trump's request, in November 2018.

I never really liked Sessions. I considered him timid socially and just not very personable. Not my kind of guy.

Chapter 12
Talking Turkey

Flynn's actions might have been a major headache for Trump, but they had been advantageous for me, or so I thought. With both Russia and Turkey badly needing good press and friends in Washington, I was sure that Ballard would get rich on contracts from them.

And he did, but I didn't.

I was at home on May 11, reading the news on my phone when I came across a story with the headline: Amid Complicated Relations with U.S., Turkey Hires Longtime Trump Lobbyist Brian Ballard." The story said that Ballard's firm had just signed a $3.5 million contract with Turkey after adding it to the Dominican Republic and Albania on its roster of clients.

Ballard was making $125,000 a month on a contract that I delivered to him by introducing him to the right people and vouching for his abilities and connections with them.

Where was my cut? I was sure that Ballard owed me $25,000 a month and I was determined to get my part.

I called Ballard. I demanded to know where my commission was. I fulfilled my part of the deal and I wanted my money.

I spoke with Ballard several times and never did gain satisfaction. He told me that he had gotten his deal with Turkey on his own, through other connections he had there. I called bullshit. If he had his own people, why had he been so desperate to get to Akhmedov through me? And there was no way in hell that Erdoğan would have even seen such a deal if Mevlüt Çavuşoğlu, the Turkish Minister of Foreign Affairs hadn't signed off on it. And I had introduced Ballard to Çavuşoğlu and Akhmedov.

Ballard stuck to his narrative, but told me we could figure out something later on. You know, something for my efforts.

Mere days after our confrontation, another exploded. Erdoğan, now totally assured of continuing as Turkey's unquestioned leader, came to D.C. to meet Trump and Ballard.

There were many issues on the table — including the U.S. supplying Syrian Kurds with weapons while the Turks were bombing them and the status of two Turkish nationals in the U.S., Fethullah Gülen and Reza Zarrab — but many observers in the media opined that the Washington visit was an attempt by Erdoğan to get some international validation for his role as the nation's supreme leader.

Arriving at the Turkish ambassador's residence on May 16, 2017, Erdoğan's motorcade met with a group of protesters, some of who were displaying the flag of the PYD (Partiya Yekîtiya Demokrat or Democratic Union Party), a Syria-based Kurdish political party — one that is considered an enemy by Turkey. Erdoğan said that "extermination of the PYD" was on his government's agenda back in August 2016.

Videos quickly appeared on social media that seem to show a member of the Turkish security detail, known as the Police Counter Attack Team, speaking with Erdoğan in his limo, then running toward another security team member and saying something to him. After that, men in dark suits ran past the police officers who were there and began to punch and kick the protesters. The same videos show Erdoğan waiting in the car, watching.

After the brief melee, both sides were very vocal about what happened. Erdoğan claimed the bodyguards were protecting him from protesters who had provoked them and he was shocked when they were arrested by D.C. police.

Many saw it as a display of the kind of authoritarian rule they feared Trump might embrace. "They think they can engage in the same sort of suppression of protest and free speech that they engage in in Turkey," said Flint Arthur, who was at the event. "They stopped us for a few minutes ... but we still stayed and continued to protest Erdoğan's tyrannical regime."

After high-level meetings between Erdoğan and Secretary of State Rex Tillerson in May 2018, charges against the Police Counter Attack Team were dropped. However, in 2021, a court issued an amicus that determined that the bodyguards were indeed to blame for the incident.

I was sickened by the whole affair. I'd seen what can happen when authoritarian governments hold sway and now I was seeing it replayed on U.S. soil. I didn't make any connection with my work to help Turkey and the U.S. get closer and with Erdoğan's men beating up Americans. The security team did it over there all the time. This time, they did it over here.

As for the two men Erdoğan had been asking after — Zarrab and Gülen — one was likely to be welcomed home, the other would not be.

The FBI arrested Reza Zarrab in Miami in May 2016. He was charged on suspicion that he had circumvented U.S. sanctions on Iran, while performing money laundering and bank fraud.

Zarrab was a connected guy back home. Born in Iran, Zarrab moved to Turkey when he was just a toddler, he had acquired Turkish and Azerbaijani citizenship and made a colossal amount of money in shipping. His father had been close friends with Iran's former president, Mahmoud Ahmadinejad, and Zarrab's wife was a famous pop singer.

Zarrab first got in trouble during the Turkish Corruption Scandal of December 2013. While Erdoğan was in Pakistan, the government arrested 52 people in a gas-for-gold scheme with Iran. Zarrab was among them. Three of the arrested were sons of Turkish cabinet ministers and another was the son of Turkey's former top negotiator with the EU. And there was Zarrab, who was arrested after his chauffeur, Turgut Happani, was caught with more than $150 million in cash (pictures of which he ill-advisedly posted on Facebook).

Erdoğan railed against the arrests, claiming that the accusations were part of an international conspiracy and the real target of the investigation was him because people were "jealous of his success." He openly vowed to take revenge upon Gülen, a Muslim cleric and leader of a centrist political movement, who he blamed for the arrests. Erdoğan then instructed the government to refer to him and his party as "terrorists."

A month later, Erdoğan claimed that the investigation was corrupt and fired 350 law enforcement officers, including the chief of Smuggling and Battle Against Organized Crimes Department. Due to the resulting lack of evidence, the arrested were then told that they were free to go.

Although accused in 2014 of attempting to overthrow the government with an "armed terrorist group," Gülen had not been prosecuted. After a 2016 coup attempt that resulted in the imprisonment of 90,000 people, Gülen was again blamed. He fled to the U.S. He now lives in Pennsylvania's Pocono Mountains and Turkey is still seeking his extradition despite his ill health and a lack of evidence.

Gülen's name was also familiar to many Americans because ex-CIA Director James Woolsey told The Wall Street Journal that he had been briefed on a meeting Flynn had with Çavuşoğlu and Erdoğan's son-in-law, Berat

Albayrak, who was then fighting allegations that he supplied oil to ISIS. The group, Woolsey said, discussed ways to remove Gülen from the U.S. and return him to Turkey, clearly against his will.

The Turks also met with Flynn in September 2016, shortly after the coup attempt. What happened in the meeting has not been disclosed to the public, but because of what he heard about the meeting from others who had attended, Woolsey resigned from the Flynn Intel Group's advisory board and turned down their offer of more consulting work.

But by the time the Woolsey story broke on February 13, Flynn had been fired by the Trump administration, just 23 days into the job.

Ballard and Flynn were not the only Trump allies talking to Turkey.

In February 2017, Giuliani, still known at the White House as their cybersecurity expert, traveled to Turkey with old pal Michael Mukasey, who had served as Attorney General under George W. Bush. They said that they had been retained by Zarrab and were speaking on his behalf, not either country's. They had Sessions' permission for the trip and had told Preet Bharara, the U.S. attorney in Manhattan, about it.

When The New York Times asked another one of Zarrab's lawyers what Giuliani and Mukasey were doing there, he answered: "Neither the government nor even the court most respectfully has the right to know precisely what their role[s] are or may be in the future." He said, sounding not at all defensive. "If the government has the temerity to even intimate that Messrs. Giuliani or Mukasey are engaging in any inappropriate conduct, then let them come out and say it," he added. And if that were the case, he asked, why would Giuliani have personally notified Mr. Bharara before the trip? And why would Mukasey have informed Attorney General Sessions of their efforts?"

I didn't know about the trip at the time, but found out later. I thought that it was part of the efforts to free an American clergyman who was being held by Turkey, Andrew Brunson.

Tommy Hicks — a Republican supporter who was friends with Don Jr. and whose father had been part of the abortive Giuliani-for-President campaign in 2008 — had made the detained man an issue of his.

Once made public, the meeting drew attention in no small part because both Erdoğan and Çavuşoğlu claimed that Zarrab was innocent and was being railroaded by the Americans. After Bharara stood firm, Erdoğan spoke to

U.S. officials about him, calling him "malicious" and a "pawn for anti-Turk-ish forces."

On the same day, Turkey opened an investigation on Bharara as their Justice Minister, Bekir Bozdağ, claimed that the case against Zarrab was yet another "coup attempt" against Erdoğan without explaining exactly how.

Giuliani met with Trump and Tillerson to brief them on the meeting. Trump asked Tillerson to get the case dropped. He said he wouldn't do it. Trump didn't want to go public with his opinion on Zarrab because, as he said, "I have a little conflict of interest" due to his Trump Towers in Turkey and who kept them a going concern.

There might have been more to Trump's rare reluctance to speak his mind. Trump admired Erdoğan for the same reasons he did Putin. They were strongman leaders who ruled their countries with iron fists and apologized to no one. He absolutely loved and respected that. Who cares about the people?

Trump had grown up with gangsters and tough guys all his life. So did I. To the young men growing up around them, their wealth, popularity and ab-ility to get away with anything made them role models, heroes even. Trump always had a problem, all he could respect was strength and winning. It was the whole Big Man idea, it shaped his personality. I also read somewhere that it might have had something to do with his father. I'm sure it did.

It would be one thing for Tillerson, who he considered an underling, to argue about Zarrab. But what if Erdoğan didn't like him anymore? He would find that outcome horrifying.

Trump fired Bharara (along with 45 other Obama-appointed U.S. at-torneys). Bharara's replacement, Joon H. Kim, wrote that the Turks "sought to meet other officials in the U.S. government." Kim also pointed out that Giuliani's law firm, Greenberg Traurig, and Mukasey's, Debevoise & Plimp-ton, represented banks that prosecutors alleged had suffered from Zarrab's actions, it could create even more possible conflicts.

When first questioned, Giuliani vociferously denied he'd been in any such meeting, then said that he "might have" after evidence that he had piled up. The following month, Giuliani wrote to the Department of Justice, saying that he believed that dropping the Zarrab case would be "part of some agreement between the United States and Turkey that will promote the national security interests of the United States." His desire to be Secretary of State seemed to be showing.

In November, Zarrab shook up the whole deal. In a Manhattan court room, he pleaded guilty and said that Erdoğan was behind the scheme — in which Turkey sent gold, through Chinese banks, to Iran for oil — along with Deputy Prime Minister Ali Babacan and Mehmet Hakan Atilla, deputy chief of Halkbank, the Turkish state-owned bank.

Earlier that year, Ballard had signed a deal to represent Halkbank in Washington that Open Secrets reported was worth $910,000 but I remembered as $1.5 million.

I was still looking for my 20 percent.

I'd never get it. After much haranguing, Ballard eventually relented and sent me $45,000 (two payments of $22,500 each). He made it clear to me that the money was in relation to the Halkbank deal and not the original contract with the Turkish government. Still, it was far less than 20 percent of what that deal was worth. Since I was in great financial need, I decided to take what I could get.

With Turkey in the U.S. media's eye, many outlets connected the dots between Flynn and Ballard, who were both very close to Trump's ear.

Turkey's Ambassador to the United States, Serdar Kılıç, was asked about the links the lobbyists shared with his country. He stressed that their communications had been legal. "Turkey has been working with a multitude of U.S. lobbying firms for decades. Contracts are naturally being constantly re-evaluated according to evolving needs and requirements," he answered. "Turkey's dealings with U.S. lobbying firms have always been in total agreement with U.S. legal requirements."

Chapter 13
Texas to Ukraine Express

Still smarting from the experience with Ballard and remembering how easy it is to get stiffed, I kept thinking about new business ideas. After much thought, I came to the opinion that the only way that we could make real money was through trading commodities, not helping other people do it.

Igor came to me with some possible deals, one involving the Ukrainian electrical grid and another with petroleum. Quickly, we reached the same conclusion. The best commodities were oil and gas. Everybody needs them. Like an addiction, nobody can quit them without suffering. And, some of the countries in which we had contacts — the U.S. and Russia — had lots to sell and others wanted to buy. We had to get in.

My idea was simple. We would take natural gas from the U.S. (West Texas has so much that they sometimes have to burn it just to get rid of it), liquefy it, put it in tankers, sail it to Poland and pipe it into Ukraine. If that sounds like something someone should have thought of before then, maybe they did. But to accomplish something like that requires a lot of people, a lot of friendly contacts. I knew people in America, I knew people in Ukraine, so I really thought I could make it happen. All I needed was for the right people to believe in the idea enough to devote their resources to it.

We decided to name our new company Global Energy Producers, LLC. We were unaware of Global Energy Capital LLC, that — as of 2024 — has pictures of both the U.S. Capitol and the Kremlin on its website and was founded by Trump foreign policy advisor Carter Page.

Now all Igor and I had to do was find some customers. Gas and oil deals are never small, so contacts with power were essential.

***

With the Zarrab debacle over, the Russia investigation was still very much on Trump's mind. He had put one of his favorites, former Trump

Media & Technology CEO and Chair of the House Intelligence Committee Devin Nunes, in charge of the investigation.

Nunes was abrasive and caustic. He was never nice to me, or anyone that I ever saw, really. He just seemed like a nasty guy.

At first, Nunes followed the party line. He denied the widespread belief that the U.S. intelligence community had evidence of contact between the Trump campaign and Russia. He also answered his critics by declaring a dearth of evidence and characterizing any investigation as a "witch hunt." He announced to the media "at this point, there's nothing there" and that Trump would not be releasing his tax returns.

He also characterized Flynn's talks with Russia to be anything but nefarious and that he would not investigate them. "From everything that I can see, his conversations with the Russian ambassador — he was doing this country a favor," he said, "and he should be thanked for it."

Putin then decided to make the situation a touch more complicated. At a joint press conference with far-right and increasingly authoritarian Prime Minister Viktor Orbán of Hungary (a NATO member), he first accused Ukraine of "posing as a victim of aggression" to extract money from the rest of Europe. Then Putin addressed the U.S. election.

> "As we all know, during the presidential campaign in the United States, the Ukrainian government adopted a unilateral position in favor of one candidate. More than that, certain oligarchs, certainly with the approval of the political leadership, funded this candidate, or female candidate, to be more precise. Now they need to improve relations with the current administration, and using a conflict to do so is always a better, easier way to draw the incumbent administration into addressing Ukrainian problems and thus establish a dialogue."

In essence, he claimed as fact that the Democrats used the same tactics that the Republicans had been accused of, with Ukrainians in place of Russians. As one D.C insider told me: "If you want to know what the Republicans are up to, just see what they are accusing the Democrats of." The difference was that those accusing Trump actually had evidence. Lots of it.

I was then so convinced of the war between Trump and the Deep State, I didn't doubt what Putin said. I knew the Clintons were against Trump, so I thought they were using Ukraine to set him up. I was also solidly of the belief that the Ukrainian government was corrupt beyond repair. My opinions had been nurtured by the billionaires and the politicians they'd bought. That didn't mean that Russia wasn't corrupt, or even that America wasn't inching closer to such a status as I watched from inside, just that Ukraine's government was really, really bad and what they had to say wasn't to be trusted. Besides, if Trump didn't fix things, I believed, the Deep State would just operate as usual. I'd picked his side.

After Trump falsely claimed that the Obama administration had been "wiretapping" his phones in Trump Tower, Nunes admitted that he had received information that the communications of "some members of Trump's transition team, including potentially the President himself" were "incidentally collected" by intelligence operatives. Further, that it had been "widely disseminated." He did say that the leaks were legal and "not related to Russia and the Trump transition team." They were.

Nunes was deeply criticized, even by old-school Republicans (by that point, Trump was already calling any Republicans who dared criticize him "RINOs," which stood for "Republicans In Name Only"). Many Democrats and much of the media accused Nunes of simply protecting Trump and not actually investigating. The top Democrat on the House Intelligence Committee, Adam Schiff, called for Nunes, as a once-and-perhaps-future Trump employee, to recuse himself from the investigation.

He refused at first, but relented on April 6. The House Ethics Committee then started an investigation of Nunes for potential ethics violations (the probe was dismissed in December).

Carter Page, who Trump told The Washington Post's editorial board was one of his primarty foreign policy advisers, admitted to the FBI that he had joined the Trump campaign to use his knowledge of, and contacts in, the former Soviet Union to help improve relations between the U.S. and Russia. Page is the founder and CEO of Global Energy Capital, a fund that focuses on oil exploration in Russia and other former Soviet nations. He had been questioned in relation to a Foreign Intelligence Surveillance Act warrant issued in 2014.

Page was an interesting guy and probably someone who did not belong in politics, at least not in foreign policy. As soon as his name started showing up in the media, there was a backlash. His former employer, Ian Bremmer of the Eurasia Group, called him "whackadoodle" on Twitter.

Russian relations expert Stephen Shestakovitch described Page as sympathizing with Putin and his position on the U.S. One unnamed official even called him "a brazen apologist for anything Moscow did." Indeed, Page appeared regularly in Russia media as an expert on relations with the U.S., often giving opinions that were more favorable to Putin than the Americans.

Further, convicted Russian spy Evgeny Buryakov testified that he had tried to recruit Page as an asset, with the aid of Igor Sporyshev. A recorded call between Viktor Podobny, a prominent Russian banker, and Sporyshev, who has also been charged with spying by the U.S., went like this:

> "[Male-1] wrote that he is sorry, he went to Moscow and forgot to check his inbox, but he wants to meet when he gets back. I think he is an idiot and forgot who I am. ... He got hooked on Gazprom thinking that if they have a project, he could rise up. I also promised him a lot ... This is intelligence method to cheat, how else to work with foreigners? You promise a favor for a favor. You get the documents from him and tell him to go fuck himself."

BuzzFeed News revealed that Male-1 was Page, And he said that what he handed over "did not include anything sensitive." Gazprom is Russia's state-owned oil and gas company.

According to the Mueller Report: "The investigation did not establish that Page coordinated with the Russian government in its efforts to interfere with the 2016 Presidential Election," they could not find "evidence or testimony about who Page may have met or communicated with in Moscow" and "Page's activities in Russia — as described in his emails with the [Trump campaign] — were not fully explained."

Once these revelations were made public, close Trump allies Nunes, presidential campaign communications director Jason Miller, Kellyanne Conway, Sean Spicer and even Trump himself all denied that Trump had ever met Page. In May 2016, Trump had personally told The Washington Post that he had named Page as one of his foreign policy advisers. Nunes later intimated on Sean Hannity's Fox News show that Page might have been working in secret for the Democrats (and, one can project, the Ukrainians), despite presenting no evidence to support that idea.

I was unaware of Page or his company with a name nearly identical to my own. People walked in and out of my professional life, If he wasn't a major player, I wouldn't have known him. He wasn't on my radar.

A few days after saying "the concept of Russia with respect to [the 2016 campaign] is a total phony story," Trump played host to Russian Foreign Minister Sergey Lavrov. Media were not allowed inside the meeting (as was becoming habitual with Trump), but sources close to it reported that the President told Lavrov that he was unconcerned about Russian interference in the election because the U.S. has interfered in other countries' elections in the past. More damning, Trump shared classified intelligence about ISIS with the Russians, despite it being very ill-advised to do so (even with America's allies). He is also said to have told them that he fired FBI Director James Comey specifically to take pressure from the Russian Collusion investigation off his back.

The FBI director had been a sore spot for the President since the first week of his term. On January 26, Priebus told Trump that Flynn was being investigated by the FBI about his ties to Russia.

The following day, Trump had dinner with Comey. Trump asked him to promise his "loyalty." Comey replied with a pledge of "honesty."

Under oath, Comey said that, on February 14, the President — in what appeared to have been a desperate measure coming the day after Flynn left his post — told him to back off from investigating Flynn. Mike Pompeo and Dan Coats said that they received the same order, but as Secretary of State and Director of National Intelligence, they felt they had the right to decline. But Comey's refusal got under Trump's skin so completely that, in March, the White House Counsels Office began writing a memo giving reasons for his dismissal months before it actually happened.

I was all for getting rid of Comey, who I did not trust. First he investigated Hillary, then he investigated Trump. Whose side was this guy on? I was so caught up in the partisan politics that I no longer had any concept of impartiality in government. Some of that probably came from my experiences on the streets of Brooklyn and in the former Soviet Union.

Relations with, and potential interference by, Russia and Ukraine were at or near the front of American political discourse in no small part because they were involved in a low-intensity war at the time. The Russians had annexed Crimea by force three years earlier and had armed pro-Russian paramilitary groups in the Donbas and Luhansk Oblasts (analogous to U.S. states). Most of the world was convinced that Russian soldiers were fighting there as well. Ukraine fought to try to regain their eastern territories. By the middle of February 2017, more than 10,000 people had died in the conflict and no end appeared to be in sight.

On February 17, Poroshenko delivered a speech at a security conference in Munich, warning the West not to engage in a policy of "appeasement" toward Russia. He picked the very word that had been famously used by British Prime Minister Neville Chamberlain, when he explained in 1938 why he would take no action against Hitler's Germany after its annexation of the Sudetenland, part of Czechoslovakia. Hitler used the guise of protecting the German-speaking minority there, eerily similar to Putin's own arguments about the Russian-speaking minority in Ukraine.

Chapter 14
Peace in Our Time

F lynn, still in Trump's favor, received a sealed document. It had been hand delivered to Trump's personal lawyer and longtime fixer Michael Cohen by my old pal, Felix Sater. It was an unsolicited peace plan for Ukraine and Russia that would result in the lifting of U.S. sanctions on Russia. Its authors ("amateur diplomats," The New York Times called them) were Sater and Andrii V. Artemenko. Artemenko described himself as one of Putin's "top aides," despite having held senior positions in Ukraine's government.

It was called the Rovt-Weldon Plan, after Republican Pennsylvania Congressman Curt Weldon and New York City real estate developer Alexander Rovt who he had introduced Andrii Artemenko to. Both had documented ties to Firtash.

Weldon, in fact, was a Moscow favorite. He sought to eli9minate sanctions of Russia and met with Alexander Bortnikov. head of the FSB and the Russian army's chief of staff, in Lubyanka, the notorious headquarters of the KGB on Felix Dherzinsky Square. Weldon also convinced Congress to send $97 million to Kremlin-backed IEG Group, which then emplyed Bortnikov. Weldon finally lost his seat in 2006 under suspicion in several investigations that included an FBI raid of his daughter's home. She had been hired by the Russian-owned gas company Itera International Energy Co. for $500,000 to do PR. After she started there, Weldon steered U.S. government contracts to Itera. Weldon was never charged with any crime.

Rovt, known as the Fertilizer Baron after becoming wealthy in that business in Russia, went into banking after he sold his fertilizer concerns to Firtash. Originally from the Carpathia region of what is now Ukraine, he lives in a reinforced concrete-and-brick house in Manhattan's Upper East Side that is reported to have bulletproof shades on the windows.

Artemenko was a former Mayor of Kyiv, a major critic of Poroshenko and just as big a fan of both Putin and Trump. He had been telling anyone who would listen that he had hard evidence of Poroshenko's corruption, but never presented it.

He had been so fawning in his praise of Trump that many Western media outlets have suggested that Artemenko saw himself as a Trump-like future President for Ukraine. He had never met Trump, but said that his wife was an old friend of Melania's from back in her modeling days.

He was known in Trump circles after he allowed Manafort and Kilimnik to use his private jet for a flight to Frankfurt.

Although Artemenko had been in Ukraine's parliament, he had no foreign policy experience.

Valeriy Chaly, Ukraine's Ambassador to the U.S., said that he was "not authorized to present any alternative peace proposal on behalf of Ukraine to foreign governments, including the U.S. administration."

Artemenko disagreed. "A lot of people will call me a Russian agent, a U.S. agent, a CIA agent," he said. "But how can you find a good solution between our countries if we do not talk?"

Artemenko said that he knew Cohen through Alex Oronov, a Ukrainian-born Manhattan art dealer with residences in Florida and on Long Island, whose niece Oksana was married to Cohen's brother, Bryan.

Sater, who had never held political office and was better known for his arrests, added: "I want to stop a war, No. 1; No. 2, I absolutely believe that the U.S. and Russia need to be allies, not enemies. If I could achieve both in one stroke, it would be a home run."

Still, Artemenko and Sater said they gave the plan to Cohen in the lobby of the Loews Regency with instructions to pass it to Flynn.

The substance of the plan was that Russia would agree to withdraw its support for the rebel forces in Donbas and Luhansk in exchange for a 20- to 100-year lease of Crimea and a lifting of U.S. sanctions. If adopted, it would tilt things heavily in Russia's favor. Crimea is strategically valuable for many reasons, but especially for the Russians, who have long sought warm-water ports (not to mention that three-quarters of the Ukrainian Navy, which had been seized there) and because of its proximity to and territorial claims on underwater natural gas deposits that are worth trillions of dollars.

News of the plan was greeted with outrage in Ukraine. The Kremlin, despite Artemenko's claims, denied any knowledge of the plan.

Media suggested that the Trump-Artemenko relationship was a back channel to Putin, just as many later believed that the Ballard-Mansimov one had been to Erdoğan and Ballard-Akhmedov had been to them both.

It was amusing. It was total bullshit. Artemnko was in no position to offer such a thing. The plan had zero support in Washington. Nobody I knew took it seriously — except maybe Don Jr.

Chapter 15
Whose Side are We On?

In 2018, I couldn't stop thinking about how Ballard was making piles of money off Turkey after I had greased the wheels for him, and all I got was a lousy $45,000. While I was busy trying to get Global Energy Products off the ground, I really thought that Fraud Guarantee was an idea that also had legs. I firmly believed that if I could find a way to get into investors' consciousnesses, I'd have a big winner on my hands.

In the period between the germination of the Fraud Guarantee idea and my ascension to unofficial-but-critical Trump advisor, I couldn't really have moved forward with it. It wasn't that I didn't have investors or potential clients, what I needed was a corporate underwriter for such a big lift. Insurance companies, I knew, were by nature cautious and probably not ready for such a radical idea. Still, I believed that with my connections, I could get it off the ground. What I needed was a face of the franchise, someone famous who connoted trust.

The feeling in and around the White House was not quite as hopeful.

Manafort was arrested by the FBI in October 2017. He and his deputy for the Trump campaign, Rick Gates, were charged with engaging in a conspiracy against the U.S., engaging in a conspiracy to launder money, failing to file reports of foreign bank and financial accounts, acting as an unregistered agent of a foreign principal, making false and misleading statements in documents filed and submitted under the Foreign Agents Registration Act and making false statements. The primary accusation was that Manafort laundered in excess of $18 million, which had come from Ukraine.

At about the same time that Manafort was assuring Gates that "they" were "going to take care of us," in early 2018, he filed a suit against the Department of Justice alleging that it broke the law when it appointed Mueller to the investigation. The Department of Justice, probably stifling yawns, responded that "the lawsuit is frivolous but the defendant is entitled to file whatever he wants."

At the time, I didn't know much about Manafort other than that he was on our side. I was sure that Manafort was being railroaded by the other side. Like many within Trump's gravitational pull, I saw people in strict terms of us, who I had to protect, and them, who I had to fight at every turn. That view was altered by Manafort's case, though not seriously challenged, after Igor filled me in on many of Manafort's activities in Ukraine that he heard about from patrons of his nightclubs.

Meanwhile, Sessions had been asking staffers for disparaging information against Comey and told them that he expected to see at least one anti-Comey article in major media every day.

CNN reported that former Press Secretary Spicer and Priebus had tried to pressure Sessions not to recuse himself from the investigation.

Despite the distractions, Mueller continued apace.

Emin Agalarov's close associate, Roman Bemiaminov, told the FBI that he had warned Aras Agalarov employee Ike Kaveladze that — in a notorious 2016 Trump Tower meeting that included Kaveladze, Kushner, Manafort, Don Jr. and Russian lawyer Natalia Vesilnitskaya — the subject of "dirt" against Hillary Clinton could come up. Kaveladze said that he attended the meeting as a translator and that he thought it would be about sanctions. Beniaminov was an old friend of Emin's from Tenafly High School in New Jersey.

The Daily Beast then dropped a major bombshell, reporting that Kevin Harrington, a senior National Security Council official, had proposed a plan in which the U.S. would reposition its forces in Europe in a way that would clearly be more amenable to Putin.

The shock value was based on a number of factors. First, the fact that Harrington was in a position to make such a proposal. He had no military experience nor even any notable experience in government before the White House tapped him to become a senior official for strategic planning. He was, however, a hedge fund manager for a company owned by, and named after, Peter Thiel, a prominent Trump donor and supporter. Another is that the proposal appeared to be much more in line with Putin's interests than those of NATO or even the U.S. Trump had already made his view on NATO clear, angering many allies, even calling the alliance "obsolete."

The fact that Harrington specifically asked for U.S. forces to be moved out of Lithuania, Latvia and Estonia — which had been part of the Soviet

Union, had remnant Russian-speaking minorities and had joined NATO over Putin's fierce opposition — further hinted at Russian involvement.

In that same vein, Flynn had pushed to strengthen cooperation with the U.S. and Russian militaries, despite Congress opposing it, and Trump himself had backed a Putin peace plan for Syria that proposed allowing Bashar al-Assad to remain in control of the country (the U.S. had called for his resignation as early as 2011 over human-rights abuses) and for Russian forces to remain in Syria as American ones pulled out.

The anonymous administration official who reported Harrington's actions said he or she smelled a rat. "I sensed we were giving something and it wasn't clear what we were gaining in return," the source said. "I did not take it to the President because the White House is the leakiest ship possible and can you imagine how that would have looked."

While I knew that The Daily Beast story and other revelations made it look as though Trump was repaying a favor for Putin or was under extortion, I could not support that idea. When people asked me if Putin forced Trump to do his bidding, I always tell them: He didn't need to. Trump's agenda lined up with Putin's, and Trump would serve as his useful fool until the end.

As if on cue, a Democratic Senator, Ben Cardin of Maryland, published a scathing report called Putin's Asymmetrical Assault on Democracy in Russia and Europe: Implications for U.S. National Security. It not only detailed evidence of Putin meddling in other democracies, but it acknowledged that he had also affected the 2016 U.S. election. Cardin didn't implicate Trump, but did call on him to change policy. "As the extent of Russia's obvious meddling in the 2016 U.S. election continues to be investigated, it is imperative that the American people better understand the true scope and scale of Putin's pattern of undermining democracy in Russia and across Europe. That is why I commissioned this report shortly after the 2016 election," he wrote. "This threat existed long before President Trump took office, and unless he takes action now, it will continue long after his administration. While President Trump stands practically idle, Mr. Putin continues to refine his asymmetric arsenal and look for future opportunities to disrupt governance and erode support for the democratic and international institutions that the United States and Europe have built over the last 70 years."

Trump's opponents hypothesized that the Russians had funneled money to his campaign through the NRA and that his company was actively laundering money for the Russians, a story that didn't gain much traction.

Meanwhile, news broke in the Netherlands that did not make much of a ripple in the U.S., either. Amsterdam-based de Volkskrant reported the AIVD, the Dutch intelligence service, had infiltrated the Russian hacker group Cozy Bear in 2014. Their moles were reported to have actually witnessed active attacks on the DNC and State Department servers.

AVID sent their observations to U.S. intelligence agencies, who did not act in any meaningful way. Cozy Bear is believed to be closely associated with Russian intelligence.

On January 29, 2018, Trump made a move widely criticized by much of his own party — one that would clearly make Putin's life easier. Although the Countering America's Adversaries Through Sanctions Act — which Trump railed against but reluctantly signed into law — called for additional sanctions against Russia for its involvement in the election, Trump refused to impose them. "Today, we have informed Congress that this legislation and its implementation are deterring Russian defense sales," Heather Nauert said for the State Department. "Since the enactment of the ... legislation, we estimate that foreign governments have abandoned planned or announced purchases of several billion dollars in Russian defense acquisitions." In other words, the law calls for new sanctions, but they will not be enacted because the existing ones were effective.

The backlash was quick and overwhelming. Treasury Secretary Steven Mnuchin pulled a quick 180 and released a list of 114 Russian politicians and 96 Russian oligarchs, affected by the law. He just made it. His list came out 12 minutes before the deadline set by the law.

In a rare move, Putin commented on the list. He called it a "hostile step," but he also joked that he felt "slighted" because he was not on it.

While the investigations were constant and the drumbeat got louder. Nunes released the Foreign Intelligence Surveillance Act Abuses at the Department of Justice and the Federal Bureau of Investigation, better known as the Nunes Memo. The main gist of it was that the FBI "may have relied on politically motivated or questionable sources" when they got a warrant to interview Carter Page.

Trump, never one to avoid claiming victory, pointed to the Nunes Memo and proudly announced that he was "totally vindicated" in regards to all of the Russian collusion investigation accusations.

Nevertheless, the investigation continued.

And it bore fruit. In February, Mueller indicted 13 Russians and three Russian organizations for interfering with the election. Most of them were involved with the Internet Research Agency (IRA), a St. Petersburg troll farm. The IRA was accused of having waged "information warfare" on the U.S. and of falsely posing as Americans on social media "to sow discord." Specifically, the IRA was accused of "supporting the Presidential campaign of then-candidate Donald J. Trump ... and disparaging Hillary Clinton."

Again, Trump claimed vindication, announcing that, although the Russians might have tried to sway the election, there was no evidence mentioned of his or his staff's involvement. He probably would have liked to have been part of something like that, but I'm certain that he wasn't.

At February's Munich Security Conference, National Security Advisor H.R. McMaster said that the evidence showed that Russian election interference is "now incontrovertible." Russian Foreign Minister Sergey Lavrov called the indictment "just blather." Trump would later impose financial sanctions on the 13 people on the list.

Putin even weighed in. In an interview with NBC's Megyn Kelly — who had left Fox News after sexist comments by Trump — he tried to undermine the idea that Russia was behind the attacks. He seemed to have confirmed that they happened — by hinting that the accused were not truly Russian. "Maybe they are not even Russians," he postulated, "but Ukrainians, Tatars or Jews, but with Russian citizenship, which should also be checked." Then, he said that even if Russians were behind the acts, their impetus could well have come from Americans. "Maybe they have dual citizenship or a Green Card," he went on. "Maybe the U.S. paid them for this. How can you know that? I do not know either." He appeared to believe that Russian citizens who were not ethnic Russians were not really Russian and that the U.S. would provide the impetus for Russian actions.

Any hope that there had been no collusion died for many after The New York Times reported that the State Department had not spent a penny of the $120 million fund Congress allocated it near the end of the 2016 election to fight foreign interference.

Further evidence of Trump's long-lived desire for Putin's attention was made public at the beginning of March 2018. Mueller had been given a letter that Trump had written to Putin in 2013. According to The Washington Post, the letter personally invited Putin to the 2013 Miss Universe Pageant in Moscow, promising "beautiful" women.

The Post interviewed Aras Agalarov about any communication between Trump and Putin at the show. "That was a very complicated situation then, because I promised Trump he would meet Putin," Agalarov said, pointing out that the two did not actually meet in person. He believed Trump was satisfied with a "friendly," small gift from Putin. "So he was leaving with very warm feelings," Agalarov said. "He was very happy."

Trump might well also have been happy that the majority Republicans of the House Intelligence Committee ended their investigation of Russian influence on the election, despite calls from the Democrats to continue. The committee's final word acknowledged Russian interference, but said that "there was no evidence of collusion" with themselves or the Trump campaign and that the Russians did not help one candidate more than the other.

Ranking Democrat Adam Schiff said that the Republicans' report was "little more than another Nunes memo in long form." Committee Democrats vowed to draft their own report that pointed out what they believed were remaining targets in the investigation.

On that same day, March 12, Sater was outed by BuzzFeed as a spy, but not for who many might have believed. Citing leaks from the government, their article listed acts he had done on behalf of the U.S. Some might have even found the my mutual friend with Trump to have been heroic.

Just after 9/11, Sater managed to get five of Osama bin Laden's phone numbers and to convince Mullah Omar — bin Laden's personal secretary and leader of Afghanistan's Taliban — to provide information for the U.S. He also foiled al-Qaeda plans to assassinate George W. Bush and Colin Powell that involved shooting down their planes, as well as a scheme for operatives in the Senate Barbershop to poison Bush or Dick Cheney.

His work was not limited to the Middle East. He convinced a GRU agent to hand over the name of a North Korean military officer who had been buying equipment for his country's nuclear advancement.

Sater even went undercover in Cyprus as a Russian-American who was looking to launder money in that country's notoriously loose banks. His job was to unmask actual money laundering suspects.

When BuzzFeed spoke with Sater, they saw him living a life of luxury and he seemed to be making a point of being conspicuous, driving a flamboyant convertible around Miami Beach. He told them that he felt that he needed to come out with his secret activities because the media had been dragging his name through the mud after finding out about his peace proposal with Artemenko and his involvement with the Trump Organization. "I am being given no choice because of the ongoing Trump investigations," he told them. "The media lies about me."

So he went to the media.

Later, the Justice Department would confirm that Sater did work on the government's behalf in several countries. He was thanked for risking his life to "combat terrorists and rogue states," and they added that he was instrumental in helping several of their operations against the Italian Mafia.

I won't deny any of Sater's accomplishments, but I still find the idea of him as a spy to be amusing. I think that he was just using his contacts, the way we all did. He was playing the Justice Department to avoid jail for securities fraud, cutting a deal with them in 1998 after he was implicated in a pump-and-dump scheme involving the Bonnanos and Gambinos. The lead prosecutor in his case was Andrew Weissmann, again.

On the day after Sater's revelations, Trump fired Tillerson and Steve Goldstein, the fourth highest-ranking person in the State Department. Trump nominated CIA Director Mike Pompeo to be the new Secretary of State. He had been a U.S. Army platoon leader and, as CIA Director, had met with several high-ranking foreign politicians, including Erdoğan.

Meanwhile, more information on Trump's relationship with Putin came out when The Washington Post reported that, in their initial conversation, Trump went very much off script. Not only did he congratulate Putin on his recent election win — despite briefing materials that said in all-caps "DO NOT CONGRATULATE" — he also failed to mention the poisoning of double agent Sergei Skripal and his daughter, Yulia, in England, although his advisors stressed how important it was that he do so.

The National Security Council recommended that Trump expel certain unnamed Russian diplomats due to the Skirpal Incident. Like many other Western leaders, he did. But he was alone in informing the Russians that they would be allowed to replace the expelled people.

Chapter 16
Giuliani Time

T rump frequently shook up his staff. Someone was always getting in trouble or falling out of his favor, so they had to be replaced. After The New York Times reported that John Dowd, Trump's personal counsel for the Mueller campaign (who would later serve briefly as my lawyer after my arrest), discussed with Trump a plan to pardon Flynn and Manafort should they be convicted, Dowd resigned his position soon thereafter, but remained very much in Trump's orbit.

Dowd's absence left an opening for a personal attorney for Trump. His first choice was Joe diGenova and Victoria Toensing, who were also well-known Fox News personalities. It had been reported that Trump didn't feel any "chemistry" between himself and the pair, but that wasn't it. He loved having them around. They didn't have to be working for him, they were always there. Trump was especially impressed when they would say things on Fox News like, as diGenova once offered: "There was a brazen plot to illegally exonerate Hillary Clinton and, if she didn't win the election, to then frame Donald Trump with a falsely created crime." Their hiring had been announced but almost immediately canceled due to a conflict of interest arising from a client of theirs having once accused an aide of Trump's of planning to obstruct justice.

With them out of the running, Trump offered the position to Giuliani, as his personal attorney for the Russian Collusion case. He jumped at the chance. It wasn't Secretary of State, but it would be a better gig than he had. I found it hilarious that Giuliani — who seemed perpetually looking for more money — wouldn't be paid for the job. But we all knew that was Trump's standard method of doing business. Still, there were benefits in the job for Giuliani. He could travel the world and stay in the limelight. And, he could keep everything he said to Trump confidential as it would, he believed, all fall under attorney-client privilege.

While it appeared that Trump was cozying up even closer to Russia,

Giuliani was becoming more familiar with Ukraine. In 2017, Giuliani made a couple of trips to Kharkiv, an eastern Ukrainian city about an hour's drive from the Russian border that had become Ground Zero for clashes between pro-Russian and pro-Ukrainian demonstrators.

Officially, he was there to see the city's eccentric mayor, Hennadiy Kernes. He was well known for having given himself a 25 percent raise and for having been alleged to have sent in titushky — hired thugs who blend in with members of crowds to provoke them into violence or start it themselves — to disrupt pro-Ukrainian demonstrations. He'd survived an assassination attempt in which he was shot in the back — it left him in a wheelchair — and then came out against pro-Russian separatists. He shared his office with a boisterous parrot named Johnny who would speak Russian to guests, including Giuliani, who didn't understand a word of the language. The local papers trumpeted Giuliani's presence as a visit from "one of Trump's advisors," although that was neither an official or paid role of his, and his company said he was there to talk security on behalf of Giuliani Partners, not for the White House.

While in Ukraine, Giuliani also met with Kharkiv-born billionaire Pavel Fuks. He'd made his money in Russia, first in oil and then in real estate. It's been reported both in Russia and the U.S. that Fuks and Trump had been negotiating in 2004 to license Trump's name for a Moscow skyscraper until Fuks balked at the cost — a 20 percent share of equity.

But there was more to it than that. A lot more. In July 2023, FBI agent Jonathan Buma sent a 22-page letter to the Senate Judiciary Committee that was later leaked by a conservative blogger and published by Insider. In it, he revealed that Fuks "was a co-opted asset" for the Russian Intelligence Service (the FSB). Buma also wrote the FBI had been trying to end Fuks' relationship with Giuliani.

They didn't. Fuks paid Giuliani $300,000 to lobby for Kharkiv. The deal was publicly known. "I would call him the lobbyist for Kharkiv and Ukraine — this is stated in the contract," Fuks said. "It is very important for me that such person as Giuliani tells people that we are a good country, that people can do business with us. That's what we would like to bring to America's leaders." That does not sound like Giuliani was brought in to train Kharkiv's police force.

Once he realized that he was not allowed to lobby, Giuliani said that the

$300,000 was for his company's security consulting services. Immediately, Fuks changed his tune to agree with Giuliani's claim.

Buma wrote that Russian intelligence used Fuks to launder immense amounts of money through Russian organized crime and to hire some thugs to spray-paint swastikas all over Kharkiv in an effort to support Putin's claim that Ukraine being full of Nazis forced him to invade. Fuks, of course, denies it all.

The FBI managed to get Fuks' U.S. visa revoked (he now lives in London) and recommended that the Treasury Department apply sanctions. They didn't.

In his letter, Buma pointed out exactly how compromising it was for an asset of Russian intelligence like Fuks to be doing business with one of the President's top advisors in Giuliani.

Of course, there was a great deal of outrage from the Democrats and the media, but both Fuks and Giuliani tried to put out the fire by claiming that their work together ended before Giuliani became Trump's lawyer (ignoring the fact that he was a top advisor well before that).

Buma acknowledged that they had officially broken ties in 2018, but also pointed out that Fuks hired a functionary named Andrii Telizhenko to "establish contacts with U.S. politicians." To nobody's surprise, one of those politicians was Giuliani, who also hired Telizhenko. Notably, Telizhenko had previously worked for a contractor for Burisma.

The FBI managed to get his visa revoked and for the Treasury Department to invoke sanctions on him because of his involvement with Russian "disinformation narratives that U.S. government officials have engaged in corrupt dealings in Ukraine."

Of course, almost everything that was said in the U.S. about corrupt Ukrainians came out of Giuliani's mouth.

According to Telizhenko, it was all just a big misunderstanding. He acknowledged working for Fuks and Giuliani at the same time, but maintained that the two jobs were absolutely "unrelated" and that the fact that Giuliani was saying exactly what Russian intelligence wanted him to say was just coincidental.

Giuliani also met with Poroshenko on both of his 2017 Ukraine visits. He later claimed that the two spoke "about increasing American support for the Ukrainian military, cybersecurity and financial reforms." Of them, only cybersecurity could be construed as part of Giuliani Partners' area of expertise, but that also happened to have been Giuliani's unofficial role at the White House.

Almost as soon as he was installed as Trump's lawyer, questions were being raised about Giuliani's overseas engagements. Although not officially representing the White House, he was omnipresent there and it was widely known that nobody was closer to Trump.

The word from the Trumpverse was that Giuliani's work in foreign countries, including Ukraine, was for his private business and had nothing to do with the White House. Still, the connection was inevitable.

There are plenty of cybersecurity firms, but only one whose principal spent most of his time in the White House. Giuliani was in high demand everywhere, particularly Ukraine, because the big-money guys there wanted access to the President. Not only did Trump hold the most powerful office, he appeared to be someone whose opinion could be swayed, even molded.

While it looked to many that Giuliani was serving as a shadow ambassador for Trump (and plenty made that accusation), all such criticism was deflected by the explanation that Giuliani was serving only as Trump's lawyer for the Mueller Investigation and was free to conduct business that wasn't directly related to that task.

Chapter 17
Cannabis and Candidates

Giuliani and I had been growing closer. In fact, our relationship had evolved from mere acknowledgment to a deep friendship. It made sense. Both of us were natural showoffs who liked to be shown off to, we both were chatty and liked to make jokes, we both came from Brooklyn and we knew many of the same people. We both enjoyed a fine cigar and we had both linked our future success to Trump.

It was never boring hanging out with Giuliani, but it was expensive. Giuliani absolutely loved traveling by private jet — but only if he wasn't the one paying. He stipulated that he required "a Gulfstream IV or bigger" on his rider for all of his speaking engagements. Giuliani would often try to get me to get us private jets to go wherever we went. Frequently, he'd ask me to fly in from Florida to D.C. or New York, to take in an event or just hang out.

Giuliani had plenty of responsibilities, although none were official, aside from those as Trump's personal attorney regarding the Russia investigation. But, just as he had been in the campaign, Giuliani was tasked with spreading the Make America Great Again mantra throughout the entire land, especially in states with important midterm races. Still widely seen as the hero of 9/11, Giuliani was always in demand and I came along to work my magic and help every Republican candidate that I could.

But it wasn't all work. Being friends with Giuliani had its benefits. He had more or less free use of the Owner's Box at Yankee Stadium and would often take me to ballgames. We even once flew to see the Giants play the Cowboys in Dallas. We did all kinds of things together, like golf outings, hanging out at exclusive cigar bars or just taking in the sights. I once even watched Rudy sing New York, New York with Joe Piscopo at the Statue of Liberty. I still have a video of it.

We were seeing each other pretty much every day and were always seated at the other's side. It must have looked like I was his son.

Giuliani had a habit of giving lavish gifts to people he was close with, sometimes well out of proportion to the event (or lack thereof). I was surprised at some of the items I received. Once, for no special reason, he gave me a watch right off his wrist. Who does that? Another time, he just handed me a pair of cuff links that he had been wearing on 9/11. These were not things of little worth. It certainly made me feel like he valued my friendship a great deal.

While I have been around luxury and the trappings of wealth for much of my adult life, this was different. I wasn't sharing a private jet with some pop star manager, but with the World's Mayor, the city's hero. And we weren't just having dinners and private luncheons with some lucky investor, but with the President of the United States of America, the Leader of the Free World. The man who would change everything, make it better for guys like us.

As much as I was drinking the Trump Kool-Aid, I still hadn't lost sight of what I was really after — a way to get at least one of my business ideas off the ground. While I was hyping Fraud Guarantee and Global Energy Producers, I really thought my ticket to big money was cannabis. It was the perfect business, profiting off something I loved and believed in. I had been trying to get into the industry for years, but hadn't found a viable opening.

As close as I was to Giuliani, I was gaining some notoriety of my own among Republican movers and shakers. I had to figure out a way to use that. I decided that I could multitask — while I was campaigning for Trump-friendly candidates, I would also see if I help my businesses germinate and still be an advocate for cannabis.

There were benefits to being seen with Giuliani. Not only was he famous, powerful and connected in his own right, everybody knew that he was a direct conduit to President Trump. He knew him better than anybody.

Those same people started to see me as a way to get to Giuliani on their way to Trump. Tell me something and maybe I'd tell Giuliani and maybe he'd tell Trump. Considering how hard it was for anyone to get any access to Trump now that he was in office, I was in an advantageous position.

There was no shortage of people in line to get to Trump, so I quickly became very popular around D.C.

The group that sought me out most often were the MAGA-faithful candidates running in the 2018 Midterm Elections.

One of the most persistent was Congressman Ron DeSantis, who was running for Governor of Florida. At the time, he wasn't well known outside

the state, but he had a reputation as a hard-right, almost theocratic conservative, opposing gun controls, voting against any bill about countering Climate
Change, receiving the lowest rating from LGBQT organizations, opposing all
immigration reforms as well as sponsoring a bill that would allow states to
determine their own education criteria. He often invoked his deep Catholic
faith when describing his opinions political and cultural issues. He'd had an
abbreviated run for Senate in the short period between the day Marco Rubio
started his ill-fated Presidential campaign and the day he ended it.

DeSantis was definitely someone who could use some Trump magic, or
even just recognition, to jump-start his campaign.

His poll numbers were not outstanding (actually, not good at all) and he
was clearly trying to secure a Trump endorsement, going as far as introducing a bill to end the Mueller investigation, citing a dearth of evidence.

As a politically active Republican in Florida, I knew who DeSantis was,
but I kind of wrote him off early because I knew he was against cannabis
legalization.

When we first met in May 2018, DeSantis was just another Republican
candidate looking for a favor.

He approached me in the lobby of the Trump International and handed
me his card. He told me that he was running for governor of Florida, and that
he really wanted to somehow get Trump's endorsement, Trump's support.
He told me that he was aware that, because of my relationship with Trump
and with Rudy, I could make something like that happen.

At that point, I still supported one of his Republican opponents, Adam
Putnam, who had a more cannabis-friendly platform. But Trump didn't like
him because Putnam had spoken out against him in 2016. Trump would
never forgive or forget something like that. So I knew it would be a good
idea to switch my support to someone else. I had been around long enough to
know how to run Washington's quid pro quo game.

I knew that DeSantis was anti-cannabis, so I said to him, listen, Ron, it's
very difficult for me to support someone who goes against the things I'm going to need, want, in the state of Florida. Although I was a confessed cannabis aficionado, I wanted it to be legalized not just so I could get it, but so everybody could. At that point, I could see no easier way to make money than
selling legal cannabis. I didn't think I could have made my point any more
clear to DeSantis.

He understood. DeSantis turned to me and said: "I would be open to thinking differently about cannabis if you were to get me Trump's support." It was as easy as that.

A few weeks later, Trump endorsed DeSantis. Trump would later re-count the event as DeSantis coming to him "on his knees," sometimes adding that he was in tears, begging for his endorsement. I remember it somewhat differently. I spoke to Giuliani, told him that, if DeSantis was elected, he'd be a 100 percent Trump guy — so he told the President. And Trump endors-ed him. No real discussion. He just did it.

It was DeSantis' only major endorsement (Democrat Gwen Graham had 74). Neither Trump nor DeSantis mentioned me, but I was essentially the on-ly person who knew them both, other than Giuliani.

Six weeks later, DeSantis' PAC received a $50,000 donation from what SDNY prosecutors and the media later described as "a Delaware-incorpor-ated shell company" owned by Igor and me, that was "dedicated to funneling money to candidates."

I'm offended by that. The company was Global Energy Producers, which we had been fighting to get off the ground. Sure, we hadn't made any deals yet, but it's not like we were selling used cars — these were petroleum deals between countries, which are in the billions — it takes time and we always felt like we were getting closer. People who knew me complained that I would never stop talking about it, trying to get funding and trying to make deals for it. A shell, it was not.

Now that I had a Republican candidate who supported cannabis, I went to work, did my magic, for DeSantis. In our relationship, it was not just one thing: a) I was helping him with the Trump endorsement, b) I was helping him with a lot of the fundraising, c) I was helping him with people in Florida because I'm a Florida guy and I know a lot of important people in the state.

But what DeSantis wanted most, besides Trump's nod, was help finding him big-money donations. DeSantis was absolutely voracious when it came to campaign donations. Immediately, I steered him to all the well-heeled con-servatives in the state. I actually did a lot of the legwork myself. I got him money from a lot of wealthy donors, even people who had donated to him al-ready. I'd go out and ask them for more money. I threw three fundraisers for the guy, I helped deliver the Cuban vote and the Jewish vote for him with my events and my magic.

Like a gangster, DeSantis had two phones — one official and one off the record, a burner. He often texted me about a potential donor, saying things like: "Would it be reasonable for me to ask him for $50,000? I think he did six figures for Trump" and "Make sure Robert gives a lot."

Still looking for a way into the cannabis market, I was at a party at Igor's apartment in Florida when I went out on the balcony for a smoke. Igor had said he wanted to introduce me to a guy who had a thriving cannabis business in California and was looking for more opportunity. He was Andrey Kukushkin. We liked each other immediately.

Like me, Kukushkin was born in Odessa to a Jewish family. The Kukushkins emigrated to San Francisco in 1993, when Andrey was still in his teens. He grew up American, but, like me, had some important contacts back in Eastern Europe. The primary things we had in common was our shared love for making money and, of course, smoking weed.

Kukushkin told me about his cannabis business in California, but he also complained that the market was exceedingly crowded there. He wanted to check out Nevada. Recreational cannabis was legal there, and he thought he might be able to get in before the market was flooded.

I liked Kukushkin and the idea of running a cannabis business out of Las Vegas. But I admitted to Igor that although he was very smart, he was a little "loosey-goosey" when it came to business. You know, the creative type, I told him. Not a real businessman.

Igor laughed and told me that that's exactly what he was, the heavy lifting in the business was done by his partner, Andrey Muraviev.

I knew who he was. Muraviev was a Russian oligarch, although his fortune might have been in the hundreds of millions, rather than billions.

Muraviev was one of many international investors who wanted to get in on the action as U.S. states began to relax their regulations on cannabis. He had recruited Kukushkin to help him find Americans who could help him get into the business legally, and Kukushkin would lead him to me.

I had what might have been the perfect contact. Adam Laxalt was Nevada's Attorney General and also happened to be the son of former governor and long-time senator Paul Laxalt, a Nevada institution.

Adam was a Republican running for governor and, despite all the name recognition he inherited, could use all the help he could get.

He was Trump's kind of guy. Laxalt opposed same-sex marriage and allowing LGBQT people to serve in the military, he was against red flag laws — until the NRA changed its mind and he quickly followed suit — supported bans on various abortion terms and procedures and was part of a lawsuit attempting to keep the identities of political donors secret. He fought to keep fraud investigators from scrutinizing ExxonMobil's role in downplaying Climate Change along with several organizations funded by the Koch brothers, who then donated $2.5 million to his 2018 campaign.

By then, Nevada was no longer the safe Republican seat it had been in his dad's time. Lots of people had moved to the state from other parts of the country and the Democrats were steadily gaining steam there.

And Laxalt had not seemed to have made enough important friends. Before he met me, Laxalt had just one notable endorsement. It was *Adam Laxalt talked with us about cannabis while running for governor of Nevada.*

from Storey County Sheriff Gerald Antinoro, who was accused of sexual harassment by numerous women, including his top deputy. Laxalt stopped touring with Antinoro, but declined to charge him in his position as attorney general. Notably, Brian Sandoval, the outgoing Republican governor, made a point of publicly refusing to endorse Laxalt.

One notable friend he did have was DeSantis. They had served together in the Navy's Judge Advocate General's Corps. DeSantis told me that he was more than happy to introduce me to Laxalt. He told me that he thought that I could give Laxalt's campaign in Nevada the same marked boost I had given his in Florida.

Like DeSantis, Laxalt was against cannabis; but, again, it wasn't a deal breaker. I flipped DeSantis on the issue, so why not Laxalt? No matter what they say, these guys are far more interested in getting elected than they are about policy.

Our introduction was over the phone. We got along well and his interests seem to align with mine, so I told him I'd think about throwing my support behind him.

We actually met in person at a mobbed-up Italian restaurant on the Las Vegas Strip. That's one of the things I noticed about all these Republican wannabe tough guys — even, maybe especially, Trump and Giuliani — they love to be around organized crime. It's like they're living out a fantasy.

Like DeSantis, Laxalt pulled a complete 180 on a core issue, softening his stance on cannabis after having made a big show of how opposed he was to it earlier in the campaign. It made me wonder how voters never seem to notice. They always seem to get away with it.

I immediately called Kukushkin and told him to come to Las Vegas, so I could introduce him to the next governor of Nevada. Since Laxalt was already the state's attorney general, I asked him, who could possibly know more about the intricacies of getting a cannabis license in Nevada? Even if Laxalt himself didn't have the greatest advice for us, he could certainly introduce us to the people who could help our cause.

Kukushkin quickly agreed, his excitement was obvious, and he brought Muraviev with him.

Kukushkin, Igor and I met Laxalt at a restaurant in the Wynn Las Vegas hotel. He had brought along his friend Wesley Duncan, who was running to replace him as attorney general.

Muraviev stayed in a hotel room with Correia.

We spoke, of course, about our primary mission in Nevada, to throw our support behind Laxalt. It can't be underestimated how important we felt it was to get as many Republicans elected as possible. Especially those aligned as closely with Trump as Laxalt was.

We agreed to work to help get Laxalt elected and to counsel Trump to give him an endorsement. As a show of goodwill, Igor pledged $10,000 to Laxalt's campaign and another $10,000 to Duncan's.

After that was finished, we spoke about cannabis licensing. Laxalt and Duncan told us that we had missed the boat, the period to apply for a license had already expired. They didn't offer any concrete help, but they promised to put us in touch with the right people.

Later, many — including the Justice Department — would accuse us of trying to bribe Laxalt to give us a cannabis license. But that's ridiculous. Not only were the cannabis licenses assigned by "randomly generated blind numbers would be used for these digital drawings" (according to the law itself, and something Laxalt later testified to as well).

We went to Laxalt's rally and pledged our support. He was utterly grateful. We took pictures with the candidate and posted them on social media.

Kukushkin told Muraviev that Laxalt looked like the man to beat and then told us that Muraviev was pleased.

We then met with Duncan and an ex-legislator who he said was an expert in what we wanted to know about cannabis licensing. They reminded us that the license application period had closed.

Kukushkin asked if there was anything we could do.

Duncan told us that we could try to buy someone else's license or apply when the licensing period opened up again. They did say that they would introduce us to some more lawyers and legislators who could give us some more specific pointers.

I can't take all the credit, but I was a major player in getting Laxalt endorsements from both Trump and Pence.

It didn't help enough, though as Laxalt lost to Steve Sisolak, who became the state's first Democratic governor in 20 years.

Four years later, Laxalt would announce a run for the Senate in a video in which he claimed that "the radical left, rich elites, woke corporations, academia and the media" were "taking over America."

He lost to incumbent Catherine Cortez Masto, a Trump critic who holds views diametrically opposite of Laxalt's on many issues.

In between, he was co-chair of Trump's 2020 campaign in Nevada, a state he lost to Joe Biden. Laxalt was also one of many Republican officials who made accusations of widespread voter fraud in 2020 but produced not a shred of evidence.

Chapter 18
Fear of a Deep State

A t a time when the Democrats were flinging Trump-Russia collusion stories around, the Republicans had their own conspiracy theory that they obsessed over. Every time they got together, the conversation was always about the Deep State. Nobody ever had to bring it up, it was just expected, it was all they could talk about. I was still under the same belief at the time.

The Deep State hypothesis maintains that everything in the world is under the control of secret and non-elected groups who operate in the shadow of government, making all the decisions and controlling everything. Many interpretations identify the Deep State as a notorious cabal that is said to include the British Royal Family, the Rothschild banking family, the Clintons, Amazon founder Jeff Bezos, billionaire philanthropist George Soros, the Pope and other boogiemen. Soros is particularly feared and despised by Deep State believers. Many of them have even accused him of having been a Nazi stormtrooper, although his Jewish family survived Hungary's German occupation while he was a small child. Faith in existence of the Deep State concept often dovetails with antisemitism, QAnon and other fringe beliefs.

Although the same people throwing around Deep State conspiracies as truth wielded immense power, none ever seemed to mount a serious attempt to expose, let alone fight, their all-encompassing fear. Republicans often invoke the Deep State in elections, usually when they are in danger of losing, but they use the same kind of code words and phrases that DeSantis did in his video, like "woke," "elites" and "radical left." The media is also seen as a tool of the Deep State, rather than a watchdog on politicians, and academics are also said to be in on the whole thing. The Deep State believers will also blame billionaires, even if they actually are billionaires themselves.

DeSantis and Laxalt were hardly the only dog whistling B-List Republicans I came to know. My travels with Giuliani frequently led to my crossing paths with such GOP luminaries as Pence and Kevin McCarthy. Although I stayed unfailingly polite, I didn't like either of them on a personal level.

Pence struck me as creepy, there's something about how his eyes never seem to focus on anything, and McCarthy was rude and self-centered, didn't ever seem to have time for anyone but himself.

Some of the guys were pretty friendly, though. There was a group of Texans who kind of ran things for the RNC and America First Action behind the scenes. There was, of course, Joseph Ahearn, finance director of the pro-Trump super PAC America First Action, his pal Roy Bailey, who was big in natural gas, and Tommy Hicks, co-chair of the Republican National Committee. Of course, they all were friends with Donald Trump Jr., who just always seemed to be around.

It was kind of their job to introduce me around and make sure I made the right connections. I knew it would help Global Energy Partners to know important people who had links to Texas' abundant natural gas.

There was so much money going in and out of America First that it was hard to keep track of it all. And I know more than a few Republicans who hoped nobody would.

I'll give you an example of how it works. There was this one guy, Barry Zekelman. He was Canadian, but did most of his business in the U.S., selling steel tubes. In fact, he had 14 factories in the U.S. But he was having a hard time because the American steel tube market had been flooded by cheaper imports, primarily from South Korea and Turkey. Zekelman did what he could legally, filing lawsuits and complaints, but saw little if any action from the government. He started a marketing campaign and hired big-name lobbyists. Still nothing.

Since he was making and selling steel in the U.S., Trump's protectionist policies stood to make him a lot of money. So, like many successful people, he wanted to donate to Trump's campaign.

But — even though his company is based in Chicago, he employs hundreds of Americans and his hometown is connected to Detroit by a bridge, a tunnel and shared history — he's a foreigner, and that's just not allowed.

America First Action did, however, receive a large donation, $1.75 million, from Sharon, Pennsylvania-based Wheatland Tube, a division of Zekelman Industries. Wheatland's president is American. It looked to everybody involved, they said, to be legal.

Zekelman and his wife had a private dinner with Donald Trump and Donald Trump Jr. They spoke about how foreign steel was harming Zekelman's ability to compete. They also discussed a monitoring system that stops long-haul truckers from spending too much time behind the wheel. The system is designed to ensure truckers' safety by preventing them from driving while drowsy. "Say someone is half an hour from home on their long haul truck — they literally have to pull over on the side of the road and stop," he told Trump. "They can't go home." He complained to Trump that he can't find enough drivers because they felt that the potentially life-saving system was so irksome that they'd rather not have jobs. "They don't even want to do it anymore," he said.

Trump told him that he was unaware of such a system and that he was surprised that trucks can be shut down after being on the road too long.

I know all this because I was at the dinner too.

The donations occurred on April 5, June 4 and October 17, 2018. Trump imposed a debilitating 25 percent tariff on foreign steel and aluminum on June 1, 2018. At about the same time, a bill to exempt some trucking companies from the driver monitoring system was sponsored by no fewer than 12 Republican lawmakers.

While that sounds shady, none of it's illegal, or at least it wouldn't have been if Zekelman was born a few miles to the west of where he was (but he wasn't, so he was fined close to $1 million). But if he were an American, he would simply be a businessman donating to a candidate he believes in and telling him about his opinions. It's not a bribe, it's a show of solidarity.

That's exactly how politics works. It always has. And it still does. Nobody would have ever heard about Zekelman's donation or his dinner conversation if he wasn't from another country.

My feeling about it at the time was that it was a pretty good system. It's important for politicians hear what their constituents had to say. The fact that the wealthiest and more powerful people had more, maybe only, access to them, I believed, was just natural.

The reason that non-Americans are not allowed to donate is because of the belief that they might not have America's best interests at heart.

Chapter 19
Good or Bad?

That's how Trump likes to conduct business. He collects small groups of people he trusts and then finds out which way their opinions were going. That was easy for me. I knew right away that Trump thought I was a real stand-up kind of guy. For his whole life, Trump has been working with people and money. The only way to do that is to determine who you can and can't trust. I know Trump, he divides everything into two opposites — it's either one or the other. To him, a person is loyal or they aren't. He decided I must be loyal because I looked, talked and acted the way he expected a loyal person to. Like a mob boss, he demanded loyalty, but didn't feel a need to reciprocate.

When I first started going to these events, I was all eyes and ears. All I wanted to do was learn. And to make contacts. My brain was recording everything so that I could sift through it all for what was valuable.

I remember it all vividly, but I don't have to — it was all recorded. Although we weren't officially allowed to take pictures or video, Igor surreptitiously caught it all on his phone without anyone realizing it. Even me.

All he had to do was keep the phone out of sight. Because of that, all his videos contain long shots of things like the backs of chairs, ceilings and water glasses. It was far more important to him to record what was said and who was there rather than it was to make it look any good.

Back in Ukraine, he'd play the videos to important people in his bars. To the people there, Igor was just a nightclub owner. So, when he said that he was spending time with Donald Trump and Rudy Giuliani, nobody believed him. But with the videos, he could prove that he had access to the very top. It made for good business.

Before Trump arrives, the video is all niceties and introductions. Many important people, including Ronna McDaniel Romney, recognize me and say that they're happy to see me. I'm offered a tour of Mar-a-Lago, but turn it down because I'd been there before (many times, in fact).

Trump enters to a standing ovation. He begins by claiming that he's recording his "highest" polling numbers. He introduces Representative Pete Sessions, who praises Trump as the "President who wants to make America great." I was glad to see that Sessions was there. No relation to Jeff Sessions, Pete was a Republican from Texas with some major pull in the House and among wealthy Republicans. He was Chair of the critical House Rules Committee, and he had also been considered a challenger to McCarthy for House Majority Leader in 2014. I made a mental note that he could be a valuable ally for my natural gas plan.

The main thrust of of Trump's address is about the midterms. Trump says that many representatives are leaving government and it was the audience's duty to replace them all with Republicans.

"Not without donations," Sessions chimes in.

McDaniel Romney then repeats what he said and adds that people stop her on the street to tell her that, because of Trump, their wages have gone up or that they've landed a job. She also claims that the RNC had raised a "record number of money," and tells the donors that their money is going to be used against a fearsome and "energized" Democratic party that has "no message" and will "turn back the clock to the Dark Ages of Schumer and Pelosi."

Trump then interjects and asks about a House race in suburban Phoenix. Debbie Lesko was running against Democrat Hiral Tipirneni to replace Republican Trent Franks, who was best known for calling Obama an "enemy of humanity" and left office after sexual harassment accusations. Sessions says that he knows "her father and husband" and they are "very Christian."

Another speaker then appeals for the Republicans to pursue the Hindu vote. Trump said that he already is.

Then the original speaker tells Trump, still talking about Hindu voters: "they love you."

McDaniel agrees.

The speaker, joined by another, complains about the backlog of legal immigration cases. "They should just walk across the border," Trump jokes.

I laugh and say to myself before the wall goes up.

Trump turns the conversation to Syria. "I was with the king of Saudi Arabia two months ago he said that Syria was one of the greatest cultures — you wouldn't know this — on Earth," Trump recalls (actually, I did know that). "He said that, before all this horrible problem, he used to take his vacations in Syria." There is then a discussion, with laughs, about the idea that Syria has the most beautiful women in the region. Trump mentions Syria's dictator, Assad. "So, to you Assad is very horrible," he asks.

"Assad's a very bad man," a woman tells him, as though speaking to a small child.

Trump then blames Obama for Syria's recent woes.

McDaniel Romney adds: "you wouldn't have this refugee problem."

I agree as well, and say out loud: He basically let Russia in.

The conversation turns to "middlemen" who are helping Assad and making huge profits brokering petroleum, paying $10 a barrel and then selling it at market prices.

When Trump asks where that was happening, she responds "Ukraine, eastern Ukraine" (the same area Russia would later invade). "They don't have a lot of oil, but they have oil," Trump then laments, most of his knowledge of the situation coming from me. "I hear it's horrible what's going on."

I was actually happy to hear Trump was thinking about Ukraine. It would give us something to talk about.

Trump then jokes about the incompetence of his generals, especially in regard to knowing who's profiting from what. "They have no clue."

A questioner then begins with how many Americans "are loving President Trump" then says something not entirely comprehensible that appears to be about how people write "we love you" on his picture. That might sound excessive, but there's no too much when dealing with Trump and flattery.

Then she says that it was "dangerous not getting rid of Assad, [he] will definitely create another ISIS." The questioner says all 300,000 Syrian-Americans love Trump, but there is discussion as to whether that number is correct. "There's a lot in Michigan," McDaniel offers. The room finally back in her control, the questioner again criticizes Assad, claiming that Assad was "a magnet for ISIS."

Trump says that Assad was against ISIS, but he makes it sound more like a question.

The questioner and an ally try to disabuse him of that idea, saying that "he sends them to Iraq to kill Americans." She goes on and on about how Assad bombs this or that civilian facility, but never asks a question.

McDaniel then invites Bill Edwards, who made his money by refinancing veterans' loans but claimed to be out of that business by then, to ask a "final question." He asks about a clause in a bill that would make refinancing veteran's loans more difficult. Trump says he doesn't know anything about it. Sessions interrupts and says that he's Chair of the Rules Committee and hadn't heard anything about it either. He says that he'll "look into it."

Trump gets excited, saying that the bill's meaning was the opposite of what Edwards said and asks where the problem was. Edwards says that any bill that passes in the Senate has "bad" clauses added by the Democrats. Sessions then repeats that he'll check up on the issue.

McDaniel then thanks the audience and Trump thanks Ballard. Everyone stands and claps. Igor moves the camera up and I am clearly visible, walking toward the speakers.

After a long shot of a chair, I can be seen in the group surrounding Trump. While the camera moves around in Igor's hand, it swings around, taking in people's midsections and the backs of chairs, but also reveals me speaking with Trump face to face, with my hand on Trump's arm in a familiar way. We walk away together and I can be seen patting Trump on the back as we are talking to each other.

It then shows me, all smiles, taking a photo of Trump with Sessions and two women. Trump instructs me to "lift it up higher" and I raise the camera. Then I pose with Trump, my arm on the President's back, my other hand giving a thumbs up and there's a broad grin across my face. Trump then smiles for the photo.

The video ends with me, surrounded by guests chatting and laughing, asking McDaniel Romney where I should go to dinner. I am then shown to be talking amiably with Sessions.

Sessions shook my hand and we agreed to meet in his office.

After the meeting, I was approached by Joseph Ahearn. A serious-looking man with glasses, Ahearn was finance director of America First Action, a 501(c)(4) nonprofit organization (a super PAC) dedicated to supporting federal candidates who backed Trump's policy agenda.

Ahearn had heard of me through our mutual friend, Stephen Katz. A veterinarian from Upstate New York, he also sat in the state assembly. I remembered that our common tie was a business venture called Therabis that would provide cannabis, as CBD, for dogs. I was interested and looked around for some venture capital for the project. Therabis did make it to retail (although its Facebook and Instagram feeds have not been updated since December 2020), but I was not part of it.

Almost immediately, Ahearn started pitching me on America First Action, he told me thought I'd make a great donor. The PAC sounded interesting, so we kept talking. When I happened to mention Pereira, Ahearn told me that we should definitely stay in touch and gave me his card.

About a week later, we met in D.C. That's when Ahearn told me exactly how the PAC works and how donors of different amounts are entitled to specific perks and privileges. The most important levels were reserved for supporters who donated $250,000, $500,000 or $1 million. For a million, you'd be named a VIP donor, with carte blanche access to all kinds of events and the right to hold a private event (usually a dinner) for Trump at the place of your choosing. That last part I found very intriguing.

I knew how valuable my deal with Ballard was, so I believed that going even higher up the ladder would yield an even bigger payoff. I knew I had to get $1 million quickly.

We considered the $1 million package to be a great investment because we'd be able to pitch our our company, Global Energy Producers, in an environment studded with the kind of people who could help us. Igor refinanced some of his Florida properties to get us the money. We pledged it to America First Action as a duo and were both treated as $1 million VIPs.

Now that we were in the VIP club, we were invited to just about every important event the Republicans put on. My charisma did the rest.

Chapter 20
A Sit-Down with the Boss

I
t was easy for me to make deals with guys like DeSantis and Laxalt. I had what they wanted, so they had to give something in return. That's just how it works everywhere, in business, politics, crime, friendships, you name it. They all wanted a little bit of Trump's magic to rub off on them, and I could get it. Something for something.

It was different with Giuliani and Trump, though. What I had to give them was less tangible. They wanted me for my knowledge, they valued and respected what I knew. It was a good feeling to know that two of the most powerful men in the world wanted to hear what I had to say.

And I was getting a chance to share my thoughts with Trump himself. Igor and I had been invited to the first million-dollar-donor dinner at Trump International, set for April 30, 2018. It would be a small affair, with maybe a half-dozen or so guests; so it would be a great chance to get some time with Trump.

While I had other ideas, my intention for the dinner was to talk to Trump about cannabis legalization. It was that important to me.

The idea had taken root, even among many Republicans. I made a point to bring the subject up frequently when I was with power brokers and I was surprised to find that many prominent conservatives, including Joe Ahearn, were for legalization. But there were two problems for them. Cannabis was not truly legal anywhere because it wasn't legal federally and that wouldn't change without a big push. And none of them could get their message directly to Trump to get that push. I thought I'd give it a try.

I even put together a presentation and ran it by an old friend who also happened to be a major player when it came to criminal law and cannabis legalization, Joseph A. Bondy. Not only has the American College of Trial Lawyers named him one of America's Top 100 Attorneys and one of the Top 100 Criminal Trial Lawyers, He specializes in cases pertaining to cannabis and holds a lifetime seat on NORML's National Legal Committee.

So, I was very excited to head to dinner at the Trump International.

Again, Igor managed to catch it all for posterity despite the usual warnings about using cameras or recording devices.

The action begins with a group of guests making patter while anticipating Trump's arrival.

After the President enters the room, he is seated in the middle of one side of the long-ish table, and Igor and I are put together right across from him, definitely close enough to talk comfortably.

Trump begins by falsely claiming that his popularity is higher than it's ever been, despite nothing but "bad publicity." He continues to praise himself to cheerful laughs from the guests.

We fall silent, however, when Trump discusses his successes with North Korea and a plan to meet Kim Jong-un. He mentions a trade war with China, and the group becomes much more animated, even applauding, and one person thanks Trump for his work in that area. There is a great deal of complaining from Trump about familiar themes — asking why the U.S. is protecting other countries militarily while those very same countries are ruining our economy and laughing at us, as well as the problems with getting his wall up. He also takes some time out to criticize Democrats Hillary Clinton, Barack Obama and California Congresswoman Maxine Waters, who he says possesses a "low IQ."

I don't really join in the conversation, which is mostly about petroleum, until it turns to the vital pipeline between Germany and Russia, which goes right through Ukraine.

At the mention of Ukraine, Trump asks me how they're doing.

Bad, I told him. They love you though. I knew what to say.

Trump acknowledges that, then calls them "great fighters."

I repeated that and that they love Trump. I then tell him that that Russia has been holding a bomb over their heads for a long time and that the Ukrainians are waiting for direction. I was sure that Trump knew what I meant.

Even before the Russians officially invaded, the low-intensity war in Ukraine had already been a nightmare. I realized that Ukraine could never get on its feet as long as it was fighting Russian-backed rebels within its own borders. And Putin wouldn't stop destabilizing the country unless he was forced to. It just seemed obvious to me that the U.S. should step in and mediate a peace process.

But my attempts to further the back and forth are drowned out by other voices talking about how the Javelin missiles already being imported to Ukraine would stop the rebels, as if that were enough.

Unbidden, Trump asks me what would happen if "Russia goes in and gets Ukraine."

I pause for effect and tell him: They'd love to, but they're scared of you (I played the flattery game too). He really didn't understand the concept that the threat of an overwhelming American military reaction keeps the peace in many parts of the world. And I knew Putin didn't mind using his own military on people he didn't consider Russians, as he had with the Chechens and Georgians.

Trump insists that Russia has already gotten what they wanted, "access to the sea."

No, not really, I say, handing Trump a rare semi-contradiction. I tell him that Ukraine is actually a vast country and that their natural resources are tremendous. I turn it up by saying that Ukrainians are throwing up in their throats because the pipeline that goes through their country doesn't do anything for them.

"Ukraine has oil?" Trump, clearly surprised, asks me, even though we had spoken about it before.

Igor — silent up till then — chimes in and adds that Ukraine is "Number 1" in Europe but that they don't have any money.

The rest of the crowd advises Trump to stay away from Ukraine because it's "dangerous" and that they "supported the Clintons."

I agree that the Ukrainian government had favored the Clintons and that Joe Biden is a big thing over there. He was widely seen as an anti-corruption crusader.

Then another voice joins those of Igor (again saying "Number 1" in his deep accent) and me, comparing Ukraine to West Texas and acknowledging that Ukraine does indeed have large quantities of petroleum, but no infrastructure to get it to global markets. I then give Trump a vaguely stated offer. They're just waiting for your support a little bit, I put on the table. It made perfect sense to me.

Trump asks: "How long would they last in a fight with Russia?" It's kind of like he knew something.

Without us, not very long, I answered. Then I added that Russia, keep in mind, talks a big game but they're not, he's not, ready to play. I slipped that in to get Trump to equate Russia with Putin.

I knew at the time that Putin was working to bring Ukraine to its knees, but I really didn't think he would actually invade. Nobody did. I wasn't really that surprised at Trump's question — it didn't take privileged knowledge to see that Putin had his eyes on Ukraine's petroleum reserves — just how abruptly it came about.

After some mutterings about how a full-scale invasion could never happen because the size of Russia's economy was a limiting factor on its reach.

I then reiterate Ukraine's fondness for Trump. They very much appreciate everything you're doing, I tell him. They're gonna be okay if you support them. I then assure him that Poroshenko is a good guy and that he wants to do the right thing.

Corruption is mentioned off to the side, then the topic turns to Ukraine's support of Germany. The crowd's reaction makes that sound like a bad thing. Playing to the audience, I mention that a lot of European countries are backstabbing us. I knew he'd love that. The crowd falls silent and seems to be very interested in what I have to say. I discreetly mumble something about the U.S. taking over, then tell Trump that the biggest problem I saw for Ukrainian-American relations is the ambassador.

U.S. Ambassador to Ukraine Marie Yovanovitch was a career diplomat, serving as ambassador to Kyrgyzstan and Armenia before Ukraine. After she arrived in Ukraine, she pushed its government for serious anti-corruption measures and had the support of the Obama administration, particularly Vice-President Biden. "It is increasingly clear that Ukraine's once-in-a-generation opportunity for change has not yet resulted in the anti-corruption or rule-of-law reforms that Ukrainians expect or deserve," she said later.

She was unpopular with Ukraine's wealthy and those who planned to be. They were well aware that any serious investigations would easily expose them and their alignment, if not outright fealty, to the power brokers in Russia, not their own country (including more than a few elected politicians).

With my many connections in various fields, there was a consensus about Yovanovitch — she had to go. And, when they found out I was American, they couldn't wait to tell me about how bad Yovanovitch was for Ukraine, without giving too many specifics, of course.

Nobody actually came out to say that they'd like to do something corrupt but that she was standing in the way, just that she was sticking her nose where it didn't belong and that she was overstepping her bounds by interfering with local politics when that was not her actual job. In fact, more of the Ukrainians I knew were complaining about her than they were about Putin or the war. When I pressed them on what really made Yovanovitch a problem, they told me that she had been saying terrible things about Trump.

So, at the table, I started to tell him about her. Where we start is … we gotta get rid of the ambassador, I tell him. She's still left over from the Clinton administration. Later, I found out that she'd been a diplomat since the Reagan administration, an ambassador since the George W. Bush years and was posted to Ukraine by Obama. She's basically walking around, saying, "Wait, he's gonna get impeached," I told him. "Just wait." I knew that hearing that would bother Trump. He's obsessive about not looking like a loser, and he dreaded the idea of an impeachment.

There are a few laughs.

After some mumbling, Trump says: "Get rid of her, get rid of her tomorrow." In all fairness, he might well have sounded to anyone else like he had been joking. But I knew he wasn't. "Take her out, okay?" he then says in an undoubtedly serious tone. "Do it."

There's a bit of applause (probably one person) and some mostly unintelligible words that I could tell included "Pompeo."

The mood lightens again. After some laughing, there's a discussion about how maddening watching the media is. I concur. The man who had introduced the topic then calls it a "Deep State deal." Everyone agrees, then Trump said that the media had "stuff" about the "other side" that they were trying to conceal, but that it was "coming out."

After that, the conversation and atmosphere turns more jovial, and then I finally get to talk to Trump about cannabis legalization, my primary political concern. I ask the President if there was anything that could be done about banks and their refusal or inability to work with the cannabis industry.

"You mean marijuana?" Trump asks me. "I don't know if that's good or bad." As was usual with Trump, every issue was one or the other, lacking in any nuance.

Other voices drown out mine, including one man who says he can't find employees because of "drugs." But I persist, and point out that a tremendous amount of revenue stood to be made and that younger people are essentially all for it. I tell Trump that it's something that will happen in the near future no matter how you look at it ... you're not going to stop it ...

Someone breaks in to say that "in Colorado, they have more motor vehicle accidents ..." Colorado was the first state to legalize recreational cannabis use in 2012. And the conversation turns to how bad marijuana use is.

But just as quickly, they all appear to change their minds and support cannabis after voices say that it "helps with opioids" and Don Jr, added that it causes much less social and economic damage than alcohol. They probably took their cue by looking at the President, who was clearly interested in what I had to say.

I then recommend a bipartisan committee (that would report directly to Trump) look into the issue, and add that it would give him a boost for the midterms because many states, with a significant majority of the U.S. population, have already chosen legalization.

Someone then asks me what I was doing, presumably professionally. I introduce Igor as my partner and say that we were interested in purchasing petroleum as Ukraine was privatizing its biggest energy companies. Maybe with some help from these people, Global Energy Producers could get off the ground, I thought to myself.

I'm asked about Ukraine, so I add Poland and Turkey as countries I'm dealing with. I also say that I want to ship LNG to Ukraine, it would cut Russia off at the knees.

The rest of the conversation is made up of harsh criticisms of Clinton and Obama. Trump reminds everyone that he did much better than expected against Clinton and that he would have devastated Obama if he had run. He mentions that, of his potential 2020 opponents, the "one who scares" him the most is Bernie Sanders and that he hopes the Democrats will nominate Joe Biden, because he is sure Biden would be the easiest candidate to beat in the 2020 election.

Even though he didn't actually believe that. In the summer, Axios would be the first to publish that White House advisers told them that Trump feared a Biden candidacy more than any other. We all knew it.

After that, the group discusses how poorly electric car companies and their products have performed, which actually wasn't true (at the time, their sales had increased threefold over the previous two years), and how much people still prefer gas-powered cars. Those opinions could certainly be expected from a group made up mainly of petroleum-selling people.

Cars didn't matter to me. I wanted to talk about my plan to ship liquefied natural gas from the U.S. to Ukraine.

Igor and I can be heard talking in low voices between ourselves, using Russian. We didn't say much, just about how we can steer the conversation toward Global Energy Producers. Otherwise, we're simply agreeing with everything everyone says and laughing at Trump's jokes.

It's then that I pull out a letter from Rabbi Moshe Azman (who claims to be the National Rabbi of Ukraine and helps Republican causes in the U.S.) in which he writes that in Hebrew gematria numerology, Trump's name adds up to 424, which he shares with the messiah, and means the "anointed one" (which is also the same root of "Jesus" in Latin and "Christ" in Greek). Igor says in his heavy accent: "It's like miracle." I then describe to Trump that it means the "savior of the world."

"It can't hurt," Trump replies jovially. He then takes the letter from me and keeps it for good luck.

The video ends — but it's really just more of the same after that. As the event was winding down, I was socializing among the guests. I felt good, I had shown Trump that I had significant knowledge of the situation in Eastern Europe — certainly more than he had — and I had also introduced the concept of making money and political headway with cannabis.

Things were looking up.

Chapter 21
A Session with Sessions

M y help was urgently needed in Texas. Sessions was embroiled in a tight race for his seat against popular Democrat Colin Allred. Allred was not just a civil-rights lawyer who had earned his J.D. at Cal-Berkeley, he was also a former NFL linebacker and very charismatic. The often contentious-sounding Sessions — who has been called a poor public speaker and refused to talk to the media without a communications staffer present — would have a big challenge in front of him.

He didn't seem like someone I would get along with. My primary political issue was cannabis legalization. As Chair of the House Rules Committee, Sessions repeatedly quashed amendments that would help legalize cannabis, He even once fought hard against federal approval of allowing medical marijuana in states where its recreational use was already legal.

I started talking with Sessions at the Mar-a-Lago event. Since he was a politician from Texas, the conversation, naturally, turned to petroleum. I described the situation in Ukraine.

The problem, I told him, was the U.S. ambassador, Marie Yovanovitch. I described her with some of the things I had heard in Kyiv. It was bad enough that she was sticking her nose in everyone's business, but she was also bad mouthing the Boss. She wouldn't, I had heard, even hang Trump's picture up in the embassy. It wasn't just that she hated him, but she was telling people that he was going to be impeached.

Sessions quickly became interested in the Yovanovitch situation, but I could tell that what he really wanted to talk about was getting noticed by Trump.

He'd been energized by attending two Trump events in quick succession and he believed that if he could just get close to Trump, he'd be able to accomplish what he wanted.

Sessions knew how to operate. He'd been in Congress for a while. Sessions was an important person to Trump because he was another reliable

Republican vote in the House, a major player as a committee leader and, as a representative from Texas, a link to the oil and gas businesses that overwhelmingly supported Trump (and had a chance to make me rich). What made

recruiting all that much easier was the fact that Sessions was a dyed-in-the-wool Trumper, voting in favor of the President's position no less than 97.5 percent of the time, according to FiveThirtyEight.

Getting Sessions reelected was a priority. The fact that I could potentially benefit from that just made it all the better.

The promise of a few bucks opened up many doors for me with Congressman Pete Sessions.

We had even a common link, Trump, Giuliani and Sessions all had an interest in the continued success of the American oil and gas industry in the face of climate change activism and increasingly competitive renewable energy. Igor and I were staking our futures on Global Energy Producers even more than I was with Fraud Guarantee.

With that in mind, Igor and Correia and I went to D.C. to visit Sessions.

We spoke about what we could do for his campaign and how America First Action was definitely on his side.

He told us that he had sent a letter requesting Yovanovitch's removal to Pompeo, but had received no answer.

I told him that was disappointing.

Sessions said that he had written another letter. This one to President Trump.

Sessions' letter to Trump (in my hand).

It explained what he had said in the first letter, that he had sent it to Pompeo and had not received a reply. He asked me if I could hand deliver the second letter to Trump.

I couldn't believe my ears. Although I had been surrounded by some of the top people in the U.S. government, I was still very much affected by the gravity of the situation. Holy shit, I thought. A Congressman wants me to take a letter to the President — for his eyes only. Who does that? I really thought it was a great honor. That I held the trust of my country in my hands.

Besides, I had already introduced Trump to the idea of getting rid of Yovanovitch— I agreed to take him the letter.

After that, we decided to talk about money. To get that ball rolling, Sessions introduced us to his chief of staff, Caroline Boothe. She later remembered our visit and described it to the media vividly. She gave us a VIP tour of the House of Representatives and I had a photo taken of myself sitting in Sessions' chair while holding a gavel. Boothe said she remembered me as "nice" and chatty. And so was she. Boothe told me that Sessions wouldn't be able to make the annual Congressional baseball game, so she gave me two tickets to cheer on the Republicans and Sessions' jersey.

Boothe recognized that we were official visitors and donors, but later told reporters that she noticed that Igor and I — all open shirts and multiple gold chains — looked out of place in suit-and-tied Washington.

I turned the conversation to donations for Sessions' campaign. She said, "I'd love to talk about this further, let's take it across the street, you can't conduct any campaign or unofficial business on government property."

We all walked with Sessions to the Capitol Hill Club, a members-only Republican hangout (with no official affiliation with the party), about a block away from the Capitol. I'd been there dozens of times, and was recognizable to the staff and many patrons.

Boothe later told the media that our group was excited about making a donation, especially me, but I think that might just have been my personality. I did tell her that I wanted to max out and give more through bundling (individuals at the time could contribute no more than $2,700 to a candidate, but PACs could donate more through bundling — for example, the Koch Brothers managed to contribute $889 million during the 2016 election). Waiting a beat, I mentioned bundling around $20,000.

Of the original $1 million we had pledged to America First and been riding ever since, this would be the first actual payment we made. We sent $5,400, our combined personal maximums, to Sessions.

That wouldn't have been illegal, unless the money came from a foreign or criminal source. Since Igor and I were both American citizens and had clean records, and the money came from Igor's refinancing loan, I felt that the whole thing was above board. I did not know that the Laxalt money could have been mixed with the money from Muraviev, who was not a citizen. Igor had used the same accounts.

That's it. That's the crime.

Chapter 22
Stormy Weather

Things were also changing, perhaps to my advantage, in Ukraine. The Obama administration had been warm to Kyiv, doing its best to tilt their philosophy westward. Because of that — and the near-universal belief that Hillary would win in 2016 — they backed Clinton heavily. When Trump shocked the world and actually won, the people who ran Ukraine were caught totally off guard.

That meant they had no relationship whatsoever with the incoming administration. As one of the few people, with important contacts in both governments, I knew I could make my voice heard.

Poroshenko appeared to be trying to get on the good side of America's new set of politicians. Things were not quite as warm on the other side. Early indications that the new administration might hold back military aid from Ukraine unless it played ball emerged as early as May 2018. At least from the Ukrainians' point of view.

While Poroshenko was negotiating with the U.S. for Javelin missiles, chief prosecutor Volodymyr Ariev blocked the country's investigations into Manafort and made no secret as to why. "In every possible way, we will avoid irritating the top American officials," Ariev said. "We shouldn't spoil relations with the administration." It is important that Ariev said it was the "administration" that he didn't want to annoy, rather than the country, because Manafort was still very much under investigation in the U.S. It would appear that Ukraine could put up with behavior like Manafort's if it meant getting weapons to defend itself. That's how things work in politics, just like they do in organized crime. Don't sweat the small stuff.

Manafort might have gotten off the hook in Ukraine, but his boss was still in trouble. Deripaska — as well as Kirill Shamalov, Putin's ex-son-in-law who suddenly somehow became a billionaire after his wedding, and 15 other Russians — became the target of economic sanctions by the U.S. Treasury Department. It announced:

"Deripaska has been investigated for money laundering, and has been accused of threatening the lives of business rivals, illegally wiretapping a government official, and taking part in extortion and racketeering. There are also allegations that Deripaska bribed a government official, ordered the murder of a businessman and had links to a Russian organized crime group."

Despite the widespread belief that Trump would reflexively take it easy on the Russians, I was not surprised that he allowed the Treasury Department to go after Deripaska, Shamalov and others. He was playing to his base who wanted him to show that he was not soft on Russia. It was nothing serious, certainly nothing that would bother Putin. That was the fine line Trump walked. He made it look to his fans that he was "tough on Russia," while still bending over backwards for its leader at the same time.

He had a much harder time being as subtle in domestic politics, which had become increasingly partisan, or with his own indiscretions.

When the news of Trump's 2016 affair with adult entertainment performer Stormy Daniels broke, it was Giuliani who quickly took center stage in his defense.

The much-discussed drama first came to public eyes after an April 9, 2018 FBI raid of Michael Cohen's office at the Rockefeller Center law firm of Squire Patton Boggs, his apartment in Trump Tower and his room in the Loews Regency Hotel. The warrant had been issued by the U.S. Attorney's Office for the SDNY after a recommendation from Mueller.

The warrant allowed agents to seize emails, tax records, business records and other potential evidence in relation to any payments that he had made to Daniels just before the 2016 election as well as evidence pertaining to the notorious taped conversation with Billy Bush.

Squire Patton Boggs terminated its working relationship with Cohen.

An unnamed administration official later told The New York Times that Trump raged for hours after receiving the news. He complained loudly about the FBI, the Department of Justice in general, Sessions, Mueller's team and the annoying fact that there had been no such investigation of Bill Clinton, who he considered to be a serial philanderer.

Aboard Air Force One, Trump officially denied any knowledge of repaying Cohen for a $130,000 payment to Stephanie Clifford (Daniels' off-stage name) in exchange for her signing a non-disclosure agreement, which she did just a few days before the 2016 election.

It was huge, worldwide news and we all went into damage control mode.

Before the raid, Cohen had told the media that he would have taken a bullet for Trump. But that was before Trump surprised us all by doing something he would later do time and time again. He abandoned Cohen.

Trump couldn't deny knowing Cohen, but he said that he barely knew him — an outrageous lie — and described him as more of an errand boy than an attorney. That slap in the face effectively squandered any loyalty Cohen had for his boss. After Trump said that he wouldn't pay for Cohen's

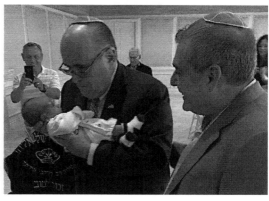

Giuliani holding my son Nathan at his bris.

legal fees, he turned and agreed to be a cooperating witness against Trump.

That, of course, made him Public Enemy No. 1 in the White House.

Other than perhaps Trump himself, nobody was more upset than Giuliani. To him, loyalty was everything. But it wasn't a two-way street. Just like in the mafia, you owed the Boss everything and he owed you nothing. You get caught? Take your punishment and keep your mouth shut. That's how you get ahead.

Giuliani thought I'd be as disgusted with Cohen as he was. He asked me how well I knew him. I told him that we knew a lot of people in common, but knew of each other more than we actually knew each other.

That's when he asked me if I knew anything embarrassing about him, something he might not want to get out now that he was in the public eye.

I told him I didn't, but I'd ask around. Giuliani told me to try to find any dirt on Cohen. He might have had his team, but he didn't have his eyes and ears on the streets like I did anymore.

A few days later, Giuliani appeared on Trump-friendly Fox News. It should have been a routine repetition of the party line, but it certainly wasn't.

Almost immediately, Giuliani denied exactly what the President had told the same network just hours earlier. Asked a leading question about the Mueller Investigation's apparent inability to find any Russian payments to Trump, Giuliani decided to bring up Cohen unbidden and totally out of context. A visibly flustered Sean Hannity appeared to be desperately trying to get back to the softie question he'd posed, when Giuliani said:

> "Having something to do with paying some Stormy Daniels woman $130,000? Which, I mean, is going to turn out to be perfectly legal. That money was not campaign money. Sorry, I'm giving you a fact now that you don't know. It's not campaign money. No campaign finance violation."

In fact, he repeated variations on that statement several times, often in shouted fragments.

Giuliani then said that Trump was actually aware of the payment despite Hannity's question inferring that the President did not. "Ah, he didn't know about the specifics of it, as far as I know," Giuliani quickly replied to what appeared to be Hannity's utter astonishment. "But he did know about the general arrangement, that Michael would take care of things like this."

I didn't let it bother me. I thought that Trump was too beloved by his fans for something as minor as a payoff for a porn star to keep her mouth shut about a dalliance to make even a tiny dent in his popularity. What did people expect? That's Trump.

Chapter 23
Land of Milk and Money

Although I was still steamed at Ballard for not paying me my rightful share of his Turkey deals, we chatted amiably the next time we met. Of course we did. I knew that I still had to do business with the guy, so why not? You know that old saying about keeping your enemies close? It applied.

I was much closer to Trump at the time. When he first met me, Giuliani was sure that I was rich. That didn't last long. As you might expect, he has a staff of security experts who do background checks on everyone he gets close to. He soon knew I was not a wealthy man.

That didn't stop him from being my friend, and that impressed me. It became clear to me that he valued my input, even though I didn't really have any money.

Still, I had the trappings of money, like the use of a private jet. The one thing about Rudy, though, is that he never asked how I had the use of a jet. No matter what the situation, he could not possibly care less about who was paying for anything — as long as it wasn't him.

I needed Rudy to promote my businesses. At the time, he was still world famous and considered by many to be a national hero (even if his image had tarnished). I thought he'd be a perfect spokesman for Fraud Guarantee. I even had a theme for the advertising. In a play on the famous American Express' line "don't leave home without it," I wanted to go with "don't invest without it." Even if some people didn't necessarily like Giuliani, he was a powerful symbol when it came to security, trust and crime fighting. He'd already done the same for LifeLock, the identity theft prevention service.

I discussed the idea of Giuliani becoming the face of Fraud Guarantee, and we both agreed it would be a great idea. With Giuliani on board, I believed, it would be no problem to find an underwriter.

There was a problem, though. Giuliani said that he absolutely had to be paid up front. That presented me with a dilemma I had grown accustomed to

— I needed money to make money. And Giuliani wasn't cheap, despite his chronic financial problems. He would not go any lower than $500,000 in two payments.

I went to an unlikely source for the money. Normally, I'd go through Igor or some Russian or Ukrainian big shot. But I knew it wouldn't look at all good for Giuliani to receive any money from foreign sources, especially Russians or Ukrainians.

Luck smiled on me, though. I found an American source for the money in, of all places, Jerusalem.

An important man in the Jewish community — Joe Frager of the National Council of Young Israel — invited me and Igor on one of a series of regular trips to Israel. The guest list was made up of conservatives, both Christian and Jewish, who had a strong interest in Israel and its security efforts.

Frager was a top-rated gastroenterologist based in Flushing, Queens, and active in Israeli-American causes, including organizing the annual Israel Day concert in Central Park and raising funds for controversial Israeli settlements and pro-Israel Republican candidates.

He drew some notice, even alarm, when he worked, from September 2017 to February 2018, as a lobbyist for the Middle Eastern nation of Qatar. The country had been seeking good press in the West, recruiting many lobbyists, because its relationships with Iran and Hamas had caused friction with the U.S., Israel, Saudi Arabia and the United Arab Emirates.

It's also a hard sell. Qatar is a monarchy with Sharia law that uses flogging and stoning for "crimes" such as alcohol consumption, adultery, blasphemy, apostasy and homosexuality. Government critics are frequently imprisoned and violently anti-Israeli sentiment is rampant.

Frager and I met in June 2018 at a Trump International America First event. He later told The Times of Israel that he saw my yarmulke and approached me. My memory is different. He knew who I was, everybody did. I wasn't just some random Jew he found who just happened to be a major donor to the Republican party and close to Giuliani.

Once we established exactly who each other were, Frager started to sell me and Igor on the idea of coming along on his next trip to Israel. "They loved Israel," he later told the media. "I was trying to motivate them, further cultivate a relationship with them that would ultimately lead to them helping a lot of causes I'm involved in, in Israel."

Most of the tour were Christians, including some big names. A former governor of Arkansas, Mike Huckabee mounted a surprisingly popular 2008 Presidential campaign and a much less successful one in 2016. He has never made an effort to hide his evangelical views or his love of Israel, which he visits "three to five times a year."

Another one was Anthony Scaramucci, who had lasted just 11 days as Trump's director of communications.

More important to me was a guy I met on the trip and got along with well. Charles S. Gucciardo was a wealthy and prominent Long Island personal-injury lawyer and a big America First donor. He was a total Trumper, saying at a 2016 RNC event in D.C. that Hillary Clinton had been "perpetrating a fraud on the American people" and that Trump had "made more people, more workers, more money than anybody on Capitol Hill."

Gucciardo also employed Christianné Allen, a bright influencer who would later become Giuliani's spokeswoman while she was a 20-year-old

Joe Frager (left), Mike Huckabee and me in Israel.

student at ultra-conservative Liberty University.

I think she was about 16 when she started working for Gucciardo, but I could be off by a bit. A social media semi-celebrity, she posted photos of four visits to the White House in April 2018.

The more I got to know Gucciardo, the more I believed that he could be a key contributor to my success. When he heard about my dilemma of being unable to find the money to pay Giuliani to be the spokesman for Fraud Guarantee, he became excited.

He told me that he wanted to make a major investment in my company. To me, the calculus around the $500,000 I needed seemed simple. Gucciardo had the money and really wanted to get closer to Giuliani. Giuliani wanted money to represent Fraud Guarantee. It appeared to be a match if not made in heaven, at least in the Holy Land.

But Gucciardo had one condition, He had to meet Giuliani in person and hear from him exactly what he was going to do for Fraud Guarantee. I told him that I could make that happen.

Me with podcaster Yair Netanyahu.

I enjoyed myself on the trip. I'd never been to Israel, and thought I should go, because I am a pretty religious person. Besides, there was some talk that we'd meet Netanyahu.

Even Rabbi Moshe Azman showed up.

The whole tour was an excellent idea I wish I had thought of. American political celebrities like Huckabee added publicity to Frager's causes and bringing rich Americans like Gucciardo and what he believed I actually was led to direct contributions.

We get a tour of the Holy Land, exposure to Israel's political movers and shakers and endless photo ops. It was a win-win.

I did not get to meet Prime Minister Benjamin Netanyahu, who was busy campaigning. But I did have a chance to get to know his son, Yair, a conservative podcaster who has found an audience among America's far right, including gaining approval from the Nazi-identified Daily Stormer.

Once we got back from Israel, I set up a private meeting between Giuliani and Gucciardo. I picked one of Giuliani's very favorite places — the luxurious Grand Havana Room in Midtown Manhattan.

They spoke at length in the cigar bar and Gucciardo must have liked what Giuliani told him, He agreed to invest the $500,000.

Later, Gucciardo's lawyer, Randy Zelin, described his client as a "passive investor" who only "invested because he believed that Mr. Giuliani — the former Mayor of New York City, former United States attorney for the Southern District of New York and, the first name in cybersecurity — was in front of, behind, and alongside the company, which would catapult the company into the world of cybersecurity and investor protection." Zelin said that, like me, he expected Giuliani to be a spokesman for the money. "He understood that he was investing in a reputable company that Rudolph Giuliani was going to be the spokesman and the face of," Zelin said of Gucciardo. "When you think of cybersecurity, you think of Rudolph Giuliani."

Things were definitely looking up. I was on top of the world because

Svetlana and I had another son,
Nathan. As is tradition, we had to have
a bris. It wasn't a huge event, maybe
20 people, and the guest of honor,
after Nathan of course, was Giuliani.
He was even given the great privilege
of holding the baby during the
procedure.

While it has been widely reported
that made Giuliani Nathan's
"godfather," that's a Christian

*Gucciardo, right, expected Giuliani to do
something for his $500,000. He didn't.*

tradition. Giuliani was actually a sandek, a role reserved for a respected
member of the community, a rare honor for a non-Jew.

Not much later, Giuliani received the second $250,000 payment. After I
paid Giuliani, I made plans to launch Fraud Guarantee. This was finally it, I
truly thought. I began to line up professionals to make the commercials and
other ads that would feature Giuliani speaking for Fraud Guarantee. It didn't
happen. It never did.

Giuliani, the close friend of mine, the sandek of my infant son, walked
away with the cash, delivering absolutely nothing. Later, when pressed by
the media, Giuliani would refer to the payments alternatively as a consulting
fee or as a legal retainer. But both Gucciardo and I are on public record, before the payment was even made, saying that the $500,000 was intended spe-
cifically for Giuliani to be Fraud Guarantee's spokesman.

It didn't matter anyway, because Giuliani delivered neither consulting
nor legal work for the company. He just stole the money. I still have no idea
how he got away with it.

Without any contribution from Giuliani at all, Fraud Guarantee failed to
launch. That put me in serious financial trouble once again.

The money went right from Gucciardo to Giuliani. That presented a
problem for Giuliani. He was desperate to hide it from Judith Nathan, since
they were going through a divorce at the time.

Later, many in the media would at least insinuate that the money had
been wired from overseas. Giuliani responded that he knew for a fact that the
money was from the U.S. and not connected with crime or criminal organizations. "I know beyond any doubt the source of the money is not any ques-

tionable source," he told Reuters. "The money did not come from foreigners. I can rule that out 100 percent."

He was right. It came from Long Island.

Chapter 24
Something in My Pocket

When I went to my next America First event in July, I was sure to remember to bring Sessions' letter. It wasn't the same letter that he had written to Pompeo, but the second letter, this one specifically for Trump. It described the first letter, complained that Pompeo didn't respond and asked for help with the situation.

I didn't know it at the time, but Pete Sessions was part of a group of old friends, mostly based in Texas, who were all involved with the petroleum business. I already knew some of them — like Ahearn, Bailey and Hicks — but I didn't know all of them. In fact, I didn't know the most important one.

As the get-together drew to a close, Aaron and I were standing in line to get our picture taken with Trump when Ahearn approached with another man I hadn't met before.

He was a billionaire, Harry Sargeant III. Although he was not really from Texas, I definitely considered him to be one of

Trump and me, just after I gave him Sessions' letter. He immediately put it in his jacket pocket.

the group that Sessions was in. Sargeant was from Florida. In fact, some published reports have said that there's a shrine to him at FSU's Pi Kappa Alpha fraternity labeled: "The Most Powerful Man That No One Knows."

And he really was powerful. A former Marine and commercial pilot, he made his money first in asphalt tankers and then by exporting petroleum to U.S. forces in Iraq — a deal he is said to have made with the aid of the government of Jordan. In Republican circles, he's not just known as a major donor, but also something of a kingmaker.

At least, when everything goes according to plan. When Giuliani ran for President in 2008, Sargeant began campaigning for him, then the Republican front-runner. But several scandals broke (and people heard him speak), so Giuliani fell off the top of the leaderboard.

Petroleum pals: (from left) Sargeant, Nigerian oil tycoon Onajite Okoloko, Trump and me.

Chronically short on money, he developed a novel strategy in which he would ignore all the small states' primaries to concentrate on the big ones. While the other Republican hopefuls all campaigned hard in Iowa, New Hampshire, Michigan, North Carolina and Nevada. Giuliani sat on his hands and fell further and further behind.

Finally, in what he believed would be a master stroke, he spent all of his money, time and energy on Florida. Once he won that, he figured, he'd have the funds and the momentum to springboard his way to the Republican nomination. He was extra confident because he had put Sargeant, a proven commodity by then, in charge of his Florida efforts.

Giuliani finished a distant fourth in Florida and gave up his Presidential hopes. Naturally, Giuliani blamed Sargeant and Sargeant blamed Giuliani. It created significant bad blood between the two and they hadn't spoken since.

But politics has a funny way of changing these things. Once Trump took office, it was clear to everyone, especially big-time Republican players, that Giuliani had suddenly become very important. Everybody knew that Trump listened to him more than anyone else. Sargeant told me he wanted to get back in communication with Giuliani because he said he had a plan. It involved Venezuela and its despotic President, Nicolás Maduro.

The only Western Hemisphere member of OPEC, vast oil reserves have brought Venezuela very little in the way of economic development, peace or good luck.

Tight control of oil revenue by a few rich families and foreign interests has led to discontent and frequent uprisings by the local population. Since oil became the country's primary export in the 1920s, Venezuela has survived dictators with cults of personality, corrupt elections, violent demonstrations (usually with looting), equally violent government crackdowns, Communist oil-industry strikes, a 1945 coup, a 1948 coup, a 1992 attempted coup and a 1994 banking crisis.

The country was approaching total economic collapse when, in 1999, it elected a charismatic but remarkably eccentric President in Hugo Chávez, a major player in the 1992 coup attempt. His governing style, which he claimed to be a throwback to Simón Bolívar's revolutionary days, was an odd mixture of Marxism, capitalism, dictatorship and conspiracy theories. It created a rare situation in which a government received harsh criticism from the left, right and center.

Another coup was attempted in 2002. The already shaky economy fell into a black hole, emergencies were essentially ignored by federal authorities and Chávez became bolder and more paranoid. He was frequently at odds with the U.S., which he blamed for the 2002 coup attempt, a foiled assassination attempt and a plot to antagonize Colombia into a war. In an attempt to embarrass the U.S., he offered free oil to "America's poor," earning him the nickname the "Oil Pimp" by the New York tabloids. A general strike helped the battered economy implode even further. Formerly middle-class Venezuelans found themselves searching through trash for something to eat.

After winning a much-criticized recall vote, Chávez amended the constitution, allowing him to be president for life. After overseeing unprecedented inflation and violent crime rates, becoming a major Russian arms importer, introducing a government-subsidized cell phone with a name that, in Spanish slang, meant "excellent penis" and publicly telling the King of Spain to "shut up," Chávez died in 2013.

He left behind a legacy of people starving in the streets of a nation blessed with enormous natural wealth. He was replaced by his vice-president, Nicolás Maduro, whose first act was to install a rule-by-decree privilege for himself, saying it was necessary to fight the nation's massive corruption (which he and his predecessor had nurtured). It was a legal move, since his party held more than two-thirds of the seats in the National Assembly. He then passed a law that allowed the military to confiscate the property of appliance retailers to sell their wares for quick cash.

Maduro won the 2018 election, but it was fraught with many complaints of corruption and acts of violence. But the opposition won more than two-thirds of the seats in the National Assembly. Massive protests ensued. The

National Assembly declared the election of Maduro invalid and named Juan Guaidó as interim president, a move that was backed by the Venezuelan Supreme Court, operating in exile from Panama. Maduro had him arrested, but he was quickly released.

The world noticed and reacted. Soon, only Antigua and Barbuda, Bolivia, China, Cuba, Nicaragua, North Korea and Russia still recognized the Maduro government, and it remained in de facto power shakily. The standoff seemed poised to lead to a violent resolution.

Naturally, that instability in Venezuela caused a great deal of alarm for American oil companies, who had already been stung repeatedly by Chávez and his attention-getting whims. Their concerns matter to any administration, especially one as dependent on their donations as Trump's.

Sargeant told me that he was pretty close with Maduro. In fact, he even said that Maduro used to refer to the American billionaire as his "grandson." Now that things were getting out of control in Venezuela, Maduro wanted a soft landing. But war hawks like Bolton wouldn't listen to anything Sargeant had to say about that. Sargeant had to get to Trump to overcome any opposition. If he could convince Trump to help Maduro exit Venezuela safely, Maduro would then repay them by allowing free elections. That way, Maduro gets what he wants, Trump gets a win with regime change and Sargeant and his guys would reap the rewards in billions of barrels of petroleum.

But to get to Trump, I told him, he had to go through Giuliani. Not only was that becoming common knowledge, but Sargeant told me that he had a close relationship with Ballard, who was in the second echelon of Trump's people. Even though Ballard had Trump's ear, it paled in comparison to what Giuliani had. What Trump heard from Giuliani, he valued.

Ballard had been hired by Raúl Gorrín, a Venezuelan lawyer and investor who had purchased Globovisión, a 24-hour all-news TV station in 2013, just after Chávez died. Globovisión had been unfailingly critical of Chávez (he even accused them of encouraging his assassination, but many just chalked that up to Chávez being Chávez). Its previous owner, Guillermo Zuloaga, said the sale came because of external pressure. Immediately after the sale, the broadcaster announced that it would be moving toward the political center, indicating that it would be cozying up to Maduro.

So Sargeant, Ballard and the whole Texas gang seemed to be on Team Maduro. The problem was that nobody else was.

Sargeant had told me that he had thought that Bolton was one of his boys, but Bolton had convinced Trump and Pompeo that Maduro was bad news and that getting involved with him would end up as a terrible mess. The White House was officially, and decidedly, pro-Guaidó. In fact, Bolton was not against the idea of sending in the U.S. military if it came down to that.

If his team had any chance of succeeding, Sargeant said that he had to get through to Giuliani — the only person, they believed, who could get Trump to override Bolton and Pompeo.

It was also common knowledge that I had a big plan that involved shipping liquefied natural gas. Even if he hadn't known, someone like Ballard or Ahearn would have gotten him up to speed pretty quickly.

So, my introduction to Sargeant didn't seem to me to be a chance meeting. It would appear that he wanted to get to know me so that I could relay his messages to Giuliani.

My first impression of him was that he was a powerful man and he liked to make people aware of it. Bingo, I thought to myself. For someone like me, who was trying to get into the natural gas transportation business, meeting this guy was like buying a lottery ticket. This guy had tankers, exactly what I needed for my natural gas plan. I felt that my chances of hitting the big time had just gone up exponentially.

We hit it off; rich guys always like me, and agreed to exchange numbers.

After he left, Aaron and I reached the end of the line. I greeted Trump and he smiled as we spoke to each other. As we were getting ready for a photo, I reached into my side pocket and — I was grabbed by the Secret Service.

Trump told them to hold on and they let me go. The President knew me, so he figured whatever I was reaching for was pretty safe.

I handed him the letter, and explained that Sessions wanted him to read it. I added that it was about Ukraine.

Trump suddenly looked a lot more interested. He took the letter from me and put it in his inside jacket pocket.

Mission accomplished.

***

Sargeant and I spoke frequently after that. Venezuela was as much his baby as Ukraine was mine. I really hadn't thought much about the country before then. I knew they had oil and that Chávez had run the economy into the ground, but it was otherwise outside my realm of expertise.

But Sargeant kept pushing the idea of me getting interested in Venezuela. I always listened, but I really started to pay attention when he said that I could make more money in a single day in Venezuela than I could in a lifetime in Ukraine.

Sargeant's ardent little group, which also included top military adviser Pete Marocco, all tried to convince me to talk to Giuliani about exactly how important Venezuela was. When I spoke with Giuliani, I told him that Sargeant, Hicks and Sessions had a solution to the tension in Venezuela in that, if the U.S. guaranteed Maduro a suitable exit strategy, we could avoid a full-

scale revolution in Venezuela and, potentially, a use of U.S. force.

Giuliani, after speaking to both Sessions and Sargeant about the dire state Venezuela was in, agreed that it would be a good idea to have a call with Maduro.

Sergeant outlined the plan. He told us that he would fly to Venezuela,

From left, Sargeant, me and Igor at the door of Sargeant's private jet. I put a lots of miles on that plane.

while Giuliani, Sessions and I would meet up in D.C. to initiate a call between Maduro, Sessions and Giuliani. There were no flights there from the U.S. because of sanctions, so Sargeant told me that he flew to Colombia, then took a smaller plane, literally flying below the radar, into Caracas.

I started dialing Sargeant's number, he was at the Palacio de Miraflores (Miraflores Palace), Maduro's residence, when Sessions stopped me. He was sure that the CIA and others were listening in on my phone. He handed me his own phone and said: "They can kiss my ass."

Just after Sessions made the introductions, Giuliani's phone rang. It was the President. We all knew he had to take the call. He excused himself and left the room.

Quickly, Maduro established what he wanted, actually expected, from the U.S. — a safe passage out of Venezuela with all of his money and some of his entourage. "I want to sit at home and watch football while I wear my Cowboys jersey," he said, indicating a preference for Texas.

In exchange, he would allow fair elections in Venezuela and relinquish control of the country. It's what is called a soft landing in diplomatic circles.

Sessions assured him that he and Giuliani would relay the message to Trump, giving Maduro reason to believe the deal might actually go through.

Giuliani returned after the call and Sessions filled him in. Giuliani thought it was a pretty fair deal.

So, he went to the White House to discuss it with the President. When Giuliani came into the Oval Office, Bolton and Pompeo were already there in a meeting about a different situation. Once Giuliani brought up the subject of Venezuela, Bolton left the room.

Just as he finished his pitch, Giuliani went outside to speak with Bolton. Giuliani, who believed that Bolton was loyal to him because he thought he had gotten him his job, expected total agreement.

He was wrong. Bolton told him to go fuck himself. If Bolton ever owed Giuliani anything, it had long since been payed off in his opinion. And, by then, Bolton was growing concerned about Giuliani's influence on Trump, especially when it came to Ukraine.

That resulted in a stalemate. The U.S., led by Bolton, officially supported Guaidó, to the point of military intervention if necessary. But Giuliani, representing powerful petroleum interests, lurked in the background, ready to fill Trump's ear about Maduro's offer. So, while the U.S. did nothing, Maduro clung to power, hastening the inevitable conflict over who ruled Venezuela.

Chapter 25
How to Win an Election

P riority Number 1 for me as the midterm elections approached was to get as many MAGA Republicans elected as possible. All the while, I was campaigning hard, particularly for DeSantis. I even brought Giuliani in to help. The two of us would tail DeSantis' plane all over the state and attend his events, usually with Giuliani as a featured speaker. And as if

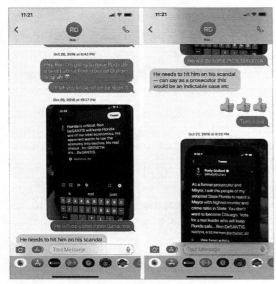

that wasn't enough, DeSantis texted me to encourage Giuliani to come out publicly against his Democrat opponent — former Tallahassee Mayor Andrew Gillum.

Gillum was soon the target of several accusations, including that: He had bought personal email software with taxpayer money (he had reimbursed the city), that his treasurer had received a government contract (he had fired him) and that he had obtained

When it came to campaigning, DeSantis always seemed to want to take the lowest road possible.

tickets to the Broadway musical Hamilton from an undercover FBI agent through his brother (he said that he simply received a gift from his brother and didn't ask him where the tickets had come from).

Of course, all of that came from our side. One of Gillum's oldest friends was his campaign treasurer, Adam Corey. They went back to their days together at Florida State. But some friends are closer than others. Sargeant and his lawyer, Christopher Kise, were also FSU alumni. Sargeant had also employed Corey for three years at his company, International Oil Trading. With a little convincing, Corey came out and told us about Gillum.

Even with all of our help, DeSantis really came close to blowing the 2018 Florida election.

Gillum knew who it was, but was powerless to stop it. "I had a trusting relationship and I felt like I allowed people around me who were acquaintances of his because I trusted him," Gillum told a reporter for The Tallahassee Democrat. "And it appears that if these guys were here for an investigation, that the only way they got to me was by leveraging my friendship with Adam."

Sensing his vulnerability like a shark smelling blood in the water, we poured in on. I texted DeSantis: "Hey Ron I'm going to have Rudy do a tweet about how crooked Gillum is."

DeSantis replied: "He needs to hit him hard on his scandal - can say as a prosecutor this would be an indictable case etc." I gave him more than he asked for. A lot more.

About a week before the election, Trump tweeted:

"In Florida there is a choice between a Harvard/Yale educated man named @RonDeSantisFL who has been a great Congressman and will be a great Governor - and a Dem who is a thief and who is Mayor of poorly run Tallahassee, said to be one of the most corrupt cities in the Country!"

The President kept it up the next night while appearing on Fox News. "Here's a guy that, in my opinion, is a stone cold thief, and his city, Tallahassee, is known as the most corrupt in Florida, and one of the most corrupt in the nation," Trump said. "The FBI offered him tickets at $1,800 apiece and he took 'em, he took a trip with the same FBI agent. I guess he was posing as a developer or something. The man stone cold took this stuff. I don't even think he should be allowed to continue on with the race."

Even with all of our help, DeSantis barely squeaked by Gillum with the tiniest of margins. Our guy took 49.586 percent of the vote, compared to Gillum's 49.191. Although I was jubilant about the win, how close it was came as a bit of a shock.

Days after the election, all charges against Gillum were dropped. Of course, both Trump and Giuliani accused the Democrats of cheating in the election, blaming Hillary Clinton, despite her party's loss.

But, years later, after I became a well-known name, many prominent Republicans, including DeSantis, hastened to say that they didn't know me or even that they had never met me. But my mountains of evidence, like photos and videos (not to mention hundreds of personal texts and emails), made any long-term denial impossible.

When pressed by media, DeSantis' office said that he had "probably" first met me at the ZOA event in May 2018. He didn't. When it eventually came to light that I had contributed to his campaign, DeSantis backpedaled unconvincingly. "This is a guy at RNC functions, Trump victory functions, he was at a lot of these things," he stuttered. "This guy was viewed as one of the top sup-porters of the President in Florida, and so it was just like any other donor, nothing more than that."

The thought of that still makes me laugh. I was more than just a donor or supporter at the time. We became friends. In fact, we had not only met several times before the ZOA event, we knew each oth-er well and I was a key contributor to his political success.

As soon as he realized that he'd won Florida, DeSantis came up to me to celebrate.

DeSantis' blatantly ridiculous claim that he didn't know me was laid bare on election night. Not only was I front and center at his campaign party, but I was the very first person DeSantis hugged after his win was called and the newly minted governor-elect whispered "we did it" in my ear.

After he was sworn in, DeSantis wanted nothing to do with me. He text-ed me, the guy who had worked so diligently to get him elected, and told me that, because of the media, we could no longer be seen in public together.

Still somehow believing that DeSantis was actually my friend, I texted back: "You're still my boy!"

Then DeSantis stopped returning my calls. I thought he was my friend, I thought he'd be a good governor, we had all these ambitions and plans, but all of a sudden, once he became governor, he didn't have time for me.

Even now, DeSantis is not someone I hold in high regard. I understand the denials about knowing me, but after experiencing an insider's look at how DeSantis flip-flopped on issues like cannabis, his going to ridiculous lengths to get elected and not caring who he used or lied to, I can't respect him. Forget the policy, forget the promises, DeSantis was all about DeSantis.

On the same night that DeSantis won Florida, Sessions lost to Allred. I wasn't exactly heartbroken. But that wouldn't be the last I would hear from him. He was replaced as head of the House Rules committee by Massachusetts Democrat Jim McGovern, an outspoken Trump opponent.

At the time, I believed that I'd won one and lost one. But it's important to remember that the reason why Ron DeSantis became governor of Florida is because of a little plant called cannabis.

Chapter 26
One of the Gang

I t was one of those days when Giuliani and I were just hanging out at our favorite place, The Grand Havana Room. Operating under the belief that Giuliani would deliver on his promises, I was still very friendly with Trump's sidekick. There was nothing like The Grand Havana. A private club with a panoramic view of Manhattan, it had the best food, the best drinks and, of course, the finest cigars. He could stay there all day, just doing nothing and shooting the breeze.

But that's not my style. I have to work. And that's exactly what I was doing. Giuliani and I might have been friends, but I also knew that he was the key to my future success. So, we were talking about ways to get my business off the ground when he excused himself for an important phone call.

It was Bart Schwartz. I didn't know him personally, but I did know that he used to be a prosecutor under Giuliani at the SDNY and the two had stayed in touch for years. Schwartz was then acting as a receiver for a hedge fund (a post that would later end with him in big trouble with the SEC), but still kept his eyes and ears open. He had a tip that he thought Giuliani might be interested in.

Giuliani told me that Schwartz had heard that Joe Biden and his son, Hunter, had been involved in something perhaps a bit shadier than mere conflict of interest in Ukraine. Apparently, there had been a couple of letters, whistle blower complaints.

Giuliani was alive with excitement. I had never seen him so happy. He's a man of strong emotions, but none more pressing than hate. He had no time for Democrats, especially the country club type he considered the Bidens to be. Making it all the sweeter, Biden was the Democrats' most likely pick to run against Trump in 2020.

And it was Ukraine! He was sitting right beside a well-connected expert on that very country. Giuliani could not believe his luck.

He asked me what I knew about Biden in Ukraine. I told him that the

Poroshenko government had supported Obama and Biden, but the people I knew hated him. Just like the ambassador, he was another foreigner sticking his nose in where it did not belong. In fact, I told him, Biden had used the threat of withholding American aid to force the Ukrainians to make changes in their government.

He was shocked. He had no idea.

I had proof. My contacts in Ukraine talked about Biden all the time. He oversaw Eastern Europe for the Obama administration, and he was, to put it mildly, an active participant. Not long before, a friend over in Kyiv sent me a video of Biden bragging about how he was the one making big changes in Ukraine. I played it for Giuliani.

It was the Vice-President's January 23, 2018 speech for the Council on Foreign Relations, Biden was asked about Ukraine, its conflicts and what he did to help quell corruption there:

> "I think the Donbas has potential to be able to be solved, but it takes two things. One of those things is missing now. And that is I'm desperately concerned about the backsliding on the part of Kiev in terms of corruption. They made — I mean, I'll give you one concrete example. I was — not I, but it just happened to be that was the assignment I got. I got all the good ones. And so I got Ukraine. And I remember going over, convincing our team, our leaders to — convincing that we should be providing for loan guarantees. And I went over, I guess, the 12th, 13th time to Kiev. And I was supposed to announce that there was another billion-dollar loan guarantee. And I had gotten a commitment from Poroshenko and from Yatsenyuk that they would take action against the state prosecutor. And they didn't. So they said they had — they were walking out to a press conference. I said, nah, I'm not going to — or, we're not going to give you the billion dollars. They said, you have no authority. You're not the president. The president said — I said, call him. I said, I'm telling you, you're not getting the billion dollars. I said, you're not getting the billion. I'm going to be leaving here in, I think it was about six hours. I looked at them and said: I'm leaving in six hours. If the prosecutor is not fired, you're not getting the money. Well, son of a bitch. He got fired. And they put in place someone who was solid at the time."

His pride in forcing Kyiv's hand really irritated the Ukrainians I knew, so did his glib, almost joking, tone. It didn't help that the replacement, Yuriy Sevruk, was a drunk who was no more ethical or moral than the guy who was fired had been. He lasted a little more than a month in the job.

Giuliani, still clearly shocked, asked me if I knew the guy who Biden had thrown out of office.

Viktor Shokin? I don't know him personally, I told him, but I know peo-

ple who know him. Of course I did. I had, by then, a huge number of important contacts in Ukraine. Not just in business, but in government as well.

"And you can get him?" Giuliani asked. "Bring him to me?" You can do
that?

I told him that I believed that I could.

He asked me if I knew anything about any Ukrainians meddling with the
2016 U.S. election.

I told him I didn't.

Giuliani grinned broadly and stared at the image of Biden as he was
proudly going on about how he forced the Ukrainians to do what he said.

Giuliani put his hands up and shouted: "We've got you!"

And that's the very moment everything changed for me. Up until then, I
had been an outsider. I was a businessman, a donor, who had been hanging
out with the guys who ran the country. Sure, it was exciting, but I was really
more of a spectator.

Now, I was on a mission. I was a participant. If I had been excited to carry a letter from a congressman to the President, it was nothing compared to
this. I, Lev Parnas, was on a mission for the United States government. An
international mission. A secret mission. I felt really important, like an ambassador. Before, I was there to make money. But this meant I was serving my
country — and had an even better chance to make money. It was perfect. It
was like I had found what I was meant to do in life.

Now all I had to do was find Shokin.

Chapter 27
Up in the Big Leagues

I could tell that Giuliani had been thinking a lot about Ukraine. And that he had been doing his own research. At an event in November 2018, Giuliani took me aside to speak privately. He showed me some letters about Ukraine that he had received and was preparing to pass along to important U.S. officials.

The first was to Republican Senator Lindsey Graham, although his name was misspelled "Lingsey," and the other to Sigal Mandelker, Under Secretary of the Treasury for Terrorism and Financial Intelligence. The letters accused several notable Ukrainians of being part of an "organized crime syndicate" that was "actively involved in the siphoning of funds appropriated by the American government for aid to Ukraine." The letters went on to say that those stolen funds were being used to buy weapons from a Russian company sanctioned by the U.S. And, perhaps most important, Ukraine's top prosecutor, Yuriy Lutsenko, knew about it and wanted to act, but could not do anything because President Poroshenko was blocking him. Mandelker, perhaps because of her job with the Treasury, received an extra line in her letter: "It concerns me, as should any fellow American, that a taxpayer's money is rudely been stolen in Ukraine."

Conveniently, the letters' writer had a plan to fix everything. The letters recommended sanctions be placed on 12 prominent Ukrainians, including Burisma chief Zlochevsky. Also on the list were the former head of the National Bank of Ukraine, Valeriya Gontareva, and her top deputy, Kateryna Rozhkova. Both women were known to be enemies of Ihor Kolomoisky.

Kolomoisky was not someone you'd want to have as an enemy. Generally regarded as the second-richest man in Ukraine, he was a successful entrepreneur even before the Soviet Union fell. His stable of companies, Privat Group, emerged when he started Ukraine's largest bank, PrivatBank in 1992. After that, he acquired massive media holdings and he controls much of what is seen and heard in Ukraine.

Of course, business in Eastern Europe is never easy nor clean. A judge in a 2013 London case involving Kolomoisky said that he had "a reputation of having sought to take control of a company at gunpoint in Ukraine" and openly questioned his overall honesty. In another London case two years later, Kolomoisky was accused of using murder and bribery to achieve his ends. He settled out of court.

During an ugly fight with the federal government over the nationalization of PrivatBank, Kolomoisky left Ukraine for a self-imposed exile in Tel Aviv. Since Ukraine does not allow dual citizenship, Kolomoisky no longer retained his and instead carries Israeli and Cypriot passports.

Gontareva and Rozhkova had good reason to be concerned. Their enmity with Kolomoisky stemmed from his attempts to retain control of PrivatBank while being investigated for money laundering. After taking on Kolomoisky, Gontareva's house was burned, a coffin with an effigy of her was sent to the Central Bank and she had been the victim of (and seriously injured by) a hit-and-run incident in London.

That the author of the letters was also kind enough to send along phone numbers for all of the supposed malefactors was interesting.

Giuliani told me that the letters had been written by Michael Guralnik, a Ukrainian-born defense and security analyst who had worked extensively in the former Soviet Union, particularly Central Asia. Before that, Guralnik attended the Soviet Military Academy and served in the Red Army for a decade. He has refused to talk about the letters, not publicly recognizing their existence, let alone his supposed authorship.

While I didn't think the letters would make any difference even if they got to Graham and Mandelker, they made me realize that Giuliani was all in on Ukraine. And that meant it was important to the United States.

If I was excited about my mission before, now I just couldn't wait to go. While I was tasked with finding Shokin and given access to what I was sure were top secret letters, I wondered how this would affect my standing among the other people in power. If I really was one of them.

I didn't have to wait long for my answer.

After former President George H.W. Bush died on November 30, his body was to lie in state at the Capitol until his December 5 funeral at the Washington National Cathedral. The event was expected to be huge. Giuliani invited me, and I invited Igor. I did my best to blend in. The Trumps, Pences,

Obamas, Bidens, Clintons, Gores, Cheneys and Carters were all there, as were royalty and many heads of states.

The funeral was treated by Homeland Security as a National Special Security Event, and I was among the guests, although failed Presidential candidate Jeb Bush later said that he was angered that I would be allowed to attend.

Might've been different if you'd won, Jeb.

Chapter 28
A Hanukkah Surprise

T he greatest feeling for any husband and father is to make your family happy. I had a great chance to wow my son Aaron by taking him to the White House 2018 Hanukkah Party. It's an annual tradition that gathers many of the nation's most prominent and accomplished Jews to celebrate together. The tradition only goes back to 2001, but there is compelling evidence that George Washington celebrated Hanukkah with a friend at least once.

The Bush funeral had delayed the event, but everybody was in good spirits. Of course, I had taken Aaron, who was still very interested in politics, and Igor was with one of his sons.

It was actually a pretty hot ticket. Not only would it be an enjoyable night, but it was a rare networking opportunity and an excellent chance to raise one's social status.

We met Giuliani and his guests, author Ashley Hutson and her mother, at the Trump International. I took some time to talk with Giuliani about Venezuela, using some of Sargeant's new information, and about Ukraine. He took it all in and we were ready to go.

When we arrived at the White House, Giuliani surprised us all by insisting that we go through the back entrance.

Inside, we were met by Secret Service officers. Giuliani said that he had to go to speak with Trump before his speech, get him up to speed on what we had spoken about earlier. He promised to meet up with us later. The secret service escorted Giuliani to the President's residence and the rest of us to the party.

After a few minutes, Trump came out to the party with his entourage (including Giuliani) to give his Hanukkah speech. While he was speaking, Giuliani came back to our group. He told me that he had just had a conversation with Trump and that they both wanted me to go to Ukraine and find Shokin. They were very interested in what he had to say about the Bidens.

As we were speaking, a Secret Service officer tapped Giuliani on the shoulder and told him that the President wanted to see us in the Red Room.

Inside, Giuliani made everyone uncomfortable by awkwardly putting the moves on Hutson, with her mother and the kids right there. He was clearly

trying to impress her with his power and fame, saying that he was the President's Number 1 guy and that he would introduce her to Trump.

We could hear Trump finishing his speech. Through the applause, I heard him scream: "Where's my boy, Rudy?"

When he and his entourage entered the Red Room, where we were all lined up, Trump didn't offer any greet-

My son Aaron and me at the Hanukkah Party.

ings. Instead, he made a beeline toward Hutson and, leering her up and down, asked: "Who is this?"

Men of the Red Room: (from left) Pence, Igor, me, Trump, Giuliani, Aaron and Igor's son.

Giuliani put on a boyish smirk that was at once proud and embarrassed. He was, in a way that Trump would clearly understand, telling him that she was there with him.

Without taking his eyes off Hutson, Trump said, lasciviously: "Rudy, my boy!"

At that, Melania smacked her husband on his shoulder and went off to sulk. She did not speak to Trump again for the duration.

Once he was finished with Hutson, Trump came to speak directly to me. He looked me straight in the eye and shook my hand. "Rudy's been saying good things about you," he said, adding: "Keep up the good work." Then he winked.

I didn't need any translation. It was like something straight out of a gangster movie. You know, when the boss would acknowledge a subject, without articulating it exactly, so anyone who might have heard or been re- cording would be at a loss to prove anything, even though everybody knew what he was saying. He was thanking me for going after the Bidens in Uk- raine and wanted me to keep at it.

Thank you, Mr. President, I answered.

Trump then posed for some photos — Melania insisted that they be all female or all male — then left.

The timing was intentional. Nobody would think twice about me being in attendance at the White House Hanukkah Party — I was a Jewish VIP, after all — while Trump and Giuliani would have some time with me off the pub- lic record and away from any prying eyes.

With Trump gone, I went back to the party and led a minyan — a public Jewish prayer that has its roots in the story of Abraham bargaining with God to save the people of Sodom.

After the party, I was almost busting with pride. I had always loved Am- erica, and now I was on a mission for the President himself. I could think of no better way to serve the country that I was so proud to be part of.

I booked a flight to Kyiv.

Chapter 29
A Chilly Reception

There is a particular kind of cold in Eastern Europe that most Americans can't comprehend. It cuts not just through flesh, but through blankets and coats and just about anything that humans use to try to stop it right through to the bone. To most people, it feels like the end of the world. To Ukrainians, it means winter's coming.

It was in that kind of weather that I landed in Kyiv to find Shokin. It wouldn't take long for him to turn up. Everybody who was anybody in Kyiv knew me or at least knew of me. If I put the word out that I wanted to see Shokin, it would get to him.

It didn't take long, I got a call from Nasirov. Of course he knew Shokin, he told me, they were old friends. He'd be more than happy to take me to see him. Shokin had a place just outside Kyiv.

It helped that Shokin wanted to be seen. He viewed politics the Ukrainian way, not the American way. He thought it was his undeniable right to be the top prosecutor and, if he kept fighting and had the right allies, he would get his job back. It's hard to blame him considering how lucrative his position could be, at least the way he did it.

Shokin felt that he had been wronged. And, worse yet, it had been by foreigners. Besides, it was Biden who didn't like him and he wasn't Vice-President anymore. It's not just that he wanted his job back, he felt like he deserved to get it back.

I used that greed and over-inflated sense of worth to our advantage. I let it be known that Giuliani was looking to speak to him, on behalf of President Trump.

Like all prosecutors, good or bad, Shokin had made a lot of enemies. But none he hated as virulently as he did Biden. He felt as though it was Biden who was responsible for getting him fired. That's not really true, Biden was merely the spokesman for a large group that included the Obama administration, the EU, the G7, the IMF and many others. But, since it was Biden who gave the speech, Shokin decided he was the enemy. Biden should have been minding his own business, he believed, not interfering in a country he knew nothing about.

The best way to get back at them would not just be to return to his old post, but to make friends with their enemies in America. Us.

In the meantime, I put together the information that I had about Shokin. I was told that, when he was chief prosecutor, Shokin threatened to investigate Burisma and Mykola Zlochevsky unless he was paid a hefty bribe. I think it was around $5 million. Zlochevsky refused, so Shokin went ahead with an investigation that had been started, but abandoned by his predecessor. The whole thing took a lot of time as Shokin and Zlochevsky traded threats and insults.

The Obama administration had dedicated Joe Biden to oversee its anti-corruption efforts in Ukraine. When his team evaluated Shokin, they found him to be dragging his feet on major investigations, including the one aimed at Burisma. A prime example of Shokin's notorious inaction occurred when the U.K.'s Serious Fraud Office confiscated $23.5 million of Zlochevsky's money, but had to release it because the evidence arrived from Shokin's office too late. Zlochevsky got his money back, and Shokin felt like he owed him big. Shokin put pressure of Zlochevsky, but then Biden began to pressure the Ukrainians to get rid of Shokin. It's almost ironic that Biden got him fired for not investigating Burisma.

Shokin's ouster was greeted with relief even joy, in the West. "Everyone in the Western community wanted Shokin sacked," said Anders Aslund of the Atlantic Council. "The whole G7, the IMF, the EBRD, everybody was united that Shokin must go, and the spokesman for this was Joe Biden."

In his last incredibly spiteful act in office, Shokin fired his Number 2, Davit Sakvarelidze, for attending an anti-Shokin rally, calling it "unethical."

Sakvarelidze retorted: "What exactly are their prosecutorial ethics? It's theft, corruption and covering up for each other's crimes."

After his dismissal, Shokin gave an interview to Ukrainian media in which he denied any wrongdoing and said that he was fired at the behest of "grant-eaters" — a derogatory term for NGOs, whose critics say offer fealty to the West in exchange for funding.

Bitter, corrupt and vengeful, Shokin was exactly what we needed.

I remember the trip to see him, but not fondly. Shokin's place was in a wooded area in the middle of nowhere, and there was a blinding snowstorm. The visibility did not extend beyond the window glass and the car careened around the windy, icy roads like it was on skates instead of wheels. And, of course, the driver — one of Nasirov's bodyguards — never took his foot off the gas the whole time. I wasn't sure we were going to make it there. Our trip was maybe 15 or 20 miles, but it took more than two hours.

When we finally arrived, we were greeted by two armed bodyguards who took us to the house. It was like a log cabin, but hundreds of years old. Inside, it had all the modern, Western-style conveniences you'd expect to see in a rich guy's house.

We were guided into the living room, where Shokin was sitting behind a table. After our greetings, we sat across from him. Nasirov offered to translate anything I didn't understand because Shokin was speaking Ukrainian and my grasp of the language was nowhere near my mastery of Russian. Nobody really ever spoke Ukrainian in the old neighborhood. If it wasn't English, it was Russian.

Most of the meeting was taken up by Shokin's long and loud tirades about how he was taken out of his job unfairly. He showed us a pile of documents that he said proved all the good things he had done while in office, and another pile of documents that were evidence for the lawsuits he had filed against the Ukrainian government and against Joe Biden.

I looked at them. They were mostly in Ukrainian, but some were in English. I told Shokin that I would take them to Washington and show them to Giuliani and Trump.

Then we discussed what I considered to be the most important part — why he was fired.

He told me that he was investigating Burisma and that, although he was not investigating Hunter Biden, he knew he would have to question him. That meant that if Hunter were to say something incriminating, he would have to be indicted. Joe Biden, Shokin assured us, was so scared that Hunter would say something that he had to stop the investigation, And he did that by having Poroshenko fire Shokin.

That was exactly what I needed to hear. And tell Giuliani.

Chapter 30
Everywhere You Want to Be

For all his macho blustering, Donald Trump is pretty open about his fears. If there was one thing that seemed to scare him more than any-thing, it was losing the 2020 election. He made it abundantly clear that he had no respect at all for one-termers like George Bush and Jimmy Carter. There was something that struck him as embarrassingly weak about getting the job and not being able to hold onto it. Losing in 2020 would have been far worse, in his eyes, than losing in 2016. That, of course, also went hand in hand with his opinion that term limits were a "stupid" rule. If you could do the job, he believed, you should be able to keep it for as long as you possibly can. He saw it as everybody's job to keep him in office for as long as we all could.

The best way I could help with that, we believed, would be to let Shokin speak. Of course, I knew that Shokin was corrupt. I'd spent enough time in Eastern Europe to know that pretty well all the politicians (along with police and border guards and anyone else with any power) were corrupt. It was just too easy to make money that way. And it was ingrained in the system, kind of like tipping is here, you factor bribery into your budget.

But I thought he was telling the truth when it came to the Bidens. It all just made too much sense. And since Giuliani and Trump were sure, I was sure. Not only was I close with those guys, I was still a huge Trump suppor-ter and had a great deal of respect for the office of President of the United States.

Then I brought the documents Shokin had given to me to show Giuliani. I mentioned that some of it was in Ukrainian and he told me not to worry, he had translators. Once he opened the package, the President's lawyer looked like I had given him a treasure map. "You know who's got to see this right away?" Giuliani told me, "Lindsey Graham."

The Senator from South Carolina had been ingratiating himself to Trump after previously being one of his harshest Republican critics (he said that he didn't even vote for Trump in 2016). Now re-educated in Giuliani's eyes, Graham was not only a veteran senator — he replaced Strom Thurmond (!) for his seat — but was also very persuasive in his own effete way.

In fact, Giuliani wanted Graham to have an official, closed-door interview with Shokin. That was the only way, he told me, to beat the FBI, who he didn't trust.

Giuliani wanted Shokin on the next plane to D.C. He felt that if he met him face to face, he'd know where he was coming from, what he really knew and what he had that we could use. He put me in charge of getting him to the U.S. I reminded Giuliani that Ukrainians require a visa to visit the U.S. He told me that Shokin shouldn't mention that he'd be visiting us on his visa application, that he should come up with some other reason.

It just so happened that he had a daughter in the U.S. She came to light in February 2018 when she tried to sue Biden, Obama and the DNC over the "son of a bitch" comment about her father. Apparently, the family took it literally. "The fact that he called my late mother a bitch means that a person has nothing sacred," Viktor Shokin told a Ukrainian newspaper. "I believe that a normal person who has a mother cannot speak like that. This is my deep conviction. Mother is mother." The suit went nowhere, of course, but having a daughter in California did give Shokin a reason to apply for a visa.

I called Shokin and gave him his instructions. He went to the U.S. embassy in Kyiv and applied for a visa, since his had expired.

According to Shokin, he submitted his application with up-to-date documents and a letter from his daughter that said that he'd live at her place while he was visiting. He waited a half hour and then, he said, they called him to a window and asked him about some surgery he had undergone in the U.S. He said he was told that because he had not provided proof that the surgery had been paid for, his entire application was under review.

But, like most people who are cynical and corrupt, he believed everyone else was also cynical and corrupt. He told a Ukrainian reporter that he was sure that the surgery story was a ruse. Shokin said that it was Yovanovitch; she had stepped in and prevented him from getting a visa. He told the Ukrainian News Agency that Biden had blacklisted him and that Yovanovitch had personally made it her business to prevent him from coming to the U.S.

Immediately after the visa denial, Shokin called me to do something about it. I didn't think it would be a big problem to fix. I told him, not to worry, that we'd take care of him. So, I told Giuliani what had happened. When I did, Giuliani said to leave it with him and he'd get it done. "It's no big deal," he told me. "Pompeo will fix it."

It was a big deal. Shokin called back and angrily told me that they had declined his visa again.

I immediately called Giuliani.

He was incensed; angry that Pompeo had broken a promise to him. He told me to wait. He called back and told me that he had spoken with the State Department (by which, he probably meant Pompeo) and that it was all cool now, that I should tell Shokin to try again.

I called and Shokin was still upset.

If Giuliani and I were as powerful and close to Trump as we said we were, why couldn't we just get him a visa? Was Yovanovitch more powerful than the President?

I assured him that things work differently here in the U.S. and that he should just be patient. He

Giuliani repeatedly told me he could get a U.S. visa for Viktor Shokin. But he couldn't.

told me that he had already booked his flight, and was getting anxious for a resolution.

I couldn't just call Giuliani because he was golfing at Augusta. So, I texted him, and told him that Shokin was getting edgy. I also told him that Shokin has bought tickets for next Saturday but still doesn't have a visa.

Giuliani replied: "It's going to work I have no 1 on it." That meant that the President himself would see to it that Shokin got his visa.

The following day, Shokin told me that he had been turned down for a third time.

He said that the embassy called him and told him to cancel his tickets, he was not going to get a visa.

I told Giuliani. He shot back: "he will get one." Then he told me that he had given Jay Sekulow, another of Trump's lawyers, my number and that he'd take care of it.

The following morning, while on a flight back to Florida, I told Giuliani that Shokin had just called me and he still didn't have a visa.

Giuliani texted back: "Still trying."

After I landed, I shared some important news with Giuliani. Pompeo had just tweeted that the U.S. considered Maduro to be an illegitimate ruler of Venezuela, and called upon the people there, particularly the military, to take their country back.

But Venezuela had to wait, Ukraine was a more pressing matter and it was my project. I was tired of Giuliani's failed assurances over the visa and I knew Shokin was too. Giuliani looked to me for a solution.

The answer came to me almost immediately. We could hold the meeting and any subsequent interviews via Skype. Not only would Shokin not have to get on a plane, he wouldn't even have to get off his couch.

We met in Giuliani's office at Park Avenue and East 56th. Giuliani, to my surprise, had invited an ex-FBI agent along to take notes. Igor, as always, was there to videotape everything. Nasirov was on the other side, with Shokin in Ukraine, in case there was a language problem.

Immediately, Shokin started in on who had wronged him, what they were all up to and why they should be our enemies too. After an eternity of his self-indulgent rambling, Giuliani interrupted him. "Did Biden do anything illegal in Ukraine?" He asked point blank.

"No," Shokin answered, and then went on another tirade about if he had only been allowed to interview Hunter, he knew he would have caught him on something.

He was still droning on when Giuliani turned to me and said: "That's okay, he broke American laws … bribery."

Looking back, I can say that it was classic Giuliani. Shokin had just told him, in no uncertain terms that Biden had not broken the law in Ukraine, and still he believed that he did and that he could catch him. Either he was trying to fool me (and the nation) or he really was that deluded.

At the time, I believed him. But I started to wonder what had happened with the visa. I knew that the powerful Giuliani had used all of his influence on Pompeo, the Secretary of State, and been sent home wanting. It had to be powers beyond even his preventing the visa. We were the guys, we were in charge, we got what we wanted. Watching Giuliani run into so many obstacles helped convince me there were powers beyond those we all knew about. The Deep State. That's how conspiracy theories are born.

Giuliani was more than distraught, he was raging. While he was going on about the Deep State, he fixed on one enemy in particular — Yovanovitch. The very thought of a non-elected official using government to further their own agenda enraged him. Who the hell did she think she was? Of course, sensing irony was not one of Giuliani's strengths.

From then on, Yovanovitch was on his enemies list.

There was no way in hell he was going to let her keep her job.

Chapter 31
Let's Make a Deal

Giuliani continued the questioning, asking how the Bidens became part of the investigation. Shokin — a jowly fellow with a bright red complexion, snow white hair and a chin that hides in his neck — told us that he had been investigating Burisma when he was fired. His primary interest, he told us, was in Zlochevsky. However, Hunter Biden was one of Burisma's other board members and he would have to come under questioning. If he was doing anything illegal, Shokin assured us, he would have caught him.

He also told us Yovanovitch was close to Joe Biden and she had denied him a U.S. visa because she did not want him letting the American public know exactly what was going on with the Bidens in Ukraine.

Between what he said and what my Ukrainian contacts told me, I knew that Shokin had inherited the investigation of Burisma from his predecessor, Viktor Pshonka, and took it up again when he thought it would lead to a big payday. The investigation was into accusations of money laundering, tax evasion and other charges against Zlochevsky, but it was really just a shake down. More important, it was limited to a period from 2010 to 2012. Hunter Biden joined the company in 2014, so the investigation wasn't about him at all. Shokin was resting his entire case on the concept that Hunter Biden must have been doing something illegal (otherwise, why would he be in Ukraine?) and would crack and spill it all under questioning, even though the questions would not actually be about him.

My image of Shokin came into better focus. He was doing his best to get Giuliani on his side. He looked liked he'd say just about anything if it would prompt Giuliani into helping him get his job back (or at least punishing his enemies). Shokin was desperate, bitter and stuck in self-preservation mode.

Regardless of the veracity of Shokin's claims, they fell on welcoming ears. Giuliani hated the Bidens almost as much as the Clintons, and knew that Biden would likely be the Democrats' choice to run against Trump in

2020. Certainly, Biden was the opponent he feared the most. It was Giuliani's duty, and his pleasure, to expose any information that could compromise Biden's character, credibility and his campaign.

The job offer accepted, Shokin was also clear that he expected to be paid. He knew the Americans couldn't give him any money, but we could do him a favor. He wanted help to get his job back — it wasn't just the money anymore, he wanted a chance to mete out his concept of justice again. In exchange for public support from Trump, he would hand over every scrap of evidence of every dishonorable act either Biden had ever done in Ukraine.

I was all in for the deal, even though I was aware that Shokin wasn't the most reliable source. The cynic in me realized that all Giuliani needed was for an important Ukrainian official to accuse the Bidens of wrongdoing. It didn't matter if they had done anything or not.

Although one Ukrainian official looks pretty much like any other to most Americans, it helped that Shokin at least claimed he was fired for fighting corruption. Even better, it was against the Bidens, who many Trump supporters saw as leading the charge to bring the Deep State back into control of the White House.

While there has been a remarkable number of unsubstantiated rumors about Hunter Biden that I have personally been able to debunk. At the time, we were all absolutely sure that we were right about Hunter. We thought nobody could get that much money in Ukraine and not be crooked. And the timing was suspicious — his father was in charge of U.S. policy in Ukraine and ordered the Ukrainians to fire the guy who was investigating his company. We didn't need any more information to decide that he was guilty.

If that wasn't enough circumstantial evidence, which dovetailed perfectly with our near-religious belief in the Deep State, every one of my contacts on the ground in Ukraine was telling us the same thing. I never thought they could be lying. Sure, I knew they were all corrupt, but I didn't think they'd play that game with the U.S. But they did.

Everyone on our side, Giuliani, Lindsay Graham, Ron Johnson, Nunes, even Trump, worked diligently to push that disinformation. Any information their staff received that fit in with their agenda wouldn't even be vetted, just distributed to Congress, while anything that didn't was buried and never seen. The Trump crowd believed what they believed because that was all they ever knew or even saw.

To all of us, it just seemed like a matter of time until the Bidens were proven guilty. I knew that the evidence against them was circumstantial, but that was only the evidence that had been found so far. Somewhere out there, there had to be a smoking gun that we hadn't been able to find. I believed it because the President did. I had a great deal of respect for the office back then, and I believed everything the President said, even if what he was saying was something I told him. The whole thing just made absolute sense to me.

Like most changes in Ukraine, this situation was prompted by people struggling to get out from under the hold of the oligarchs. Spurred by protests, the government was cracking down on corruption, and settling a few old scores. Zlochevsky — founder and president of Burisma Holdings and, conveniently, a former Minister of Ecology and Natural Resources — was worried when he saw reforms sweeping Eastern Europe. He didn't want any increase in transparency in his business and he'd heard that Poroshenko wanted to get rid of him with a money laundering investigation. But he had a plan. Over there, if you wanted to stay safe, you loaded your board with heavy hitters. So he went and got one.

Zlochevsky was friends with Vitaly Pruss, a Brooklyn-based Russian investor, and asked him for help. Pruss knew some important people. He'd worked with Rosemont Seneca Partners, an international investment advisory company that was founded by Yale school chums Devon Archer and Christopher Heinz (stepson of former Secretary of State John Kerry and heir to the Heinz tomato-based family fortune), along with Hunter Biden, another Yalie. Pruss introduced Archer to Zlochevsky, who offered him a high-paying post on Burisma's board if he could recruit his better-connected partners as well. The timing was really, really bad. The offer came in March 2014, just after the invasion of Crimea, a crisis that Joe Biden was handling for the Obama administration. Still, Hunter Biden made the decision to come aboard.

Heinz did not. He thought it was a very bad idea. So bad, in fact, that after warning Archer and Biden not to take the Burisma offer and being rebuffed, he severed his professional ties to them. He even emailed State Department officials — Special Assistant Matt Summers and Chief of Staff David Wade — about their decision, saying:

"Apparently Devon and Hunter both joined the board of Burisma and a press release went out today. I cant speak why they decided to, but there was no investment by our firm in the company."

It's been widely stated as fact that Hunter had no experience or credentials to deserve a job at Burisma, but that's not entirely true. His role there was to be in charge of international regulations compliance, which he had handled at previous posts — just not in the oil and gas industry. Later, NBC News would quote two unnamed sources "close to Burisma" who said that Hunter's work actually did provide value to the company.

The people who actually run things over there saw Hunter coming a mile away. Obtaining kompromat on the son of the U.S. Vice-President, who was also the public face of American foreign policy in Eastern Europe and could well be President in the future, looked like a goldmine. It certainly didn't hurt that Hunter had a hard-earned reputation as a party boy and to have been rewarded handsomely, maybe a bit too handsomely, while serving on the board of China's BHR Partners.

Not long after, Pruss told me, Hunter was taken to Kazakhstan for a meeting with a prominent cabinet minister. His hosts encouraged him and fed him a steady, perhaps even overwhelming, banquet of booze, drugs and hookers. It's not like he didn't want them. Hunter might have enjoyed himself or been chasing any of a number of possible addictions, but what he was not aware of at the time was that every second of it was recorded — photo, video and audio.

But it was widely known that Hunter had struggled with addiction, so the kompromat that had been gathered had not been of great value. Trump had already tried the old if-he-can't-control-his-son-how-can-he-run-the-country? thing, and Joe had deflected it adroitly to his own advantage.

While Hunter was busy partying, his hosts spirited away his laptop and they did something — copied it, altered it, put evidence on it, I don't know exactly. They didn't do it without a reason and a plan. And when I say they, I mean the FSB.

The laptop was returned to Hunter without him ever knowing it was gone. They had something better than kompromat. They had evidence — real or constructed, it didn't matter. As long as people believed it.

Of course, the laptop was something we had no idea existed during the Skype call. It didn't matter, though, we were already hooked.

As well as an endorsement from Trump, Shokin wanted something else before he would help Giuliani besmirch the Bidens. He wanted Yovanovitch gone. I wasn't surprised. She was just the kind of meddling Westerner that the old school Ukrainian politicians hated. It bothered them that some know-nothing outsider would come to Ukraine and try to tell them what to do. And, of course, she encouraged a kind of political movement that could put their lifestyles and livelihoods in jeopardy. That's why Shokin thought she had stepped in and denied his visa. Getting rid of her was an absolute must if he was to agree.

It was a deal.

Chapter 32
New Prosecutor, Same Result

After the Skype meeting, I began to be more confident, Not only was Ukraine an issue of great importance to Giuliani, he was making concrete plans about how to leverage the people there to find compromising evidence against the Bidens, thereby gaining Trump an advantage in the 2020 election. We didn't think it was unfair at all. We sincerely believed that they had been up to no good over there and that revealing it was not just good for Trump, but for the whole nation. It would certainly show my contacts in both Ukraine and the U.S. that I had some power.

And that's when a gift dropped right into our laps. At the end of January 2019, about a week or so after we spoke with Shokin, I learned from Igor that one of his friends — Gyunduz Mamedov, the Prosecutor General of Crimea — was in New York on personal business with the current top prosecutor in Ukraine, Yuriy Lutsenko, and Glib Zagoriy, a member of the Ukrainian parliament and a pharmaceutical tycoon.

When I told Giuliani, he became visibly excited. We had just spoken with Shokin and he could see his plan unfolding To get the current prosecutor to agree to open an investigation of the Bidens in Ukraine would be even better than anything Shokin could give us.

We arranged a meeting at Giuliani's office on Park Avenue. Mamedov, Zagoriy and Lutsenko on the Ukrainian side of the table, and me, Giuliani and the ex-FBI agent friend of his (there to take notes) on our side.

Lutsenko made his intentions clear. His goal was a meeting with Barr. He suspected that some wealthy individuals were laundering money through Franklin Templeton Investments and using it to buy real estate in the U.S.

He was still explaining when Giuliani stopped him. He told him "we're not interested in that" and what we really wanted to know about were the Bidens, Burisma and the Black Ledger (Manafort's secret files, which included a list of bribes he had taken).

Lutsenko was taken aback. Then he approached those subjects, but used such broad strokes that he wasn't really telling us anything we didn't already know.

Still, Giuliani was rapt. I could tell that he believed that Lutsenko could be the key to reopening the Burisma investigation and, this time, including the Bidens.

But as Lutsenko got off topic, back to his desire to speak to Barr, Giuliani interrupted him again. He told him: "If you want a meeting with Barr, you have to give me evidence against the Bidens."

This time, Lutsenko looked more than surprised. In fact, he seemed a bit offended. He said that we should take a break. He needed to think about what had been discussed so far.

We agreed to meet the next day.

When Lutsenko came back, he was prepared to talk to Giuliani about what Giuliani wanted. He brought some documents related to the investigation about Burisma. They were mostly about Zlochevsky and the company itself, but it made Giuliani instantly delighted. Lutsenko also said that he had a prosecutor from the National Anti-Corruption Bureau of Ukraine (NABU) who would testify not only that there was a second Black Ledger, but that the first one was a forgery.

Giuliani looked over the documents excitedly. I could tell that he was treasuring every moment. Finally, he told Lutsenko that President Trump would appreciate it if he would open an investigation of the Bidens' activities in Ukraine.

Lutsenko told him that he couldn't do that without President Poroshenko's okay. Then he added that he could set up a meeting with him.

Giuliani asked Lutsenko to hold on for a second and then left the room with his phone in his hand. When he came back, he was smiling and gave us a thumbs up while still on the phone. We could all hear him saying good-bye to the President. He then told us all that Trump happy to hear the news.

He added that if Lutsenko wanted to meet Barr, he would have to go through a lobbyist. And, despite the many times he has publicly denied ever having worked as a lobbyist, he offered his expert lobbying services to Lutsenko. For $200,000.

Again, Lutsenko was shocked. He didn't know why he, the top prosecutor of Ukraine, needed to pay someone just to see the top prosecutor of the

United States. He reminded Giuliani that his Templeton investigation was a serious issue for both nations.

Later, a reporter would ask Lutsenko if their was any ambiguity in what Giuliani wanted from him. No, Lutsenko said, he "understood well" what he was being asked to do, and added: "I have 23 years in politics. I knew ... I'm a political animal."

We agreed to break again and meet later. After several phone calls back and forth, we decided that the next meeting should be in Poland. There was an international conference in Warsaw, and Giuliani was going. Not to the conference itself, he had business on the side. Digging up dirt on the Bidens.

For the meeting, I picked an expensive cigar bar (I've since forgotten the name) in the old Ochota district of Warsaw because it provided a decent level of privacy and it was someplace that both could plausibly walk into without knowing that the other was there. Just two guys who happened to be in Warsaw at the same time. With plausible deniability. Just like the Hanukkah party.

Chapter 33
Iran, Poland and Ukraine

G iuliani's official reason to be in Warsaw was that he was giving a paid speech to Iranian dissidents there. It was one of the causes he said he sincerely believed in. Ever since the world-shocking 1979 revolution that brought Ayatollah Ruhollah Khomeini and his fundamentalist Islamic regime into power in Iran, the country has been something of a bugaboo for Trump. Before he was President, he would speak out against Iran frequently, even go so far as to suggest illegally invading the country, not for a regime change, but to "take some of their oil."

In his hatred of the Islamic Republic of Iran, he found another connection with Giuliani. In fact, Giuliani had met several times with Iran's largest opposition group — the People's Mojahedin Organization of Iran (actually, they are known by plenty of names but call themselves Mojahedin-e-Khalq or MEK). The group began, like Khomeini's, as an Islamist movement to overthrow the U.S.-backed Shah, and even fought alongside them in the 1979 revolution. But after Khomeini sidelined them politically, the MEK took up arms and aligned with, of all people, Iraq's Saddam Hussein. Much bad luck befell them after that mistake, including being bombed by the U.S. In 2013, the Obama administration donated $20 million to help MEK leadership resettle in Albania, must to the chagrin of many locals.

Many members of the Trump administration were decidedly more pro-MEK. A year before he became National Security Advisor, Bolton promised a MEK audience that they would "celebrate in Tehran before 2019." Further, noted investigative journalist Seymour Hirsch reported that MEK has been using U.S. support to carry out covert operations in Iran aimed at destabilizing the government.

There was no bigger American MEK fan than Giuliani, who spoke before them several times and referred to them as Iran's "government in exile," suggesting that they would receive U.S. support to rule the nation should the standing Islamist government fall. All that made me believe that MEK was the good guys, not the terrorists that some people had said they were.

So, we went to Warsaw while a conference called the Ministerial to Promote a Future of Peace and Security in the Middle East was happening. Giuliani and I flew in — and so did Lutsenko. Giuliani still didn't have an official position, so he was not part of the U.S. delegation. Neither was I. Lutsenko wasn't there on Ukraine's behalf either.

Although many in media believed the conference had been prompted by the Saudi-ordered murder of journalist Jamal Khashoggi, it turned out mainly to be a simple rebuke of Iran. The Iranian delegation was not invited, of course. MEK was there, not as an official participant, but on the streets of Warsaw protesting.

Giuliani gave the group, which is not officially aligned with the U.S., a paid-for rah-rah speech. "If we don't have a peaceful, democratic Iran, then no matter what we do we'll have turmoil, difficulties, problems in the Middle East," he told them. "Everyone agrees that Iran is the No. 1 state sponsor of terrorism in the world. That has to tell you something — Iran is a country you can't rely on, do business with, can't trust." It was a page torn right out of the Trump playbook.

When a reporter asked him if he was part of the U.S. delegation, Giuliani snapped back that he was there "as a private citizen — thank God I can still do that."

A few months later, Giuliani would claim that he had never worked as a lobbyist for foreign states or organizations and, certainly, he had not register-ed to do so. "Despite all of the contrary, false, Democratic rumors, I have never lobbied for anyone," he told Roll Call, adding that he had missed out on roughly $10 million by not doing so and repeated: "I do not lobby, I do not do foreign representation." He did, however, acknowledge that he had consulted on physical and cybersecurity issues for foreign clients and had represented them in U.S. courts.

NBC News found that the National Council of Resistance of Iran, of which MEK is a member, had recorded an official meeting with "Mayor Rudy Giuliani to discuss Iran's nuclear weapons as well as Iran's terrorism in the region, including Iraq and Syria." You know, lobbying.

When Roll Call pointed that out and that he had given speeches sup-porting MEK, Giuliani told them he had "no idea" why they would have said that and that the speeches were not lobbying.

I wasn't concerned about who Giuliani worked for other than Trump. Besides, anyone trying to bring down the Ayatollah has to be considered the good guys, right? I had bigger fish to fry.

Once we were comfortably away from prying eyes, we felt free to meet with our Ukrainian counterparts to try to hammer out the nuts and bolts of the deal.

By the time they arrived, Giuliani had already had too much to drink.

Still, he offered the Ukrainians absolutely unfettered access to Trump through him via me.

In return, the Ukrainians would announce an investigation into the Bidens. My part was to meet with Poroshenko and speak to him directly.

Giuliani and me, just two guys in a Polish cigar bar.

That's where the problem was. They told us that Poroshenko just didn't trust Trump.

By then, the Ukrainians knew that I spoke on behalf of the President. We decided that I would speak with Poroshenko, try to clear the air and tell him what we wanted and what we could give.

We ended the meeting by agreeing that if Ukraine would open an investigation into the Bidens, we would back Poroshenko for reelection. If you support us, we'll support you. The very definition of quid pro quo.

So, Giuliani sent me to Kyiv and he went back to New York.

Since Poroshenko was busy campaigning for the upcoming election, I had to wait until he was free. In the middle of the night, I received a phone call. It was Lutsenko. He told me that he'd pick me up in 15 minutes.

He arrived with a fleet of security personnel and we were driven to his office building downtown.

Once inside, we got on the elevator and, instead of going up to his office, we went down for four floors.

He led us into a conference room and poured some shots for himself and Igor.

When Poroshenko arrived, we exchanged pleasantries and talked about the rigors of a long campaign. Then, like a politician, he praised himself for 30 or 40 minutes, listing off all of his accomplishments as President.

I mentioned that we had met before and that reminded him about our mission.

"America has a big problem … with corruption," he said. "I want to get to the bottom of what happened with Joe Biden and his son Hunter."

I explained that I had a wealth of circumstantial evidence against them, that Biden had gotten Shokin fired for investigating Burisma.

Poroshenko stayed silent. It lasted long enough that I was pretty sure I must've made some kind of mistake with my delivery.

But I continued. I told him that we wanted him to say that Yovanovitch had been meddling in Ukrainian politics. As an incentive, I told him that Trump would be very appreciative and throw his support behind Poroshenko's campaign.

He stopped me there, and said that he wanted to tell me a story. He recounted his visit to the White House in which he got a handshake and some photos, just like a tourist, before he was hustled out. Just outside the White House, Poroshenko was surprised by a Trump staffer who told him that the President would be very appreciative if Ukraine would buy some West Pennsylvania coal. Figuring that's how business was done in America, Poroshenko's government purchased $100 million worth of Pennsylvania coal, even though it was much more expensive than their other sources. The following week, Trump announced the coal-to-Ukraine deal to a frenzied West Pennsylvania crowd.

After that, Poroshenko told me, it was like he was put on some kind of pay-no-attention-to-this-person list. He never heard from Trump or his people again. Until our meeting.

To put it plainly, he just didn't trust Trump to hold up his part of the bargain. He added that he didn't want to appear to be involved in U.S. politics, that it really wasn't in his best interest. He closed by telling me that he wasn't saying no, but he wasn't saying yes, either.

We agreed to keep the lines of communication open. The whole thing took maybe three hours.

The next day, Giuliani called me and asked me if Lutsenko had agreed to the plan. I said that he had. He asked me to call Lutsenko back. Giuliani told me that he couldn't work for Lutsenko while he was the President's lawyer for the Mueller investigation. It just wouldn't look good. Instead, he told me, the work would be done by Victoria Toensing and her husband, Joe diGenova. That's when they joined our little crew.

I was truly surprised. It didn't make sense. Why would Giuliani give up an easy $200,000 when he was chronically short of money and going through an expensive divorce? So, I asked him.

"Don't worry about me," he said. "I've got it all worked out with them."

Chapter 34
The 'President's Guy'

The rich donor persona that I had been cultivating went beyond the Republican party. In May, Igor and I were honored with the Chovevei Zion Award at a gala held by the National Council of Young Israel. Frager was their first Vice-President. Igor, Giuliani and I got to know Frager better on a trip to the Chabad-Lubavitch Ohel — the sacred burial site of the last two rebbes of the Chabad-Lubavitch dynasty, Menachem Mendel Schneerson, and Yosef Yitzchok Schneersohn. The Ohel is in the Montefiore Cemetery in the Cambria Heights neighborhood in Queens, and is visited by thousands every year.

When we were finished, we went to Frager's for lunch.

Giuliani came along for the optics. A neo-Nazi terrorist had just shot up the L'Simcha (Tree of Life) Synagogue in Pittsburgh, killing 11 and injuring 6 more. It made good sense for Giuliani to be seen showing solidarity with Jews, especially since many admitted and suspected antisemites had shown unwavering support for Trump.

Once Igor and I became known to national media, Frager join everyone else in distancing himself from us. He explained to the media how we ended up at his house. "They needed a place to go for a light meal afterward," he said. "My home was not far from the Ohel." He said that the three of us were among 20 or so people he was courting as potential donors to his causes. "It sounded like they were wealthy."

We were not. But I had definitely become used to the trappings of wealth and found ways to get them. While working for Giuliani and Trump, my flights on private jets were always paid for by wealthy Republican contributors. But it was rarely my flight. Generally, I would ask a donor if Giuliani could use his jet for a flight here or there. He did not like to fly commercial.

But even they had their limits. "Just becoming expensive flying u guys everywhere LEV," Harry Sargeant III texted me. I knew it was, but it was important business we were taking care of.

When asked about the text later on, Sargeant (through his diligent lawyer, Chris Kise) said that the flights for me he paid for were actually loans extended to an acquaintance he found "funny."

As is often the case with prominent Republicans, I remember it differently. He gave me free use of the private jet as long as he could justify the trip as being for Giuliani. Sargeant said he wanted to keep Giuliani happy.

I was just too excited to keep my assignment to myself. I told a few close friends that the President had sent me on a James Bond mission. I was still deeply steeped in the Cult of Trump and its valiant war against the Deep State that it made me proud of myself. If the President had assigned me to a co-vert mission in Ukraine, it

Giuliani loved to travel by private jet; if he wasn't paying.

must be part of a greater effort to help the American people. I had no reason to believe otherwise. Having an important role felt good. I believed I'd received a major promotion in the fight against everything that was wrong with the world. I really was the President's guy in Ukraine.

First on the agenda Giuliani had set out was getting rid of Ambassador Yovanovitch. If we had our guy in there instead of her, we could accomplish all of our goals in Ukraine. Giuliani even had the perfect candidate — Pete Sessions. He was definitely still looking to get into Trump's good graces and he had just lost his election in Texas. I felt like it would be easy to get him to do what we wanted. He was on our side.

Hindsight makes it perfectly clear that Trump was simply, and illegally, looking for dirt to discredit his likely opponent in the 2020 election, but I didn't see it that way at the time. Believing that Biden was a key part of the Clinton-Obama branch of the Deep State, I had a dogmatic belief that it would absolutely be in America's best interest to know if he or his son had done anything illegal in Ukraine, where they would have been essentially safe from the prying eyes of the American media and law enforcement.

After the Hanukkah Party meeting, Trump and I became much more friendly. Of course, after the arrest, Trump was first in a long line of shameless Republicans who claimed they had never met me, but few claims were as ludicrous as his. Not only were there staggeringly high piles of photos and

From left, Igor, Correia, me, Giuliani, his lawyer John Sale and Sale's wife. Sale introduced me to Giuliani.

videos of us together (which Trump dismissed with the excuse that he takes pictures with many thousands of people he might not actually know) but there are also dozens of incidents like when Trump opened up a Q and A at an August 2018 fundraiser by calling me by my first name although I'd neither been announced nor was I wearing a name tag.

At least Giuliani owned up, admitting that he knew me, although he claimed that we were introduced by an "important investigator" he won't name. I will. It was John Sale. He had worked for Giuliani at the SDNY. I knew him after we were introduced by a Republican donor in Florida. Sale had ambitions of becoming U.S. Attorney for the Middle District of the state,

At the time, I was spending a lot of time with people like McCarthy, Ballard, Sargeant, Bailey and Hicks — all members of the Republican elite and all people with close ties to Trump.

Once Giuliani introduced me to Toensing and diGenova, they became almost constant companions of mine. They introduced me to John Solomon, who was already doing his research on the Bidens' activities in Ukraine. He told me that he had a lot of information about them, but he needed me and Igor — since we were his feet on the ground in Ukraine — to vet it all. I had no problem adding that to my duties.

With that, the BLT Team was born. We quickly evolved to be within the innermost of Trump's circles, becoming the source of, or sometimes certifiers of, most of his information.

Chapter 35
A Soft Landing

Venezuela was still simmering. In fact, it was falling apart. Since Maduro had taken over, more than 7 million people had fled the country, many of them as refugees. The 30 million or so who stayed were helpless, at the whims of the gangsters and corporations, as the government did nothing to stop them. In fact, most of the people close to Maduro were drug dealers or crooks of one kind or another.

I saw the beginning of the end of the Soviet Union, and Venezuela looked like it was going down the same path

The official White House stance was to support Guaidó, even at great cost, and to denounce Maduro. Giuliani was on board with the U.S. giving him the soft landing he desired, but Bolton and Pompeo clearly had gotten to Trump's ear first. They must've convinced him that Maduro wasn't on his side (after all, he had been an ally of Castro's Cuba, something Trump truly hated). Trump has a reputation for believing the last thing he's told, so we felt like we still had a chance to change his mind.

That, of course, was where I came in. Sargeant was a big-time Republican donor, but he didn't have a lot of sway when it came to the top dogs. Trump listened to Giuliani most of all. And who did Giuliani listen to? Me.

Bolton couldn't stand Giuliani, but it was easy for him to go over Bolton's head and straight to the President. Sargeant knew that and acted accordingly.

Sargeant wasn't just try to help an old friend. Maduro was so scared that he was hiding in the palace. He promised Sargeant billions of barrels of oil if he could get him his soft landing. With his family. And the money he stole. And a few close friends.

That's an unbelievable amount of money. At the time, oil had climbed to $71 a barrel, in no small part because of the instability in Venezuela. But to get it, he had to keep Maduro safe and sound. It was understood that Sargeant would take care of the team helping with the solution.

I was no expert on Venezuela, but I was familiar with the situation of powerful people desperate to escape the wrath of the people they'd gotten rich off. I had lots of connections in the international petroleum industry and a lobbyist here and there.

I saw it as a way to show how important I was to the administration and to get Global Energy Producers off the ground.

The clock was ticking. And in April 2019, the alarm went off.

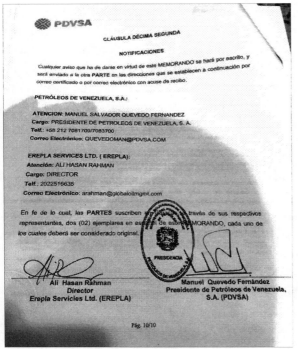

A page from the contract signed by Sargeant's company, Erepla, and the Venezuelan government.

With Maduro's authoritarian rule hanging by a thread, the head of his intelligence service, Manuel Cristopher Figuera, denounced him, left his post and went into hiding. A petulant Maduro then expelled 54 members of his staff and military who he deemed loyal to Guaidó.

Guaidó acknowledged that he was more popular among the Venezuelan people than Maduro, but had not received sufficient military equipment to unseat the entrenched leader. He called for non-violent demonstrations, and asked members of the armed forces to join them.

The next few days were not exactly non-violent. Lieutenant-Colonel Illich Sánchez, the highest-ranking officer to defect to Guaidó's side, gathered his soldiers and blocked the country's most vital freeway. Former opposition leader Leopoldo López — who had been under house arrest after receiving a 13-year sentence in 2015 for delinquency, arson, damage to public property, incitement to riot and terrorism — was freed on the morning of April 30 by military forces loyal to Guaidó and joined him on a livestream.

Guaidó announced the start of what he called Operation Freedom.

Shots started firing. López hightailed it to the Chilean Embassy and, after finding no help there, to the Spanish Ambassador's residence.

Playing to American public opinion, Trump announced: "Maduro's grip on tyranny will be smashed and broken," even though his administration and its supporters had enriched and emboldened him, as Russia, China and Iran increased their footholds in the incredibly resource-rich nation.

Making matters worse, Trump had very little knowledge of Venezuela or what was going on there. Most of what he knew came from Bolton, Ballard, whose sources were Gorrín (a close friend of Maduro's who was later placed on ICE's Most Wanted list for alleged money laundering) and Mauricio Claver-Carone (a Cuban-American lawyer and lobbyist who was as steadfastly pro-Trump as he was anti-Castro). To put it in terms Trump could understand, Gorrín essentially said Maduro good, Guaidó bad, while Claver-Carone countered with Guaidó good, Maduro bad (although Gorrín might also have been secretly working with Guaidó's people).

Things got tense on the ground in Venezuela and many in the administration felt like they had to do something after Trump said that "some aides are more openly teasing military intervention." One of these aides was Bolton, who often held opinions contrary to the Trump crowd and who I felt was all too ready to use force in any situation. Aware that Maduro was being propped up by as many as 20,000 Cuban soldiers — a position reinforced by the opinions of many high-ranking members of the U.S. military — he convinced Trump to threaten sanctions on Cuba if its forces did not "promptly and peacefully return to their island."

Behind the scenes, Bolton pushed for an invasion, even though Guaidó had made it clear that he did not want that. "We think it's still very important for key figures in the regime who have been talking to the opposition over these last three months to make good on their commitment to achieve the peaceful transfer of power from the Maduro regime," Bolton told the media. "All agreed Maduro had to go."

As the tension reached a peak, Maduro fled for Simón Bolívar International Airport. Even he, it seemed, thought the end was near. In an indication of whose side Maduro was really on, Simón Bolívar had housed two Tu-160 Blackjacks (supersonic Russian heavy bombers with nuclear capability) and had daily flights to Turkey (through Havana) on the only airline operating there during the hostilities — Iran's Mahan Air. Of course.

Not everyone agrees on what actually happened that day. Pompeo and the U.S. media said that Maduro was on the tarmac, preparing to get on a Russian military plane to Havana when "two unnamed Russian officials" talked him out of it. Maduro, of course, claimed that he had not gone to the airport, that he was bravely directing the anti-coup effort on the front line and that Pompeo was slandering him to justify an invasion "so the empire could get its claws into Venezuela."

The American story is close to the truth. When he arrived at the airport, two FSB agents told Maduro not to worry, that the Russians would safeguard his return to power. It's exceedingly unlikely they gave him the option of getting on the plane alive. Faced with the prospect of fighting Guaidó with the help of Russian soldiers or getting into a plane with those same soldiers, Maduro made the predictable decision and returned to Miraflores Palace.

When Maduro's forces — Venezuelan or otherwise — fought back with Chinese-made armored cars and news spread of López less-than-heroic response, the coup attempt fizzled out. Soldiers loyal to Guaidó shed their uniforms and were seen knocking on the doors of foreign embassies, hoping for refuge.

By evening, all was quiet and Maduro blamed the disruption on "the obsessive efforts of the Venezuelan right, the Colombian oligarchy and the U.S. Empire." Absolutely untrue, but that stuff still plays big down there. It also helped Maduro deflect any blame as he held onto power.

I was disappointed that I didn't get the big prize, but not heartbroken. I was never sure of what would happen in Venezuela and had not really planned on cashing in on Sargeant's offer. Besides, I had Ukraine on my mind then. It was more important.

Chapter 36
Smear Campaign

Yovanovitch went about her business as usual. At the start of March, She gave a strident speech to the Ukraine Crisis Media Center, an NGO dedicated to distributing uncensored news in Ukraine. She spoke about, and gave her approval for, the case for unseating an anti-corruption prosecutor, Nazar Kholodnytskyi. A few days earlier, a video emerged of Kholodnytskyi literally teaching witnesses tricks to avoid prosecution. Yovanovitch, as was her style, didn't hold back. "To ensure the integrity of anti-corruption institutions, the Special Anti-Corruption Prosecutor must be replaced," she delivered to a positive crowd. "Nobody who has been recorded coaching suspects on how to avoid corruption charges can be trusted to prosecute those very same cases."

Not everyone in the audience was appreciative. Lutsenko found the ambassador's intrusion into his department's business dangerous. He wanted to save his ally, Kholodnytskyi, and his own office's reputation.

Immediately, Lutsenko texted me.

Lutsenko was as viscerally against Yovanovitch as anyone. But he told me that the speech might actually be a good thing for us. We could position it as Yovanovitch's attempt to tell the Ukrainian government what to do. Even if she was right, it wouldn't play in Kyiv and it wouldn't play in D.C.

I knew Kholodnytskyi and thought of him pretty much the way I did all Ukrainian officials — craven, mercenary and blessed with rat-like survival skills — more of an ambivalent man making his way through a corrupt system than a malevolent one. Giuliani instructed me to tell Lutsenko to do what he could to further that opinion.

Part of Lutsenko's plan was to have Kholodnytskyi talk to me and, if I thought he would be useful, then to Giuliani and perhaps the American media. Three days after Yovanovitch's speech, Lutsenko texted me in Russian: "Nazar is waiting, I explained everything, He's ready to tell you about the bias." I heard Kholodnytskyi out, but didn't pursue him any further. When

Yovanovitch had called Kholodnytskyi out as an example of Ukrainian corruption, she was right. His record and reputation would not have stood up to even the most half-hearted scrutiny.

Lutsenko was growing ever more impatient with us as the deadline for his job was looming. He had earlier told me to tell Giuliani that he wanted to

speak with Barr. Giuliani said that could be arranged — for a $200,000 lobbying fee (even though he was not legally allowed to lobby at the time). Lutsenko balked, but it was clear that an audience with Barr was his ultimate goal. "We would dangle Barr over his head to get him to do things," Giuliani told me.

Little Dimitri met with Giuliani and me, and Giuliani was delighted to learn that we could work with Firtash.

The always nervous Lutsenko was clearly angry when — three days after I met Kholodnytskyi — he texted me in an urgent tone: "I'm sorry, but this is all simply bullshit. I'm fucking sick of all this. I haven't received a visit. My [boss] hasn't received jack all. I'm prepared to [trash] your opponent. But you want more and more. We're over." The boss he was talking about was Poroshenko, the "opponent" was Joe Biden. He felt that he had lined up people, including Poroshenko, who wanted to talk, but had seen no progress on his desire to speak with Barr.

In fact, I had managed to set up an interview of Poroshenko for U.S. media so that he could announce that he would investigate the Bidens and ask the U.S. to recall Yovanovitch. If he wanted support from Trump, he'd have to play ball. I had it all ready, cameras, interviewer, live feed back to New York and an hour before it was to start, Poroshenko got cold feet and canceled, just walked out. Lutsenko went on instead, but it wasn't the same.

Still, videos of the interview would later be used as the basis of several opinion articles about Ukraine by John Solomon.

Furious, I asked Lutsenko for an explanation. He didn't have one. So I sent him to Giuliani. Giuliani, never one to shy away from conflict, laid into Lutsenko pretty hard. He called him and his boss "a pair of two-bit liars" and promised that he was not going to forget their ineptitude and lack of guts. I knew that Lutsenko was absolutely seething, but that he had no choice but to bite the bullet and keep helping. So, whenever Lutsenko complained, I just ignored him.

Giuliani, perhaps not thinking the whole thing through, made no secret of his meetings with Ukrainian prosecutors (both sitting and expelled) or that he was looking for controversial information on the Bidens on behalf of President Trump.

Still, the operation didn't make even a tiny ripple in American news. The media was paying paltry attention to Ukraine after they signed Minsk II — a ceasefire deal with the Russian separatists in Donbas. Much of the active violence had stopped, but Russian proxies still occupied a big part of the country. Americans felt like it wasn't really a war, just an internal conflict, nothing to worry about.

The U.S. government, however, was keenly aware of the strategic implications of Russia's semi-covert foray into Ukraine. On February 15, 2019, Congress approved a $115 million military aid package for Ukraine. Administered by the State Department, the funds were part of the Foreign Military Financing Program (FMF), which helps friendly countries defend themselves against aggressors. Since there was still $26 million of funds earmarked for Ukraine leftover from the previous year, the total aid package was then $141 million. Not an insignificant amount of money, but in national defense terms — the U.S. pays about $10 million for each Abrams tank — it was not a game changer.

About two weeks later, John C. Rood, Under Secretary of Defense for Policy, Department of Defense, announced that the first half ($125 million) of an earlier aid promise that had been approved in September 2018, was ready to be moved. Notably, this package included lethal weapons.

The news was greeted positively by the American public, who recognized Putin's aggression. Everybody was happy. Trump was making it look like he actually supported Ukraine; he pointed out that he was the first one to actually give them any ammunition.

Things seemed to be looking up for Yovanovitch. Just as the plot against her was assuming a coherent shape, the State Department asked her to stay on in Ukraine for another three years. Not surprisingly, she agreed.

Shokin's name didn't surprise anyone who knew him. Career diplomat and Deputy Assistant Secretary of State for European and Eurasian Affairs George P. Kent said that the former prosecutor was "well and very unfavorably known to us."

Shokin was recognized because of the way he did his job. "There was a broad-based consensus that he was a typical Ukraine prosecutor who lived a lifestyle far in excess of his government salary, who never prosecuted anybody known for having committed a crime and having covered up crimes that were known to have been committed," added Kent.

Shokin and Yovanovitch had never been happy to see each other. It's not like Lutsenko didn't have an axe to grind, either. The embassy's David Holmes was informed that Lutsenko was telling people that Yovanovitch had "destroyed" him by, as Holmes put it, her "refusal to support him until he followed through with his reform commitments and ceased using his position for personal gain." Kent said that he wasn't at all surprised at the efforts of Shokin and Lutsenko. Their motivation was simple. "They were now peddling false information in order to extract revenge against those who had exposed their misconduct, including U.S. diplomats, Ukrainian anti-corruption officials, and reform-minded civil society groups in Ukraine," he said. "You can't promote principled anti-corruption efforts without pissing off corrupt people." Yovanovitch, it would appear, was getting the unjust rewards for doing her job well.

Nobody at the embassy knew what the game was. Yovanovitch was too professional to have said disrespectful things about the President, certainly not that he was going to be impeached. But I had been the source of a constant flow of slander against her. It was a big playground game. We'd go visit important people in Ukraine and tell them how bad Yovanovitch was. That would be followed by a visit by someone from the State Department who would tell the same people that we were lying. I would then double back and talk to the same people again, assuring them that Yovanovitch was anti-Trump and could be dangerous for Ukraine. Then the embassy staff would visit those same people again, telling them that we were nobodies who didn't know what we were talking about. I had more time, so I usually got in the last word. I actually made it hard for the embassy staff to have time to do their actual jobs by keeping them so busy. As Holmes said:

> "Beginning in March 2019, the situation at the Embassy and in Ukraine changed dramatically. Specifically, the three priorities of security, economy, and justice and our support for Ukrainian democratic resistance to Russian aggression became overshadowed by a political agenda promoted by former New York City Mayor Rudy Giuliani and a cadre of officials operating with a direct channel to the White House."

Yovanovitch, naturally, was upset. Things would get worse for her before they got better. On March 19, I spent much of my day on the phone with Solomon. I wasn't just badmouthing Yovanovitch, I was also gathering as much information as I could about her and the Bidens. Some of it might actually have been true. I fed Solomon that information, although he said his major sources preferred to remain anonymous.

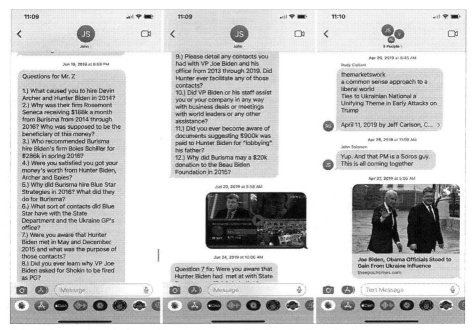

John Solomon provided me with questions for Zlochevsky about Burisma and the Bidens.

The next day, Solomon kicked off his part of the Yovanovitch smear campaign with an article for The Hill. It was based on my information and the videotaped interview with Lutsenko. He was an odd choice, considering that he acquired his important position in the Ukrainian government despite not having a law degree and was best known in the U.S. for being accused of hindering the investigations of Manafort and Kilimnik, allowing the Russian to get off Scot-free.

But he was Ukrainian and had a title. That made him credible to U.S. audiences. The article and accompanying video — called As Russia Collusion Fades, Ukrainian Plot to Help Clinton Emerges — opens by insinuating that the Russia investigation into Trump was old and tired, while the new hotness was an investigation into how the Ukrainians allegedly helped Clinton in 2016. Lutsenko told Solomon that he was opening an investigation into "an illegal intrusion into the American election campaign."

Solomon then portrays Lutsenko as an anti-corruption hero, as he had been instructed. Although along with letting Kilimnik sneak away, Lutsenko had been fired, dismissed, suspended, jailed (he was pardoned, officially for health reasons) and gotten chummy with Manafort.

Lutsenko also produced a letter from Kent to the Prosecutor's office that he characterized as warning them to back off any investigation of Clinton (Kent would later call that "poppycock" and say that the letter was about concentrating on anti-corruption efforts that had been, at best, relaxed).

Solomon also made public Pete Sessions' letter to Pompeo about removing Yovanovitch for her "disdain" of Trump.

Minutes after the article was published, Solomon called me, he was giddy with excitement and thanked me profusely for all my help.

That evening, Trump promoted the story on Twitter. The tweet received 49,600 Likes. Giuliani had even more to say, tweeting two days later: "Pay attention to @dbongino for an analysis of some real collusion between Hillary, Kerry and Biden people colluding with Ukrainian operatives to make money and affect 2016 election." Don Bongino is a former NYPD officer and secret service agent, who had become a conservative radio show host and Fox News contributor. Not officially a member of the Trump Administration, but a loud supporter.

On March 22, Bongino tweeted: "Joe Biden is going to have A LOT of explaining to do regarding Ukraine. A LOT." Later that day, he tweeted: "What was Joe Biden doing in Ukraine during the month his son Hunter was named to a key board position in an influential Ukrainian company?"

It was all part of a multi-pronged media campaign aimed at raising awareness that Joe Biden's troublesome son, Hunter, was working at a somewhat suspect job in Ukraine at the same time that Joe was calling the shots over there. It wasn't untrue, but it was open ended. We didn't say Biden took a bribe of X amount from such-and-such on whatever date, we just hinted that the pair of them were no good. It was just like the gangsters again, It's easy, and often more effective, to get your message across without articulating it directly. And — as another example of Republican projection — many of our guys started calling them "the Biden crime family."

By then, Giuliani was free to shoot his mouth off on any topic that was on his mind. On March 25, Giuliani appeared on Fox & Friends, and threatened to determine the identity of the person who instigated the FBI to start the Russian collusion investigation. Repeating Trump's dubious claim that the Mueller Report showed no collusion (falsely claiming that Trump "has been absolved, vindicated, exonerated," and given "complete vindication"), he said that some Trump-hating individual made the whole thing up. "Now the question is if there were three investigations — no evidence of collusion — who made it up?" he asked. "It didn't just come out of thin air. I want to know who did it. Who paid for it? Who fueled it? Because the person that did it, and the group that did it, knows it's untrue because they invented it." While it seemed undemocratic to some that a de facto Trump representative would seek punishment for an individual who might have spread false information (if Trump's claims were true), the hosts appeared to agree with what appeared to be a partisan threat of revenge. Giuliani ended the interview by saying that the Democrats should apologize for advocating due process regarding an alleged crime. "Shame on them! Shame on them!" he shouted.

He appeared on CNN the next day, arguing that they should apologize to the President for reporting on the Russia collusion investigation. "You guys on this network have tortured this man for two years with collusion and nobody's apologizing," he snarled at host Chris Cuomo. "Before we talk about obstruction, apologize."

Cuomo said that Giuliani was "not being fair," and that CNN reporters were asking questions that needed to be asked, even if to absolve Trump. That cast Giuliani as a mouthpiece who wanted absolute immunity for the President. He did manage to get Cuomo to conduct the interview as though his false claim that the President had been cleared was true.

Satisfied, Giuliani turned his attention back to Ukraine. While Giuliani was overseeing the operation, I was the hard-working sergeant. Both Shokin and Lutsenko were pushing me hard on their Yovanovitch problem. Getting rid of the ambassador, for whom we used the code name "Madam," had to be tied into any deal. In fact, Lutsenko sent me a message on WhatsApp saying: "It's just that if you don't make a decision about Madam — you are calling into question all my declarations. Including about B." B stood for Biden. I understood Lutsenko's messages (and others on the topic) to mean that if the Giuliani team wanted dirt on the Bidens, they needed to get rid of Yovanovitch first.

That put me back on the phone with Solomon. On March 19, we spoke with each other six times. I was telling him what was happening in Ukraine and he was asking me more questions.

The next day, an article, Top Ukrainian Justice Official Says U.S. Ambassador Gave Him a Do Not Prosecute List, was released by The Hill. It was a hit piece on Yovanovitch in which Lutsenko was again the main source of information. And he delivered a whopper: "Unfortunately, from the first meeting with the U.S. ambassador in Kiev, [Yovanovitch] gave me a list of people whom we should not prosecute. My response of that is it is inadmissible. Nobody in this country, neither our president nor our parliament nor our ambassador, will stop me from prosecuting whether there is a crime,"

Lutsenko was lucky that most viewers had no idea of his history or what his near future looked like. To them, he was a guy with an important job recounting a narrative with authority. In his statement, he portrayed himself as a crusader against corruption who was broadsided by an intruding ambassador who was trying to order him to maintain the corrupt state by saying who he could and could not prosecute.

The article was popular, and most of those who read the piece were outraged. Their impression of Yovanovitch was not positive. The thought of an American, a non-elected one yet, giving a do-not-prosecute list to a foreign government was atrocious.

Giuliani, the BLT Team and other Trump World members — including Fox News — pushed the article on social media. Even Don Jr. got into the act, tweeting (using the family's trademark poor attention to grammar):

"We need more @RichardGrenell 's and less of these jokers as ambassadors.
Calls Grow To Remove Obama's U.S. Ambassador To Ukraine.

https://dailywire.com/news/45035/calls-grow-removeobamas-us-ambassador-ukraine-ryan-saavedra"

Solomon wasn't the only one Lutsenko was talking to. On March 26, Lutsenko texted me to tell me the investigation of Burisma, was "progressing well." And then he added exactly what I wanted to read: "There is testimony about transfers to B." B again meant Biden, in this case, Hunter. He followed that up with a message about Yovanovitch, who he had called the "fool" many times before. Expressing our shared frustration at her unwillingness to stop her anti-corruption support, he wrote: "Here you can't even get rid of one fool." Lutsenko and I had been texting back and forth about why an investigation into the Bidens hadn't happened. Lutsenko's excuse was that Yovanovitch was in the way and he was powerless to do anything about it. I knew Yovanovitch was deeply entrenched. I texted back: "She's not a simple fool trust me."

I was certain that she had a lot of important friends in the Deep State. Many believers were sure that boogieman Soros was behind all of the liberalization movements in Eastern Europe, including Ukraine. I was among them. It all started in 2014 when Soros told CNN interviewer Fareed Zakaria: "Well, I set up a foundation in Ukraine before Ukraine became independent of Russia. And the foundation has been functioning ever since. And it played a — an important part in events now." Since then, every change in Ukraine could and would be discredited by saying that Soros had done it. I was among many who believed that Soros had gotten Yovanovitch and other liberal women ambassadors placed in Eastern Europe.

Aware that ending the conversation on a negative note might discourage Lutsenko, I added: "She's not getting away."

Over the next couple of days, Giuliani emailed Pompeo several times. They were part of a strategy to overwhelm him with negative portrayals of Yovanovitch. Giuliani expressed hope was that Pompeo would help, or at least not stand in the way, of any operation to displace her.

Smearing Yovanovitch was a big job and Giuliani was actively re-cruiting. One eager participant was Robert Hyde, a Connecticut business-man, QAnon enthusiast and big-time donor to Trump, Nunes, America First Action and the Tea Party Majority Fund as well as other Republicans and their causes. He entered the fold through Igor, one of his long-time drinking buddies from the Trump International. He was seriously getting ready to run for office in his home state, so a Trump endorsement could be dangled in front of him. At the hotel, he overheard everything because he was trying desperately to be relevant. From that, he developed a hatred for Yovanovitch. He even texted me: "Fuck that bitch." and "Wow. Can't believe Trumo hasn't fired this bitch. I'll get right in that."

Giuliani had me handle him. I didn't like the idea because I didn't like the man. He was strange right from the start,. He seemed to me like he was drunk all the time. I knew I couldn't trust drunks. But that wasn't what really worried me about Hyde. A former Marine, Hyde seemed to love playing spy, more than a tad too much. He told me that he had operatives on the ground in Ukraine who were monitoring Yovanovitch's every movement.

Stalking the ambassador with God knows who did not appeal to me at all. But I really knew that I'd had it with Hyde when he texted: "They are willing to help if we/you would like a price. Guess you can do anything in the Ukraine with money ... what I was told."

All I could text back was: "LOL." I was hoping that Hyde was joking. Look, I try to be nice to everyone, even those who had wronged me, like Ballard and Giuliani. I just didn't want to get involved with this guy.

Later, Hyde would disturb me by describing what seemed like his own little military operation. He texted: "If you want her out they need to make contact with security forces. From Ukrainians." The next day, he seemed to be stalking Yovanovitch. He texted: "Nothing has changed she is still not moving they check today again," adding "It's confirmed we have a person inside." On the day after that, Hyde gave a terse sit rep: "She had visitors." After a long time with no answer from me, he entreated: "Hey broski tell me what we are doing what's the next step." I never answered. Later, some people in the media would say that Hyde was offering to get Yovanovitch killed, but I don't believe that. He just liked to talk big. Hyde soon faded into the background, much to my relief. He did not get Trump's endorsement and lost his election. The fact that he owed back child support, had been charged with reckless endangerment, was detained by police under the Florida Mental Health Act, was reported to police for allegedly trespassing at a church, was issued a restraining order after a political consultant he knew said he was stalking her (which forced him to give up his guns) and made a nastily vulgar reference to Kamala Harris and oral sex in a Twitter post probably didn't help either. He's a lobbyist now.

Chapter 37
Sending a Message

L
ess than a week later, Solomon pulled the Lutsenko tapes out once again for an opinion piece for The Hill called U.S. Embassy Pressed Ukraine to Drop Probe of George Soros Group During 2016 Election. Trying to sell the prosecutor hard, Solomon said that he was "widely regarded as a hero in the West" for spending two years in prison on what he characterized as dodgy, politically motivated charges. The article is a sequel to the first, and adds new characters to get the Deep State believers excited.

Solomon wrote that Yovanovitch specifically told Lutsenko not to investigate the Anti-Corruption Action Center (AntAC), which was funded by Deep State all-stars George Soros and the Obama Administration and their alleged co-conspirators, the FBI. No major figure had ever accused AntAC of any wrongdoing. In fact, when the International Monetary Fund and the European Union asked for a report on corruption in Ukraine in 2015, they chose AntAC's over one from Poroshenko and parliament, believing it to be more accurate and reliable.

While there's certainly nothing illegal about Soros or the Obama Administration funding NGOs in Ukraine, mention of them was enough to send many Trump fans into a rage. That was, of course, our intention.

Solomon's next shot was fired on April 1 with another article for The Hill — Joe Biden's 2020 Ukrainian Nightmare: A Closed Probe is Revived. In it, he demonizes Biden's pride in helping get Shokin fired, then turns the subject to Hunter Biden. In a statement to summarize his point, Solomon wrote a sentence that was technically true, but misleading: "Ukrainian officials tell me there was one crucial piece of information that Biden must have known but didn't mention to his audience: The prosecutor he got fired was leading a wide-ranging corruption probe into the natural gas firm Burisma Holdings that employed Biden's younger son, Hunter, as a board member." While Shokin was (sort of) investigating Burisma and Hunter Biden was on Burisma's board, the two did not overlap. It's as though he wrote that the President won a Nobel Prize; Donald Trump is President. Trump didn't win a Nobel, Obama did, but it's still a technically true pair of statements, just misleadingly arranged.

Those "Ukrainian officials," of course, were the people I had been visiting. Solomon's sources knew Hunter Biden worked at Burisma and that Joe Biden had gotten Shokin fired, so they reported their reactionary conclusions as fact. In effect, the article argues that Joe Biden used pressure to get Shokin fired to save his son Hunter. Solomon makes the case that Joe Biden is too compromised, perhaps too corrupt, to run for President.

Another week, another Solomon jab at Yovanovitch and, of course, the Bidens. The day before his next article came out, my phone records say that I called Giuliani 16 times and Solomon 10.

The article was given the beseeching title Ukrainian to U.S. Prosecutors: Why Don't You Want Our Evidence on Democrats? Lutsenko gets dragged out again (smart observers probably noticed that he was wearing the same shirt and tie in every video), but this time Solomon also had a second source: Kostiantyn Kulyk, deputy head of the Prosecutor General's International Legal Cooperation Department — Lutsenko's Number 2.

Lutsenko actually hated Kulyk because Kulyk liked to characterize himself as this hardcore investigator, making it look like he had gotten all of the evidence in every case and anything Lutsenko had, he had come from Kulyk. It's not like Kulyk was Mr. Clean, either. Two years earlier, he was indicted for taking bribes. The primary evidence against him was that his lifestyle far exceeded his reported sources of income. When his assets were collected by investigators, they were 1,615 times what he should have been able to have afforded on his salary. He had two apartments in Kiev and his primary ride was a Toyota Land Cruiser of dubious provenance. "In any other country a prosecutor like this would have been fired a long time ago," said anti-corruption lawyer Andrii Savin. "But what happened in this country? The prosecutor general promoted him." Kulyk was also known to be a friend of Yevhen Zhylin, leader of a group that regularly sent thugs into protests to start violence so he could blame it on the protesters. But to most Americans, he was simply a high-ranking Ukrainian official, to be given the same amount of trust as the rest of them.

In the article, Kulyk complains that he and "other senior law enforcement officials" were denied visas for a planned visit to D.C. They were hoping, Kulyk said, to share evidence on wrongdoing by "American Democrats and their allies in Kiev." The villain? Who else but Yovanovitch. "We were supposed to share this information during a working trip to the United States," Kulyk told Solomon. "However, the ambassador blocked us from obtaining a visa. She didn't explicitly deny our visa, but also didn't give it to us." He listed some of the things he said he would be bringing to D.C.:

- A statement by two high-ranking Ukrainian officials admitting that they tried to help Clinton's 2016 campaign; in part, by releasing Manafort's famous Black Ledger
- Evidence of Democrats looking for "dirt" to use against Trump
- Records that reveal that Hunter Biden received more than $3 million from Burisma
- Evidence that the U.S. State Department and U.S. Embassy pressured prosecutors not to investigate key people
- Records of $7 billion in misappropriated funds, some sent to the U.S.

Kulyk said he had to deliver the evidence personally because all of the FBI agents in Ukraine were in league with Yovanovitch and the National Anti-Corruption Bureau (NABU), one of the few Ukrainian institutions with a positive reputation around the world. "It is no secret in Ukrainian political circles that the NABU was created with American help and tried to exert influence during the U.S. presidential election," Kulyk told Solomon, citing no sources. But it wasn't too much of an exaggeration. All of the anti-corruption NGOs in Ukraine had been founded and funded by Americans. To most Ukrainians, they were vassals of the Americans trying to rule the country and bring in unwanted changes by proxy.

Kulyk, of course, was working from the same package of evidence that we had gotten from Shokin and Lutsenko. He denied it, but look at what he said and look at what we said at the same time. It's no coincidence that they're virtually identical.

That same package was getting around. The next recipient was Secretary of State Pompeo. Giuliani told the media that he "hand delivered" the dossier into Pompeo's hands, but it's been widely reported that he merely sent to to the White House to forward to Pompeo. The first one is true. I prepared the package with him.

Trump ally Laura Ingraham dedicated the March 29 episode of her show to discuss what its tagline called "Joe Biden's Ukraine Connection," although it was the revelations of Manafort's activities that had put Ukraine into the news at the time. In her first sentence, Ingraham deflected any attention to Manafort and concentrated on other "bad actors" in Ukraine, then she referred to Sessions' "urgent letter imploring" Pompeo to remove Yovanovitch. She characterized the ambassador as "part of Obama's orbit" and pointed out that Greg Craig — a lawyer for Obama and Bill Clinton and an adviser to Democrats Ted Kennedy and Madeleine Albright — lied about his work for Yanukovych, although she failed to mention that he did so while working directly for Manafort. And, to sweeten the pot, she pointed out that Biden had visited Ukraine just 10 days before Trump was inaugurated.

Sessions' letter to Pompeo about Yovanovitch.

Her guests included Peter Schweitzer — a Bannon associate and a Breitbart editor — and diGenova.

Schweitzer's 2018 book Secret Empires first brought the concept of the Bidens and their ties to Ukraine into public consciousness. A few days earlier, Schweitzer had given an interview to the Kyiv Post on the same subject.

At the start, diGenova introduced Yovanovitch to American audiences for the first time. "She is known and reported by people there to have badmouthed the President of the United States, Donald Trump, to have told Ukrainians not to listen to him or obey his policy, because he was going to be impeached," he announced with what appeared to be great pride. "And finally, her activities have caught up to her."

Of course, the President's primary source of information was me, either directly or through Giuliani.

Once again, the guy from the streets of Brooklyn with no related education or professional experience in the area found himself dictating America's foreign policy with an important ally.

At hearing the news of her recall, Ingraham switched tack from the idea that Yovanovitch should be removed from office to "should have been removed a year ago, that's a separate story, what's going on in the State Dep-artment." The show must go on.

And many Americans heard the names of Hunter Biden and Burisma for the very first time. Schweitzer said that a bank account "connected to" Hunt-er received $3.1 million "from the Ukrainians" at the same time he was wor-king for Burisma. Schweitzer then went off the rails of journalism, straight into speculation. "Dare I add that Hunter Biden has no background in Uk-raine, he has no background in energy policy, and his — and his job, report-edly — his job reportedly was regulatory compliance. What Hunter Biden knows about that in Ukraine, who knows?" He then decided for us: "So, it's — it's a very, very troublesome issues, and I think has all of the markings of payoffs going to the Bidens."

Instantly, diGenova joined in, also reporting speculation that supported a pro-Trump narrative as fact. "There's no question about it, that this has all the markings of bribery and extortion, and it's something that deserves a full-blown investigation into the conduct of the Biden family in Ukraine," he said. "There's some very disturbing details about it that are about to come out in reporting by John Solomon, and I think once those details come out, I think there's going to have to be a full-fledged criminal investigation."

This is exactly how our plan worked. Shokin had admitted the Bidens hadn't broken the law, but we made it sound like they did — or something bad, at least. It's a blueprint Trump and his people used over and over again. Accuse someone of being underhanded, but keep it vague, not even the slightest amount of detail. Then hold your supposed evidence away from anyone's examination. The evidence could be blank sheets of paper, it doesn't matter. It's like a street-corner card game — the suckers are the only one who don't know it's rigged.

Ingraham, sounding a touch less than impartial, egged them on, asking if such an investigation would be aimed at "revealing, perhaps, deep connec-tions to how the Mueller probe started?"

Then diGenova made a paper-thin attempt at defending Manafort, while accusing Yovanovitch and unnamed others in being part of the reason behind the Mueller Probe, with no evidence to back it up. "Oh, absolutely, because what happened was, the ambassador there, who has been removed, was in-volved in generating false information about Manafort, other information that went into the so-called black, black binders," he said, referring to the

Black Ledger, Manafort's list of accounts received. On it were $12.7 million from the Party of Regions (which, of course, he helped create and included Yanukovych, Manafort's personal project).

As president, Yanukovych had brought Ukraine closer to Russia on the oil and gas trade (angering the European Union), he leased Russia the naval base in Sevastopol from which their invasion of Crimea was launched, clamped down on media, allowed cronyism and corruption to run wild in his government and even cut social benefits for Chernobyl rescue workers.

Yanukovych had also angered the Obama administration, who banned his visa over the jailing of Prime Minister Yulia Tymoshenko. In what I now see as a compelling display of mental gymnastics, conservatives claimed that the Black Ledger implicated Biden, Clinton, Obama and Democrats in general, or that it had to be fake. We only believed what we wanted to be true, no matter what evidence was in front of us. Hell, we even had a guy who'd testify it was fake.

The show, which had a reputation for speculation and invective, was ostensibly about Yovanovitch, but the subject of the Bidens was just too tempting. For those inclined to believe in the passel of conspiracy theories that make up the Deep State concept, the idea that Biden and his son had something illicit going on in Ukraine — which had already been implanted earlier — was like catnip.

So, Team Trump kept the heat on Yovanovitch. According to emails between their staffers, Giuliani and Pompeo had been discussing the matter for weeks. Austin Evers, executive director of American Oversight, which sued for the documents' release, said that they showed "a clear paper trail from Rudy Giuliani to the Oval Office to Secretary Pompeo to facilitate Giuliani's smear campaign against a U.S. ambassador."

Nobody cared.

Chapter 38
Lying in Plain Sight

I f people actually did care, we could have gotten in a lot of trouble on April 18, 2019. That's when Lutsenko made what could have been a huge mistake. He actually retracted his claim of a do-not-prosecute list.

Treating the situation as though it were some kind of Disney sitcom mix-up, he told Kyiv's TheBabel that he and Yovanovitch had a simple misunderstanding that led to heated words. He told them that in a January 2017 meeting in his office, Yovanovitch expressed concern about charges brought against Vitaly Kasko, an activist former Deputy Prosecutor General, who described massive corruption and "total lawlessness" of the department under Shokin's watch. He'd been charged with fraud, dismissed from his post and had his Kyiv apartment seized just as Shokin was leaving office. The charge stemmed from the accusation that the government-subsidized apartment was in his mother's name, but she actually lived in Lviv. It looked to her, and lots of others, that Shokin was just railroading the guy.

Ever the exemplar of diligence, Lutsenko said that he was actively pursuing the case because it "had signs of abuse." Yovanovitch told him that she knew the case was bogus, it was just Shokin taking another parting shot at one of the guys who tried to blow the whistle on him.

At the time, Lutsenko said, he took that to mean that she didn't want him to prosecute any anti-corruption advocates. That's when, he said, things got heated. "I shared the details [of Kasko's case] and explained that I could not open and close cases on my own. I listed some so-called anti-corruption activists under investigation. She said it was unacceptable, as it would undermine the credibility of anti-corruption activists," he told TheBabel. "I took a piece of paper, put down the listed names and said: 'Give me a do-not-prosecute list.' She said: 'No, you've got me wrong.' I said: No, I didn't get you wrong. Such lists were earlier drawn up on Bankova Street [the seat of government], and now you give new lists on Tankova Street [the U.S. Embassy, since re-named Sikorsky Street]." The meeting, he recalled, ended with anger. Yovanovitch left. "I'm afraid the emotions were not very good," he told the interviewers.

Going by Lutsenko's own account, Yovanovitch did not give him a do-not-prosecute list and tried to correct him when he suggested that she had. Then she angrily left his office when he continued to say she had. According to Lutsenko, the only witness in the case against Yovanovitch, the claim he made against her never actually happened.

It would not have made much news in the U.S. even if Lutsenko said he and the Bidens robbed a bank because the interview in a little-known Ukrainian news portal came out on the same day — April 18, 2019 — that the first, redacted, version of the Mueller Report was publicly released by Barr.

> **Tom Winter** ✔ 🐦
> @Tom_Winter
>
> NBC News: Attorney General William Barr has been aware of the investigation into Parnas and Fruman and was since shortly after he came into office this past February, @PeteWilliamsNBC reports.
>
> ♡ 5,067   10:55 AM - Oct 10, 2019   ⓘ
>
> 💬 2,440 people are talking about this   >

Of course Barr knew all about our operation.

Everybody felt a need to read it. Knowing that and, as always, worried about his image, Trump invoked an executive order of protective assertion, which prevented Congress from being able to subpoena parts of the report.

Barr had a long and tangled relationship with the report. When the investigation was announced, he refused to recuse himself, despite his public criticism of the investigation (not to mention the fact that he would be overseeing an action against his employer and political ally). The move was widely criticized. Then, on March 24, 2019 (two days after he received a copy of the report), he wrote a four-page letter summarizing it for Congress. The letter can best be summarized by one of its final lines: "While this report does not conclude that the President committed a crime, it also does not exonerate him."

The next day, Mueller sent his own letter to Barr, writing that he had not accurately represented the report's conclusions. When he did not get an answer, Mueller sent another letter to Barr, saying that his summary "did not fully capture the context, nature, and substance" of the report and that "there is now public confusion about critical aspects of the results of our investigation. This threatens to undermine a central purpose for which the Department appointed the Special Counsel: to assure full public confidence in the outcome of the investigations."

Congressional hearings were called and Barr made some iffy statements under oath. Florida Representative Charlie Crist, a Democrat, pointed out that the media was reporting that some members of Mueller's team said that Barr's summary sent to Congress was limited in such a way as to be misleading, and asked him "Do you know what they are referencing with that?" Barr told him: "No, I don't." Perhaps he had forgotten about Mueller's two angry letters. He did it again at the next hearing. Maryland Senator Chris Van Hollen asked Barr: "Did Bob Mueller support your conclusion?" Without delay, Barr replied: "I don't know whether Bob Mueller supported my conclusion." According to the Associated Press and The New York Times (both quoted in the hearings), Barr misrepresented the report in several ways, between them saying this about his summary:

- Gave no indication that Congress could make a determination on obstruction of justice (the report actually said that "Congress may apply obstruction laws")
- Said that "these reports are not supposed to be made public" (the Attorney General had the authority to release the report to the public)
- Said that "the White House fully cooperated with the Special Counsel's investigation" (it most certainly did not, Trump frequently tried to impede the investigation)
- Misquoted a section about Trump's possible motives (mentioning one, but cutting out others)
- Left out that a portion that "twice suggested there was knowing and complicit behavior between the Trump campaign and Russians that stopped short of coordination"

Trump was over-the-moon happy. He said the Mueller Report "totally exonerated" him. It didn't. Still, all Trump's people, including me, celebrated as though it did. I had believed that the Russians had meddled with the election, but without Trump's knowledge or participation — so I thought it would turn out the way it did. Besides, Barr was in charge; of course Trump was getting off.

Chapter 39
The Changing Landscape

The mainstream media then pivoted back to Ukraine and its election. Zelenskyy destroyed Poroshenko with 73.22 percent of the vote, compared to 24.45 percent — an almost exact three-to-one ratio. Some other notables also ran, including my old pal Roman Nasirov. But it was Zelenskyy and everybody else. He ran on an anti-corruption campaign, saying he would look for bad apples to get rid of.

Lutsenko knew he was as good as gone, and Shokin's hope of ever getting back his job got even tinier.

As is tradition, Trump called the President-elect to congratulate him. Trump was aboard Air Force One after a shockingly controversial trip to Japan when he called Zelenskyy. The 16-minute call began with, and was mostly made up of, Trump congratulating Zelenskyy and Zelenskyy thanking Trump. And, of course, Trump praising himself.

After that, Zelenskyy invited Trump to his inauguration. "I'll look into that, Trump said, and added: "We will have somebody, at a minimum, at a high, high level and they will be with you." Zelenskyy tried again to get a promise out of Trump that he'd come to the inauguration, this time using the country itself as bait. "There's no word that can describe our wonderful country," he said. "How nice, warm and friendly the people are, how tasty and delicious our food is, and how wonderful Ukraine is."

Trump said that he agreed. "When I owned Miss Universe, they always had great people," he added. Then he invited Zelenskyy to the White House.

Zelenskyy accepted and thanked him again, later promising to "practice English."

The fact that the only topic of importance discussed in the call was about Trump attending Zelenskyy's inauguration demonstrated how badly the President-elect wanted the President to come. Zelenskyy wanted international credibility for his administration, even his country, and a visit from a sitting U.S. President would certainly help in that department.

Giuliani and I had to adjust to the new administration in Kyiv. We not only had to appeal to Zelenskyy, but distance ourselves from the past.

But only after Giuliani got a chance to gloat and take another shot at Clinton. On April 23, he tweeted:

"Hillary is correct the report is the end of the beginning for the second time . . . NO COLLUSION. Now Ukraine is investigating Hillary campaign and DNC conspiracy with foreign operatives including Ukrainian and others to affect 2016 election. And there's no Comey to fix the result."

Not only was he wrong about what the report actually said, his opinion that former FBI director James Comey was someone who could save Clinton was odd. Many people believe that Comey cost her the 2016 election by re-opening the investigation into her troublesome email controversy just before voting day.

The next morning, Biden released a video called Joe Biden For President: America Is An Idea that announced his candidacy for the 2020 presidential election. Much of the video's content was aimed at Trump. Regarding the Unite the Right rally in Charlottesville, Virginia, in which white supremacists openly showed their support, Biden said of Trump: "He said there were quote some very fine people on both sides. With those words, the President of the United States assigned a moral equivalence between those spreading hate and those with the courage to stand against it. And in that moment, I knew the threat to this nation was unlike any I had ever seen in my lifetime."

His actual announcement was a doubling-down on the effects of the Trump presidency: "The core values of this nation, our standing in the world, our very democracy, everything that has made America America, is at stake. That's why today I'm announcing my candidacy for President of the United States."

I was not at all surprised that Biden announced, and the announcement did make me feel that his work in Ukraine was actually valuable. Finding dirt on the Bidens would be useless for Trump — though, perhaps, satisfying — if Biden had not chosen to run.

Perhaps not coincidentally, Hunter Biden left Burisma's board at about the same time. That's all that I can say because the date of his departure from the company has never been made public. According to Hunter's legal counsel, he left "in April." They refused to answer questions about exactly when. Some in media have speculated that he left on or around April 18, 2019, the five-year anniversary of his joining the company and, presumably, the end of a five-year contract.

On the same day Biden made his announcement, Trump granted Hannity an interview. Hannity threw him such softballs that the questions essentially answered themselves. Trump did get a chance to bask in what he seems to have thought the Mueller Report said about him, announcing: "We have nothing to do with Russia except that we have been tougher on Russia than any administration in 50 years — a lot tougher than Obama." No explanation was offered of how they were "tougher."

The questioning then shifted to questionable statements about the many sins of various Trump enemies, particularly Clinton and Comey. Then Hannity brings up Ukraine, obliquely referencing Solomon's articles. Trump, who had been droning on about how the Pulitzer Prize committee chooses the wrong people, starts to pay more attention. Hannity, who had been thoroughly coached by Giuliani, asks him: "Mr. President, Ukraine is offering this evidence to the United States. Would you like the United States — with all this talk about collusion, they are saying they included on behalf of Hillary Clinton's campaign in 2016. Does America need to see that information in spite of all of the attacks against you on collusion?"

Trump's answer:

"Well, I think we do. And, frankly, we have a great new Attorney General who has done an unbelievable job in a very short period of time. And he is very smart and tough and I would certainly defer to him. I would imagine he would want to see this. People have been saying this whole — the concept of Ukraine, they have been talking about it actually for a long time. You know that, and I would certainly defer to the Attorney General. And we'll see what he says about it. He calls them straight. That's one thing I can tell you."

His statements were interesting to me — and not just because Trump referenced the BLT Team when he said "people have been saying." He also lent credibility to the Ukraine Collusion conspiracy theory and said that he intended to put Barr on the case. That probably meant more missions for me.

After Barr's summary of the Mueller Report allowed Trump to claim a victory that didn't actually exist, it seemed safe to assume the results of any investigation into Ukraine would make Trump's enemies look bad — at least according to Trump.

Biden had not been in the race for very long before Hunter was brought up in the media. The New York Times ran a story on May 1 called Biden

Faces Conflict of Interest Questions That Are Being Promoted by Trump and Allies in which his tough talk that got rid of Shokin and the fact that Hunter was on Burisma's board might have been a conflict of interest. They pointed out that Hunter was "on the board of an energy company owned by a Ukrainian oligarch who had been in the sights of the fired prosecutor general" but did not say he was under investigation.

Hunter tried to make it clear that he was never under investigation. "I have had no role whatsoever in relation to any investigation of Burisma, or any of its officers," his statement read. "I explicitly limited my role to focus on corporate governance best practices to facilitate Burisma's desire to expand globally." The article also mentions Giuliani and Lutsenko but not their connection. It did, however, hint at Lutsenko's motive and ability to change his mind on a case: "The prosecutor general reversed himself and reopened an investigation into Burisma this year. Some see his decision as an effort to curry favor with the Trump administration."

It was.

Chapter 40
Bye-Bye, Yovanovitch

T
hings had gotten real for Yovanovitch at about 10 p.m. Kyiv time on April 24. Director General of the Foreign Service Carol Perez called Yovanovitch. She said she wanted to give her a "heads up" that something "had gone off track." She didn't know exactly what was going on, but she said that "there was a lot of nervousness on the seventh floor and up the street." She was talking about the State Department's Foggy Bottom headquarters in the Harry S Truman Building and the White House.

Yovanovitch was concerned, but confused. An hour later, Perez called again. "She said that there was a lot of concern for me, that I needed to be on the next plane home to Washington," Yovanovitch later said. "And I was like, what? What happened?

And she said, 'I don't know, but this is about your security. You need to come home immediately. You need to come home on the next plane.'" She did.

One of her first meetings in Washington was with Acting Assistant Secretary of State Philip T. Reeker, a career foreign service officer. He told her that she would have to leave her post "as soon as possible." He explained that Trump had wanted her to leave since the summer of 2018 — about the time I told the President that she was "bad for Ukraine" — and that Pompeo had tried to protect her, but couldn't any longer.

Yovanovitch said that she was "shocked," but she quickly put two and two together. Reeker had previously told her that Lutsenko had given Giuliani negative information about her and she knew that whatever he knew, the President heard. She had also noticed a deluge of social media posts about her, often with negative comments, although she had almost never been mentioned on any platform before.

She then met with Deputy Secretary of State John Sullivan. He apologized and told her that she would have to leave her post because Trump had lost confidence in her. She asked what she had done wrong. He assured her that she had done nothing wrong and that he had relieved ambassadors for their behavior before and that "this was not that."

Yovanovitch demanded an explanation. Sullivan didn't have one aside from the fact that Trump had decided on it. Yovanovitch warned them about what kind of signal her removal would have to Ukraine and other countries about America's attitude toward anti-corruption efforts. Yovanovitch knew that it was Trump's decision, but believed he was easily led. He might well be offended if he knew her personal opinion of him, but it hadn't affected her job in any way that she could see. She believed that someone was influencing Trump, someone who did not approve of and could potentially suffer from her anti-corruption efforts.

Realizing that she wouldn't get anywhere with Reeker or Sullivan, Yovanovitch requested an appointment with Counselor to the State Department Ulrich Brechbuhl, who she had been told was Trump's point man on her dismissal.

He turned her down.

On the morning of the same day Yovanovitch received her call from Perez, Giuliani had appeared on Fox News. "Keep your eye on Ukraine ...," he said. I think you'd get some interesting information about Joe Biden from Ukraine. About his son, Hunter Biden. About a company he was on the board of for years, which may be one of the most crooked companies in Ukraine."

Chapter 41
Did I Say That?

T
he New York Times was onto us. On May 1, they ran an article that accused Giuliani of "fanning" the tinder of the Bidens-in-Ukraine narrative, hoping that it would catch aflame. They were right, but nothing The New York Times would ever write would change the mind of a Trump voter. Remember, he referred to the free press as "the enemy of the people." We all believed he was right.

We didn't worry about stuff like that. What we did worry about was all internal. Any group of people with a goal is only as strong as its weakest link. And a few people seemed to be nominating themselves for that honor.

Barr was being questioned about the Mueller Report when Vice-President Harris asked him directly: "Has the President or anyone at the White House ever asked or suggested that you open an investigation of anyone?"

Barr panicked. It was ugly. He stumbled and mumbled and wondered allowed exactly what the word "suggested" really means.

She asked him again, and gave him a moment to collect himself.

Finally, he came up with his brilliant answer. "I don't know," he said, for the official record.

The most flagrant was Trump himself. Just a day or two afterward, once he was convinced that everyone believed that the Mueller Report actually had vindicated him, Trump celebrated in a way only he could get away with — he called Putin.

In their more-than-an-hour conversation, he listened to a long speech about how corrupt Ukraine was, how it wasn't really a country at all and how the oligarchs totally controlled Zelenskyy's every move. It wasn't all that different from what he was hearing from Giuliani.

Of course, the State Department was giving Trump the opposite message. But that was becoming commonplace. Trump and his people would say or do one thing and the rest of the government would say or do the opposite. It happened all the time.

Just two days before Trump called Putin, Bolton had called Lavrov to complain about Russia "destabilizing" Venezuela. "This is our hemisphere — it's not where the Russians ought to be interfering," Bolton told the media. "This is a mistake on their part. It's not going to lead to an improvement in relations."

He was still pretty angry about how it all worked out.

But I was happy on the morning of May 6. As always, I read the news first and was delighted to see The Washington Post had made Yovanovitch's dismissal public.

Immediately, I shared the story with Lutsenko through WhatsApp. I told him the news was a gift.

The next day brought news, at least a Bloomberg article, that cast doubt on the idea that Joe Biden was helping Hunter by advocating for Shokin's firing. They were told by Kasko that Shokin was in no hurry to investigate Burisma or if he was going to at all. "There was no pressure from anyone from the U.S. to close cases against Zlochevsky," he said. "It was shelved by Ukrainian prosecutors in 2014 and through 2015."

In the same month that the State Department asked Yovanovitch to stay on, I was in Kyiv seeking opinions on her would-be successors. The names I had been given by my Ukrainian contacts were Pete Sessions — but I knew that, of course — and Jorge Mas Canosa.

Mas Canosa would have been quite a controversial choice, and not just because he had no noteworthy experience with Ukraine or even Russia. Born in Cuba in 1939, he told The Los Angeles Times in 1996: "I have never assimilated. I never intended to. I am a Cuban first. I live here only as an extension of Cuba. I live a Cuban life here. My friends, my social activities, they are all Cuban."

Still, he appeared to be the favorite, although I could never understand exactly why. Mas Canosa's name being bandied about as a Yovanovitch replacement came to the attention of the State Department when one of their staff heard that it was a rumor going around Kyiv's in-the-know crowd.

When the Daily Beast asked Sessions and Mas Canosa about the rumors, Sessions' people denied that he had been offered the role or vetted for it, while Mas Canosa told them that he had been "approached about taking the position."

Once the issues with Yovanovitch came to light, those who supported her made an effort to get her a fair shake. Five ambassadors, including William B. Taylor Jr., sent a letter to Pompeo in which they questioned the claims about Yovanovitch. Similarly, Democratic Congressmen Steny Hoyer of Maryland and Eliot Engel from New York co-wrote their own letter to Pompeo expressing concern over "attacks" on Yovanovitch by "Ukrainian officials." They were rewarded with a terse reply that misleadingly said that her term was set to end that summer and did not address the smear campaign.

With the 2020 election looming, Giuliani was frantic to get incriminating information on the Bidens and, if he could implicate a few Ukrainians, all the better — the MAGA faithful already saw them as having interfered on Clinton's behalf in 2016 and many Americans were sure that they were as corrupt as governments get. If it helped Putin, so what?

Chapter 42
Should I Stay or Should I Go?

On May 9, 2019, Giuliani announced that he was going to Ukraine to visit Zelenskyy and "pursue inquiries that allies of the White House contend could yield new information about two matters of intense interest to Mr. Trump."

The trip was widely believed to be part of Giuliani's efforts to pressure Zelenskyy to do what Trump wanted in regard to the Biden investigation. As The New York Times put it:

> "Mr. Giuliani's plans create the remarkable scene of a lawyer for the President of the United States pressing a foreign government to pursue investigations that Mr. Trump's allies hope could help him in his reelection campaign. And it comes after Mr. Trump spent more than half of his term facing questions about whether his 2016 campaign conspired with a foreign power."

Giuliani responded with his tendency to say a little too much. On Fox News @ Night, he said: "We're not meddling in an election, we're meddling in an investigation, which we have a right to do," he told the Times. "There's nothing illegal about it, somebody could say it's improper. And this isn't foreign policy — I'm asking them to do an investigation that they're doing already and that other people are telling them to stop. And I'm going to give them reasons why they shouldn't stop it because that information will be very, very helpful to my client, and may turn out to be helpful to my government."

At that point: a) it clearly was foreign policy, b) Ukraine had no such investigation underway, and c) nobody of note, if anyone, was asking them to stop or not to do it. And his statement, of course, ignores the thinly (if at all) veiled threat that what's good for Trump would be good for Ukraine, and what isn't won't be.

On May 10, Giuliani began the day with a post on Twitter. He tweeted: "Explain to me why Biden shouldn't be investigated if his son got millions from a Russian loving crooked Ukrainian oligarch while He was VP and point man for Ukraine." It continued: "Ukrainians are investigating and your fellow Dems are interfering. Election is 17 months away. Let's answer it now." He was being disingenuous when he wrote they we should "answer it now," well before the election. The fact is that he knew any such investigation would take many months, well into the campaign period.

Giuliani said that he would be visiting in his "capacity as personal counsel to President Trump and with his knowledge and consent." He would later deny that the President knew anything about his travels.

The Ukrainians were under no illusions when it came to the purpose of the trip. "Giuliani attempted to visit Ukraine in May 2019 with the express purpose of involving Zelenskyy in this process," Ukrainian anti-corruption activist and member of Parliament Serhiy Leshchenko would later write in a Washington Post editorial. "His aim was quite clear: He was planning to ask Zelenskyy to intervene in an American election on the side of Trump."

The timing was important because Zelenskyy was due to be inaugurated on May 26. It was of critical importance to his administration that it receive credibility by being recognized by powerful countries. The Ukrainians knew that. Traditionally, they hold their presidential inaugurations in the middle of summer, but Zelenskyy was so eager to take office, he managed to get them to schedule it for May 26. A dearth of high-profile guests, including Pence, caused them to change to May 20.

Who we sent would be an important indicator of how seriously the U.S. regarded the Zelenskyy administration and the nation it served. It was never going to be Trump. There were too many complications. He seemed to have made not angering Putin an enduring pillar of his legacy, and he still believed that Ukraine had helped the Democrats in the 2016 election and that they had allowed the Bidens to run wild.

The job, then, naturally fell to Pence. It was announced that he would go until someone, I believe it was Giuliani, got the idea that, since it was important to the Ukrainians to be recognized, his presence could be used as a bargaining chip. Without an announcement of an investigation into the Bidens, there would be no Pence at the inauguration.

Unfortunately for the Ukrainians, Zelenskyy had perhaps unwittingly tipped his hand back in April. Shortly after he won the election, he and Trump spoke briefly by telephone and he made it clear how important it was to him that Trump attend the inauguration ceremony.

In the afternoon of May 10, Giuliani was called into the office of Kash Patel, who was soon to be Senior Director of the Counterterrorism Directorate, and was a favorite of Trump's. He told Giuliani that he should not go to Ukraine. Patel said that Zelenskyy had surrounded himself with "enemies of the President," and that nothing he said would have any effect on the Ukrainians. Ever the team player, Giuliani called his trip off.

Immediately, he texted me to let me know.

In the evening of May 10, he appeared on Fox News @ Night to announce that he wasn't going to visit Zelenskyy after all. "There was a great fear that the new President [Zelenskyy] would be surrounded by, literally, enemies of the President [Trump] who were involved in that and people who are involved with other Democratic operatives," he said to interviewer Shannon Bream. "I'm convinced from what I've heard from two very reliable people tonight that the President [Zelenskyy] is surrounded by people who are enemies of the president [Trump], and people who are — at least one case — clearly corrupt and involved in this scheme." He also denied that his accusations had anything to do with the 2020 election and that he would, of course, avoid any "political suggestions."

The appearance made the Ukrainians nervous. Lutsenko called me. Ukrainian Internal Affairs Minister Arsen Avakov called me. Lots of them called me. They all asked the same thing, why was Giuliani saying such bad things about Ukraine on a national newscast?

I knew it was my job to calm them. I told them, once we got what we needed, we could smooth it all over. And the next step in that process, I told them, was for them to arrange a meeting between me and Serhiy Shefir.

Shefir had long been close to Zelenskyy. A screenwriter and producer, Shefir was one of the showrunners for Zelenskyy's prescient TV series, Servant of the People. He had not yet been promoted to First Assistant to the President, but everybody in Ukraine knew it was coming in a matter of days. If there was anybody Zelenskyy listened to, it was this guy.

We set up a meeting at the Park Café for May 12. Giuliani insisted that I be tough with him right from the start and relay the message from Trump exactly. I said that Ukraine would receive zero aid from the U.S., have zero relationship with the U.S. and no Pence at the inauguration unless Zelenskyy announced a Biden investigation and fired all of Trump's "enemies" in his government. Real quid pro quo stuff.

After my ultimatum to Shefir, he agreed, said he'd make it happen. But, the Ukrainians went dark that night. To show that my threat had some teeth, I texted Giuliani. He replied: "Now they'll see." Within hours, Pence announced that he would not be attending the inauguration.

***

My relationship with Internal Affairs Minister Avakov started in a way that shows just how cunning he can be. Avakov had been a vocal supporter of Clinton and the Democrats in 2016 and, when Trump shocked the world and won, he became desperate for a relationship with the new administration.

He thought he had found an easy way into the new D.C. establishment when he befriended Christopher Ruddy, CEO of far-far-right media outlet NewsMax. Ruddy stood to benefit because NewsMax was losing money and Avakov said that the Ukrainians were looking to perhaps invest $50 million in the company. So, Ruddy held a dinner for Avakov and several conservative VIPs to talk strategy.

Word got to Giuliani that Avakov was in town, so he had me set up a call with him. Giuliani told him that I would be coming to Ukraine with a message from him and Trump. Avakov agreed, In fact, he dropped News-Max like a hot potato. He knew nobody was closer to Trump than Giuliani.

The day before we were scheduled to meet, I sent Avakov a WhatsApp message. It read:

> "My dear friend, I would like to thank you for your help and understanding in this difficult situation and for your help personally to me. I reported about this to Respected Rudy, and he today in an exclusive interview with Inter TV Channel, expressed to you personally and separately huge gratitude. Waiting for a meeting tomorrow. Thanks!!!!!"

As soon as I walked into his office, before I could even say hello, Avakov shushed me. Then he pushed a button on his desk and metal covers slid down over his windows. Still with his finger across his lips, he pressed another button and the room was filled by rain sounds that would drown out our conversation to any unwanted listeners. I felt like I was in a movie.

I put Giuliani on speaker phone. Giuliani told Avakov we were concerned with Yovanovitch's self-insertion into Ukrainian politics. Avakov sat there wide-eyed.

Avakov agreed and asked what he could do to help. Giuliani laid out his terms. The first was that my security would be "taken care of" whenever I was in Ukraine. And that Avakov help with getting Zelenskyy to announce an investigation into Joe Biden.

Avakov made it clear that he was ready to go. That's when the elephant in the room was finally addressed. Avakov had to explain his Clinton support and a few insulting opinions about Trump he'd posted on social media. Avakov explained that he had no fondness for Clinton or her policies, but —

like everyone else — was sure she would win, and he wanted his eggs to be in the right basket. He admitted that he was wrong and told him his loyalties were now with Trump, since he had won.

"All will be forgiven," Giuliani laughed. "If you do what we want." I just smiled.

We would not have been so gracious if we knew what Avakov was

Yovanovitch and Avakov in happier days.

really up to. He was playing both sides. While he was helping Trump and Giuliani pressure Zelenskyy to announce, he was also reporting our communications to the U.S. Embassy.

***

I knew that if I was going to get to Zelenskyy, the most direct route would be through Ihor Kolomoisky. He and Zelenskyy were close. Not only did he own the TV station that made Zelenskyy famous, but the president-elect's security team was mostly made up of some of Kolomoisky's bodyguards and one of his lawyers, Andriy Bohdan, later became Zelenskyy's top adviser. Early in the campaign, some observers thought that Zelenskyy was merely a proxy for Kolomoisky, who would actually run the country from Israel.

And Kolomoisky had a serious axe to grind. After accusations of money laundering and operating a Ponzi scheme, Poroshenko dismissed him as governor of Dnipropetrovsk Oblast. Later, he even nationalized Kolomoisky's PrivatBank. His anger at Poroshenko caused many to believe that he was the one who convinced Zelenskyy to run for office in the first place.

I let it be known in Kyiv that I wanted to meet Kolomoisky to talk about a meeting with Zelenskyy. I knew it wouldn't take long. The call came when I was in a synagogue. A plane would pick me up and fly me to Tel Aviv for the meeting.

When I got there, I was immediately disappointed. He was drunk and talking crazy shit right out of the gate. There was no way I was going to get anywhere with him.

He took offense at everything I said. He swore at me and told me that I was just another foreigner trying to boss him around.

The meeting turned even more acrimonious and we were standing in each other's faces and yelling at each other. I told him to go screw himself.

I took Kolomoisky's threat seriously enough to wear a bulletproof vest.

Kolomoisky's partner came running in and separated us before we could get physical. He did his best to calm both of us down. But it was clear to all of us that the meeting was over.

I got on the next plane out of there. If I was ever going to meet with Zelenskyy, it was going to have to be done some other way.

After he found out that Pence had canceled, Kolomoisky did the unthinkable. He ended his self-imposed exile and flew to Kyiv on May 15.

At Boryspil International Airport, news cameras followed him from his private jet to his limo as his motorcade made its way downtown to his hotel. He then went to the Millennium Business Center. He gave his first formal interview to Ukrainska Pravda. Kolomoisky said that he was there to visit in Dnipropetrovsk for a family issue and to Kyiv for a friend's birthday party.

On live television, he angrily said:

"Look, there is Giuliani, and two clowns, Lev Parnas and Igor Fruman, who were engaging in nonsense. They are Giuliani's clients ... They came here and told us that they would organize a meeting with Zelenskyy. They allegedly struck a deal with Lutsenko about the fate of this criminal case — Burisma, Biden, meddling in the U.S. election and so on."

Then he called Igor and me "scammers" and said that he would take us "into daylight soon." In Ukraine, that's a death threat. Not even a veiled one.

I started getting calls from Avakov. I let him wait. When I finally answered, Avakov sounded anxious. He told me that we needed to meet, to figure it all out. I agreed. Avakov suggested a meeting with Kolomoisky "out in the woods." I immediately said no, pointing out the obvious danger for me.

Avakov said that he would guarantee my safety. He'd even have a security team from the Ukrainian army escort me to the meeting. I declined again. There was no way I was meeting him in the woods. Kolomoisky was just too rich, too powerful — he could pay anyone off. There's no way I would have survived.

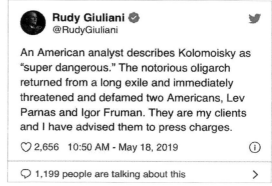

> **Rudy Giuliani** ✔ 🐦
> @RudyGiuliani
>
> An American analyst describes Kolomoisky as "super dangerous." The notorious oligarch returned from a long exile and immediately threatened and defamed two Americans, Lev Parnas and Igor Fruman. They are my clients and I have advised them to press charges.
>
> ♡ 2,656   10:50 AM - May 18, 2019   ⓘ
>
> ○ 1,199 people are talking about this   ＞

Giuliani called Kolomoisky out on Twitter, while at the same time admitting he was our lawyer.

Avakov finally agreed that we could be in danger and took us to the airport with extra security.

I told Giuliani what was going on. He instructed me to file a criminal complaint and a civil suit against Kolomoisky for the death threat and for defamation and said that he would represent me. I went to Paris to meet Giuliani. He tweeted:

> An American analyst describes Kolomoisky as "super dangerous." The notorious oligarch returned from a long exile and immediately threatened and defamed two Americans, Lev Parnas and Igor Fruman. They are my clients and I have advised them to press charges.

We did.

Chapter 44
Pinch Hitter

The team effort to discredit Ukraine in Trump's eyes shifted into high gear that week. May 13 started in the White House with a disagreement. Trump wanted to call Hungarian dictator Orbán (who is said to believe that a large part of Ukraine actually belongs to his country and is regarded as NATO's resident Putin apologist). Bolton and Senior Director of Eurasian and Russian Affairs Fiona Hill told him that it was a really bad idea. But Acting White House Chief of Staff Mick Mulvaney egged him on, and Trump called anyway.

Again, Trump was treated to a lengthy anti-Ukraine diatribe. Although most of his senior advisers sided with Bolton when it came to Ukraine, the constant flow of anti-Ukraine opinions colored Trump's view of the situation and the country in general. Giuliani, of course, was pushing the concept of Ukraine's overall corruption daily, and Trump's admiration, even weakness, for strongman leaders made him easier to sway to their point of view.

But when pressed, Lutsenko turned out to be as unfaithful to us as he was to everyone else. In a Bloomberg interview on May 14, he admitted that he had no reason to open an investigation into the Bidens. "I do not want Ukraine to again be the subject of U.S. presidential elections," Lutsenko told them from Kyiv. "Hunter Biden did not violate any Ukrainian laws — at least as of now, we do not see any wrongdoing. A company can pay however much it wants to its board." He even added that Hunter's Ukrainian taxes were in order. It was a good thing for us that nobody listened when he didn't have anything accusatory to say.

We had bigger fish to fry. Since Pence wasn't going to the inauguration, the administration scrambled to find a suitable replacement. Trump decided on Rick Perry. Before he became Trump's Energy Secretary, Perry had been governor of Texas from 2000 to 2015.

Noted conservative Jay Nordinger encapsulated the Perry plan perfectly when he wrote:

"Anyway, the administration sent the energy secretary, Rick Perry, instead. Personally, I would be just as happy to see Perry as to see Pence, if not more so. But this is diplomacy and geopolitics we're talking about. Okay, my memory of Reagan days. There was a U.N. conference that the administration wanted to thumb its nose at. Many important people were planning to attend, such as the French president, Mitterrand. But we sent Mr. Dennis C. Goodman, the deputy assistant secretary of state for international organizations. This gesture was 'intended to show contempt,' said a U.S official. ... And what did Mr. Goodman call himself? 'The traveling insult.' I had forgotten his name, until I looked up the matter — but I will never forget this self-description."

Perhaps even more insulting, Perry knew precious little about Ukraine. In the plane on his way to Kyiv, Trump ordered Perry to call Giuliani to ask him about Ukraine. Of course, Giuliani coached Perry on what he wanted — pressure on Zelenskyy to announce an investigation into the Bidens and Ukrainian meddling in the 2016 election.

Zelenskyy seemed to like Perry, and many of the photographs of the two together show them laughing or in otherwise good spirits. The pair subsequently had a positive relationship, with Perry and Zelenskyy making deals together, sending American LNG (just as I had intended with Global Energy Producers) and coal to Ukraine.

My brilliant idea didn't help me, though. Everybody knew about it by then and, although I didn't realize it at the time, it was only a matter of time before someone else took it for their own.

Perry offered Zelenskyy the names of four petroleum executives — all of them major donors to his campaign — who he said could help develop Ukraine's vast potential in the oil and gas industry. Later — two of them, Alex Cranberg and Michael Bleyzer — would form a company, Ukrainian Energy, that won a 50-year contract to explore and exploit a potential gas field about the size of Rhode Island in Ukraine, despite being outbid by the only other competitor. Bleyzer said Perry's conversations with Zelenskyy "did not play any role in Ukrainian Energy winning its bid."

More important, Perry called us and said that Zelenskyy was ready to play ball.

Chapter 45
We'll Always Have Paris

Once we had arrived in Paris, we scheduled our meeting with Nazar Kholodnytskyi, the head of Ukraine's Specialized Anti-Corruption Prosecutor's Office (and the prosecutor who was caught teaching suspects how to testify).

Before the meeting, Giuliani and I watched Zelenskyy's inauguration on French TV. Perry did not embarrass our country.

When it came to Zelenskyy's speech, we were on the edges of our seats, expecting to hear what he had been coached to say. After discussing how all Ukrainians — both inside and outside of the country — needed to help, then on to opening a dialog with Russia to end the war in Donbas, he started to talk about fighting corruption. He listed the things he wanted to accomplish, including getting rid of the chief prosecutor. That made sense. Not only was Lutsenko corrupt, he wasn't even a lawyer.

"After that, it is necessary to re-establish the national anti-corruption agency and allow the anti-corruption court to function independently," he said, as we waited anxiously. "My election proves that our citizens are tired of the experienced, pompous system politicians who over the 28 years, have created a country of opportunities — the opportunities to bribe, steal and pluck the resources." And that was it. Nothing about the Bidens, nothing about the 2016 election. It was not satisfactory. Zelenskyy had not kept his side of the bargain. Giuliani was furious. We had to keep the pressure on.

When Kholodnytskyi arrived, Giuliani played hardball. We only talked about two things: dirt on Hunter Biden and information about Manafort's Black Ledger.

He told us that we would get information on the Bidens as it became available, He also told us that the Black Ledger was a forgery and that a second one was authentic.

"The conversation was generally about corruption in Ukraine," Kholodnytskyi said. "I had a personal conversation. I told him that something wasn't right there." Kholodnytskyi had clearly expected to get a huge reaction from Giuliani and was surprised that he didn't get one. "He didn't jump with balloons," he later said.

***

At about the same time, Acting White House chief of staff Mick Mulvaney told George Kent, the deputy assistant secretary of state for much of Eastern Europe, to "lay low" on matters related to Ukraine and to concern himself with the other countries in his dossier.

Should any business regarding Ukraine emerge, he was instructed to hand it over to Perry, U.S. Ambassador to the European Union Gordon Sondland and/or special U.S. envoy to Ukraine Kurt Volker. Kent later said that he didn't approve of the plan and assumed that someone in the White House didn't like how he was doing his job. The group — which affectionately and unimaginatively called themselves the "Three Amigos" — were seen, certainly from what Kent has said, to be favored less because of their expertise and more because of their stalwart support of Trump.

Later, Kent would tell his side of the story to Congressman Gerry Connolly, a Democrat from Virginia who was on the Foreign Affairs Committee. He called Kent's statements "very powerful" and "deeply disturbing, especially the role of Rudy Giuliani."

***

After our meeting with Kholodnytskyi, we happened to run into another friend of Igor's at our hotel in Madrid. Everyone knew him as Little Dimitri because he worked for Firtash and we didn't want to confuse the two.

We spoke about why we were there and how important it was for us to get any compromising information on Joe Biden. He told us that the guy we wanted to talk to was Firtash and that he could introduce us.

He didn't need to explain to us who Firtash was. Everybody knew how powerful and connected he was. But he was surrounded by a phalanx of lawyers who didn't allow anyone near him. If we could get to Firtash, I thought, we'd be able to get everything we needed out of Ukraine.

***

We came back and assembled the BLT Team. We told them all that we were arranging a meeting with Firtash. Solomon's jaw dropped and his eyes lit up. Firtash was kind of like a White Whale for him. Not only was he one of the most well-connected people in Ukraine, he was also involved with the Mueller investigation. If we could talk to him, he told us, we might be able to discredit Mueller and his people as well as the Bidens. But all attempts to get to him had been blocked by his American lawyers, Lanny Davis and Dan Webb. We considered Davis to be part of the Democrat machine.

At a meeting of the BLT Team, John Solomon told me that we were not the first Americans trying to get Firtash to agree to a deal. Andrew Weissman had already secretly offered him a get-out-of-jail-free card when it came to his U.S. extradition, but only if he would agree to testify about the relationship between Trump and Putin, as part of the Mueller investigation. In fact, he told us that Weissmann had offered a deal before Mueller had added him to his team (he was working for Mueller in the FBI at the time).

We knew that we had to get rid of, or sideline, Webb and especially Davis, offer Firtash a better offer than the one from Weissmann that he turned down. And we also had to get testimony, or at least some evidence of the Weissmann deal, to further discredit the Mueller investigation.

Months later, when Toensing and diGenova were working for Firtash, she confronted Webb about the Weissmann deal. He reluctantly admitted that it was true.

***

In that same week, I got a text from Toensing saying that Solomon wanted me to find Andrii Telizhenko, a consultant to Fuks, who used to work at the Ukrainian Embassy until June 2016.

So, I asked around in Kyiv, talking to both sides, from the most corrupt to the least. They all agreed that Telizhenko was a Russian asset. I was warned not to believe a word that came out of his mouth. Naturally, I related that important information to Solomon and then the rest of the BLT Team.

It didn't matter, both Solomon and Giuliani met with Telizhenko anyway. While Giuliani listened excitedly in his East 56th Street office with a pen and legal pad in hand, Telizhenko told him exactly what he wanted to hear (and, I believe, what the Russians wanted him to hear: Telizhenko said, from his work at the embassy, that the Ukrainians had illegally influenced the 2016 election and the Joe Biden had ordered a stop to the Burisma investigation. Of course, the only evidence he had was his word.

Similarly, Kulyk wanted to introduce me to Andrii Derkach, a member of the Ukrainian parliament from the Party of Regions. But I did my due diligence on him and, it turned out that he was also widely believed to be a Russian asset. Not only did that convince me to sever my relationship with Kulyk, I warned the entire BLT Team not to work with any of them — Derkach, Telizhenko or Kulyk. Solomon told me not to worry he had two sources that he'd rather not name. But both he and Giuliani continued to interact with Telizhenko and Derkach.

Chapter 46
'Russia! Russia! Russia!'

Yovanovitch's quick and surprising dismissal caught the U.S. embassy in Kyiv unprepared. The next in line for her job was her deputy, Kristina Kvien. But she wasn't in Ukraine. For the week until her arrival, career diplomat Joseph S. Pennington served as chargé d'affaires and acting deputy chief. He had been one of the embassy officials who had attended at least three meetings with senior State Department officials who discussed Zelenskyy's concerns over pressure from the Trump Administration to investigate Hunter Biden even before their official phone call.

When Kvien arrived, Pennington stepped aside. Although she was not as outspoken as Yovanovitch, the administration did not see her as one of ours, so it was unlikely that she would be able to continue in the position for very long. She lasted less than a month.

Sacking Yovanovitch did not go unnoticed by the media or the opposition. The news had enough gravity to prompt Vanity Fair to publish Abigail Tracy's article There Is No Other Reason: Sources Blame the White House, and a Fox News-Fueled Conspiracy Theory, for the Sudden Ouster of Masha Yovanovitch. And the ranking Democrat on the Senate Foreign Relations Committee, New Jersey's Robert Menendez, wrote a letter to Pompeo saying: "I am extremely concerned that this suspect decision furthers the president's inappropriate and unacceptable linking of U.S. policy to Ukraine to his personal and political benefit, and potentially your own."

In an effort to quell the criticism, Pompeo reached out to veteran diplomat Taylor to take the Ukraine job, at least temporarily. Not only did Taylor have a sterling record and unassailable reputation after having served as ambassador to Ukraine from 2006 to 2009, he had also been publicly critical of Trump. With him there, it wouldn't look like we were stacking every position with our people. We were, we just didn't want it to look like we were.

Taylor took the job, but quickly became appalled at what the administration was doing to Ukraine. He would later text Volker: "As I said on the phone, I think it's crazy to withhold security assistance for help with a political campaign." In fact, he referred to the extortion of withholding aid in exchange for favors intended to discredit a potential presidential candidate to be a "nightmare scenario."

Giuliani's increasingly bizarre side of our campaign kept on chugging. He gave an interview to Yevhen Kuzmenko and Tetiana Nikolayenko of Ukrainian news source, Censor.net, in Paris on May 27.

First, they asked him why he wanted to meet Zelenskyy and what he would say to him. "Mr. President, please, don't let them talk you out of these investigations. Please go forward with it. We've got to get over once and for all," he told them. "And a critical piece in putting together the picture of how they developed these false charges on President Trump is going to be this. There are other pieces (including lot of stuff done wrong in our country and in the UK, Italy and Cyprus) — it's not just Ukraine! But this is an important piece." That was probably the first time he publicly stated his idea that the investigation into Russian meddling on Trump's behalf in the 2016 election was all part of a giant plot by the embattled Ukrainians to mask their alleged assistance on the Democrats' behalf.

When asked why he didn't go to Kyiv, Giuliani went hardcore Deep State and clearly expected the others to go along with him. "I was told by people in my country that I shouldn't go, because it was a trap that was being worked out with Democrats, people loyal to Soros. And now I see that he's put around them — Kolomoisky's lawyer and a couple of guys who work with Soros. And the message that I would send to him was: It's not a good idea to surround yourself with enemies of President Trump," he told them, without stopping for a breath. "It's one thing to surround yourself with decent people who may have a different political ideology — but another thing is to surround yourself with a guy who was the lawyer for this major oligarch who has reputed to have taken billions from your bank and then has some kind of unholy alliance between Soros and that embassy that has to be broken." As usual, the irony was lost on him. He then upped the stakes by accusing Yovanovitch of being in cahoots with Soros in an attempt to topple Trump. "Somehow, she'll go working for Soros, directly or indirectly. All I can tell you is the things I heard about her, which is that her embassy was involved heavily in finding dirty information and creating it on people in the Trump campaign. That they were heavily involved in helping Soros (including getting a case dismissed that would hurt him), and George Kent and her were the deputy," he claimed. "They actually put together that whole Special Prosecutor thing. And they put that together and then used it as a way to protect Soros, which is a horrible thing to do. If we are lecturing you on corruption we can't have our own corrupt person sitting in the background that we're doing the bidding of." As had become usual for Giuliani, he offered zero evidence to back his claims.

Then he defended moves like saying "make Ukraine great again" and the choice to send Perry to the inauguration. He assured them that he had no idea why Pence canceled. It was another lie. For a moment, things seemed to have achieved an equilibrium in the Trump administration.

Mueller on May 29 said that criminal charges against the President as a result of his investigation were "not an option." That peace did not last long. Almost lost among a deluge of his tweets, Trump posted on May 30: "Russia, Russia, Russia! That's all you heard at the beginning of this Witch Hunt Hoax. And now Russia has disappeared because I had nothing to do with Russia helping me to get elected."

While that might have been his honest belief, it fit like a jigsaw puzzle piece into my faith that everyone knew that Russia helped get Trump elected, but that Trump himself was not directly involved. Trump then told a media conference: "Russia did not help me get elected. You know who got me elected? You know who got me elected? I got me elected. Russia did not help me at all." He didn't thank the American people. He thanked himself.

Later that day, actor Robert De Niro and more than 1,000 former federal prosecutors released a video called NowThis that made a case for impeaching, and indicting, Trump.

If Trump gained any credibility by claiming that the Mueller Report exonerated him, he quickly squandered it.

On June 13, George Stephanopoulous asked Trump if he would accept any information about his opponent if it were to be offered by another country or would he turn it over to the FBI. His answer wasn't at all surprising to me, but must have made his handlers pull out their hair:

"I think maybe you do both. ... I think you might want to listen, there's nothing wrong with listening. ... It's not an interference ... They have information. I think I'd take it. If I thought there was something wrong, I'd go maybe to the FBI. ... What is being hidden?"

Pelosi answered on behalf of the Democrats, calling Trump's opinion an "assault on democracy." But she also admitted that that's where political discourse had gone. "Everybody in the country should be totally appalled by what the president said last night," she told the media. "But he has a habit of making appalling statements."

The Federal Election Commission said that what Trump outlined was illegal, but the whole matter was soon forgotten as Trump made more wild, even ridiculous, statements, like that the Queen of England had her most "fun in 25 years" during his visit and when he wished "good luck" to Flynn in his sentencing.

After increasing violence from Russia and its proxies in Ukraine, Congress approved an emergency $250 million weapons package for Kyiv. Although many observers considered the donation to be a major win in stemming Trump's series of moves that sided the U.S. with Russia, others — including the top officer for U.S. operations in Europe, Army General Curtis Scaparrotti — considered the donation to be little more of a meaningless gesture in the face of Moscow's concerted fury.

And even it wasn't safe. Mark Sandy, Deputy Associate Director for National Security Programs at OMB and the guy who signs its checks, first found out that Trump had personally shown interest in the payment on June 19. "I heard that the President had seen a media report and had questions about the assistance," He later testified, pointing out that the information came from an email to Elaine McCusker, Principal Deputy Under Secretary of Defense, from Homeland Security's Mike Duffy that he was CCed on. The email said that Trump had been inquiring about a description of the assistance. At a later meeting at OMB headquarters, McCusker gave Sandy a hard copy summary of the assistance package. He then shared it with Duffy, who was out of the office that day. Duffy then emailed a series of questions regarding the financial resources associated with the package to OMB staff. Sandy kept his notes.

On the same day that Sandy received the email, Trump appeared on Hannity's show, something he had grown accustomed to doing whenever he had something he wanted a wide audience to hear. The show began with Hannity praising Trump's rally the previous night, saying: "I actually kind of regretted not going because I wanted to hang out with the people outside because they were having a blast."

After that now-customary courtly tribute was paid, Trump laid into the "Obama-Biden" administration, quoting statistics of no real value. He spoke about how Mueller "exonerated" him after the "witch hunt," then switched to energy, mentioning Russia as a major global supplier. Finally, he said that Biden would not have been able to stand up to the scrutiny he had and that the media should be punished for reporting the Russian collusion story: "It's a terrible hoax and that should never happen to another President because many of them would not be able to handle it, I don't care who they are. Many of them would not be able to handle it. If you think Joe Biden could handle it? I mean, Joe Biden right now, he looks like he's got some big problems. But you think — can you imagine if this happened to Joe Biden? It wouldn't be good. But it should never happen to another president what happened to me and it should never happen — nobody should ever allow this to go forward again. And people have to learn — there has to be a lesson taught. There has to be a lesson taught."

And, of course, he did not fail to mention that he believed that Hillary Clinton should be in jail and that the DNC was responsible for colluding with the Ukrainians. It was nothing but negative campaigning.

Not long after, he continued to vent against and threaten the media, tweeting what many considered a call to arms:

"A poll should be done on which is the more dishonest and deceitful newspaper, the Failing New York Times or the Amazon (lobbyist) Washington Post! They are both a disgrace to our Country, the Enemy of the People, but I just can't seem to figure out which is worse? The good..........news is that at the end of 6 years, after America has been made GREAT again and I leave the beautiful White House (do you think the people would demand that I stay longer? KEEP AMERICA GREAT), both of these horrible papers will quickly go out of business & be forever gone!"

Nearly lost in the shuffle was the fact that writer E. Jean Carroll accused Trump of a 1996 sexual assault. She was the 16th woman to accuse Trump of sexual misconduct. Importantly, she had told two journalist friends about the incident at the time.

Trump denied it all, claiming in an interview with The Hill: "I'll say it with great respect: No. 1, she's not my type. No. 2, it never happened." Later, On May 9, 2023, a jury found Trump liable for sexual assault, battery and defamation. The jury found that Carroll did not prove that Trump had raped her. Carroll was awarded $5 million in damages.

The news reminded many of exactly why Trump was at war with all but the most fawning media. On the very same day, Trump announced a plan to roll back the Clean Power Plan, America's only safeguard against the unfettered use of coal. He then had the nerve to call his administration an "environmental leader."

We kept the pressure on Zelenskyy. On June 21, Giuliani tweeted:

"New Pres of Ukraine still silent on investigation of Ukrainian interference in 2016 election and alleged Biden bribery of Pres Poroshenko. Time for leadership and investigate both if you want to purge how Ukraine was abused by Hillary and Obama people."

Lutsenko saw the tweet and texted it to me, adding that he was eager to meet with me again soon because he had "2-2.5 months left" as chief prosecutor unless something big happened. Zelenskyy had introduced a bill in parliament to get rid of him. "I have a plan," Lutsenko told me.

That same night, Giuliani tweeted again, saying that Zelenskyy was "still silent on investigation of Ukrainian interference in 2016 election and alleged Biden bribery of Pres Poroshenko."

Later that week, Sondland called Taylor. By this time, Taylor had recognized "an informal channel of U.S. policy-making with respect to Ukraine, one which included then-Special Envoy Kurt Volker, Ambassador Sondland, Secretary of Energy Rick Perry and, as I subsequently learned, Mr. Giuliani." Sondland told him that he needed to ensure that Zelenskyy was not hindering any investigations.

On the next day, Taylor took part in a conference call with Sondland, Perry, Volker and Zelenskyy. All of the participants were in different places. Taylor said that he noticed a few things that were outside normal protocols. First, Sondland told him that "he did not want to include most of the regular interagency participants" and, perhaps more upsetting, that "he wanted to make sure no one was transcribing or monitoring."

Once Zelenskyy got on the line, the talk was mostly "about energy policy and the Anastasia-Luhanska Bridge" (which Zelenskyy was rebuilding after it was blown up by separatists in 2015). He also said that he was looking forward to meeting with Trump.

David Holmes, an aide to Taylor, was also listening in on the call. He said that: "it was made clear that some action on a Burisma/Biden investigation was a precondition for an Oval Office meeting." There was no more being careful about what we said. Everybody knew it. If Zelenskyy wanted to meet with Trump, he had to announce a Biden investigation. We were for-cing his hand.

Chapter 47
The Hunted

While Giuliani must have believed he was playing the Ukrainians for fools, his desire for Hunter Biden's laptop was a lure he kept striking at. The first I had heard of it was when the current top prosecutor in Ukraine, Lutsenko, introduced Giuliani to its existence in March. He told us he had access to it, but he didn't — we realized later that he was just fishing. Of course, the accursed laptop later did make its way into Giuliani's hands.

Although the connected people in Ukraine had been talking about it for a while, the first time Hunter Biden's laptop came into Western consciousness was in May 2019 when an unidentified person offered to sell its contents for $5 million to another unidentified person.

That same person was approached with the same deal again in September. Both times, the person approached said no. In an interview with Time, that person said that: "I walked away from it, because it smelled awful" (in a metaphorical sense).

When Lutsenko couldn't produce it and stopped mentioning it after a while, I was convinced it didn't exist.

Giuliani took me to Cipriani's to meet a Russian businessman he had worked with for 15 years, Vitaly Pruss.

Like many of his peers, Pruss was well connected. Only more so. Not only was he close with Zlochevsky, Burisma's founder and owner, but he had previously worked with Devon Archer, introduced him to Zlochevsky and had been the one who encouraged Archer, Christopher Heinz and Hunter Biden to join Burisma's board of directors. Just as important was the fact that he had handled Giuliani's speaking engagements in Eastern Europe.

At the famous restaurant, Pruss first told us about the laptop. Apparently, it had been made known that the hard drive from the laptop could be had, and that its contents could be seriously damaging to Hunter's reputation and could reflect quite badly on the whole Biden family.

We asked him to describe what exactly was on the laptop that could be used against the Bidens.

Pruss told us about photos and videos of Hunter clearly taking drugs and in obviously compromising positions with various women, sometimes nude.

To us, that was hardly news. We all knew about Hunter's problems when it came to drugs and prostitutes. In fact, we thought everybody did.

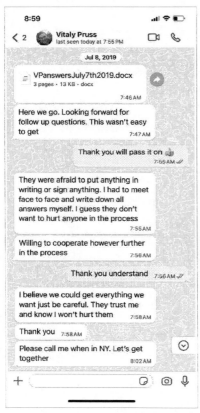

Pruss was instrumental in helping us communicate with the other side.

So, Giuliani asked him directly: Is there any evidence on the laptop that shows the Bidens doing anything else illegal in Ukraine? Did they take bribes perhaps?

Pruss answered succinctly: "No."

He must've seen my face drop. I was intensely disappointed. I believed we needed hard evidence of illegal behavior to make anything stick.

It didn't bother Giuliani a bit. He knew that the value of Hunter Biden's laptop wasn't what was on it, but what he could make people believe was on it. He decided then and there that he absolutely had to have it.

I knew that if there was anything on the laptop's hard drive that Giuliani could use against either Biden, much less a smoking gun, he would have used it the second he had it. Instead, he could keep the public wondering about what it contained and — as many have been more than happy to do in the Trump era — make decisions and declarations based on

what they'd prefer to believe, rather than what evidence dictates. It wasn't important, or perhaps even advantageous, to reveal the contents of the laptop; but it was certain to harm the Biden campaign if it could be held out as an object of mystery.

Even before the laptop became news, Pruss was still a vital resource for us. Giuliani and Solomon wrote a list of 12 questions for him to relay to Zlochevsky. Not long after, he returned with the answers. This is what we received (it came to us in all caps):

1.) What caused you to hire Devon Archer and Hunter Biden in 2014?
WE WANTED TO UILD BURISMA AS INTERNATIONAL COMPANY. IT WAS VERY IMPORTANT TO HAVE STRONG BOARD. SO WHEN WE REVIEW RESUMES OF BIDEN AND ARCHER THEY BOTH HAD GREAT RESUMES. WE ALSO THOUGHT IT WOULD HELP IN UKRAINE TO HAVE STRONG INTERNATIONAL BOARD FIGURES WITH GREAT RELATIONSHIPS IN THE UNITED STATES AND EUROPE.

2.) Why was their firm Rosemont Seneca receiving $188k a month from Burisma from 2014 through 2016? Who was supposed to be the beneficiary of this money?
WE BELIEVE AMOUNT WAS SMALLER THAN 188K MONTHLY. IT WAS SUPPOSED TO BE DIRECTED BY ROSEMONT SENECA TO PAY SALARIES TO BIDEN AND ARCHER.

3.) Who recommended Burisma hire Biden's firm Boies Schiller for $286k in spring 2016?
IT WAS LONG TIME AGO SO WE CAN'T REMEMBER FOR SURE. WE THINK DEVON ARCHER SUGGESTED WE DO IT. WE HAD COOPERATION WITH THEM IN LEGAL FIELD BUT THEY HAVE NEVER EVEN BEEN TO UKRAINE FOR BUSINESS

4.) Were you satisfied you got your money's worth from Hunter Biden, Archer and Boies?
YES. WE BELIEVE IT WAS WORTH IT. IT HAD IT OWN ADVANTAGES AND DISADVANTAGES. BUT IT GENERAL WE BELIEVE OUR COMPANY BENEFITED GREATLY FROM THIS RELATIONSHIP

5.) Why did Burisma hire Blue Star Strategies in 2016? What did they do for Burisma?
IT WAS REGULAR PR COMPANY. WE NEEDED THEIR SERVICES AND USED THEM.

6.) What sort of contacts did Blue Star have with the State Department and the Ukraine GP's office?
THIS WAS THE THIRD PARTY. WE DON'T KNOW OF THEIR RELATIONSHIP WITG DOS AND GP'S OFFICE

Question 7 fix: Were you aware that Hunter Biden had met at with State Department officials in both May 2015 (Blinken) and December 2015? What did you understand the purpose of those contacts were?
WE NEVER APPROVED OR ASKED HIM TO CONDUCT THOSE MEETINGS ON BEHALF OF BURISMA

8.) Did you ever learn why VP Joe Biden asked for Shokin to be fired as PG?
WE LEARNED ABOUT IT FROM NEWSPAPERS AND INTERNET. WE NEVER HAD

CONTACTS WITH VP BIDEN DURING HIS VISITS TO UKRAINE

9.) Please detail any contacts you had with VP Joe Biden and his office from 2013 through 2019. Did Hunter ever facilitate any of those contacts? NO ONE FROM BURISMA EVER HAD ANY CONTACTS WITH VP BIDEN OR PEOPLE WORKING FOR HIM DURING HUNTER BIDEN'S ENGAGEMENT

10.) Did VP Biden or his staff assist you or your company in any way with business deals or meetings with world leaders or any other assistance? NO

11.) Did you ever become aware of documents suggesting $900k was paid to Hunter Biden for "lobbying" his father? NO

12.) Why did Burisma made $20k donation to the Beau Biden Foundation in 2015? YES. WE MADE THIS DONATION BECAUSE WE HAVE BEEN WORKING WITH HUNTER BIDEN AND WE BELIEVED IT WAS GOOD CHARITY PROGRAM TO DONATE TO.

Giuliani, of course, was unhappy with the results. "He told me to "bury it," and make sure nobody sees it.

Chapter 48
Promises Broken

D ebate raged about Trump's upcoming meeting with Putin on June 28. One major issue was that Russia had been holding 24 Ukrainian soldiers captive, despite the fact that the two nations were not officially at war. Trump had tweeted that he was canceling a meeting with Putin in Argentina over the issue, but went anyway.

When a reporter asked Trump if he planned to bring up Russian meddling in the 2016 election, Trump was not an exemplar of transparency in government. "I'll have a very good conversation with him," he said, adding: "What I say to him is none of your business." It was.

Jimmy Carter, who has spent much of his time after his presidency as an official observer of foreign elections did not mince words responding to the announcement of Trump meeting Putin and Russian election interference. "The President himself should condemn it, admit that it happened," Carter told an audience in Osaka, where the summit was to be held. "There's no doubt that the Russians did interfere in the election. And I think the interference, although not yet quantified, if fully investigated, would show that Trump didn't actually win the election in 2016, he lost the election, and he was put into office because the Russians interfered on his behalf."

Trump responded by saying that Carter was a "nice man" but a "terrible President."

He also announced that he would be meeting Putin at the G20 Summit in Japan in July, although the Kremlin said that it was news to them. Again, lost in the news of Trump's outrageous pronouncements was the fact that he used an emergency declaration to bypass congressional opposition to his plan to sell $8 billion in sophisticated weapons to Saudi Arabia and the United Arab Emirates while the comparatively tiny $391 million earmarked for Ukraine was still frozen.

Zelenskyy made his first trip outside of Europe as President, landing in Toronto on July 1. There he met with Volker, who was referred to in media as the "U.S. special representative for Ukraine negotiations" although there were no official negotiations going on at the time. Volker again stressed how important the announcement of the two investigations was and what could befall Ukraine if they did not happen. He warned Zelenskyy of the "Giuliani factor." Do what we say and nobody gets hurt — straight out of a gangster movie. Just like always with these guys.

On July 10, a senior Ukrainian official texted Volker: "I feel that the key for many things is Rudi and I ready to talk with him at any time."

All of the bluster about the Russia-and-Trump alleged criminal activity obscured the active moves of the administration. On July 3, the OMB very quietly blocked the transfer of the $141 million in funds that the State Department had earmarked for Ukrainian "security assistance."

The dog-and-pony show went on as Trump stumbled into June attending the 75th Anniversary of D-Day ceremonies in France on July 6. After reports leaked that Pelosi wanted "to see him in prison," Trump told Ingraham: "I think she's a disgrace. I actually don't think she's a talented person. I've tried to be nice to her because I would have liked to have gotten some deals done. She's incapable of doing deals. She's a nasty, vindictive, horrible person." He also threatened tariffs on Canada and Mexico and told an Irish reporter that Brexit "wouldn't be a problem for Ireland."

To keep the soap opera running, a few days later, Trump praised Kim Jong Un after receiving a "very warm" letter from him and then prohibited U.S. embassies from flying the Pride Flag. Although the countries were officially not talking, Kim said that Trump sent a return letter that contained "excellent content."

With Biden appearing to be gaining popularity, many around Trump became more desperate for ammunition to use against him. Trump didn't help his 2020 chances, as he kept giving the Democrats their own ammo. At his Independence Day celebration, he told a massive audience: "Our Army manned the air, it rammed the ramparts, it took over the airports, it did everything it had to do, and at Fort McHenry, under the rocket's red glare it had nothing but victory. And when dawn came, their star-spangled banner waved defiant." Besides the obvious fact that there was no air travel in the late 18th Century, the references he made to Fort McHenry and the Star-Spangled Banner were actually from the War of 1812, not the Revolution.

Unknown parties then leaked cables that the British Ambassador to the

U.S., Kim Darroch, sent back home. Among other things, he said that Trump's policy on Iran was "incoherent," that he might be indebted to "dodgy Russians" and wondered if he "will ever look competent." British Foreign Secretary Jeremy Hunt reprimanded Darroch for not respecting an ally, but Trump had to get in his shots. He called Darroch a "very stupid guy," and tweeted: "The wacky Ambassador that the U.K. foisted upon the United States is not someone we are thrilled with."

Days later, on July 8, Zelenskyy released a video address to Putin about the situations in Crimea and Donbas. "We need to talk? We do. Let's talk," he said to the Russian leader. "I suggest the following company for our conversation: You and I, U.S. President Donald Trump, British Prime Minister Theresa May, German Chancellor Angela Merkel, French President Emmanuel Macron."

He also took some time to discourage the planned Russian purchase of a Ukrainian TV station by Russian state television. He called the company vital to the "information security of the country" and the purchase a "dangerous PR trick before the elections aimed to once again divide us, Ukrainians, into two camps." The seller was Viktor Medvedchuk, a Ukrainian investor and politician, whose daughter, Darya, had Putin for a godfather.

Two days later, Bolton met with two senior Ukrainian officials and several Americans (including Sondland, Volker, Perry, Fiona Hill — Senior Director for Europe and Russia at the NSC — and Lieutenant-Colonel Alexander Vindman, who was responsible for coordinating U.S. efforts in the region). As expected, the first issue on the Ukrainians' agenda was getting a date for a meeting between Zelenskyy and Trump. While Bolton was hemming and hawing, Sondland told the group that he had a deal with Acting Chief of Staff Mick Mulvaney to schedule the White House visit, but only after Ukraine initiated the investigations (everyone knew which ones he was talking about). According to witnesses, Bolton "stiffened" and immediately shut down the meeting. Sondland waited until Bolton left and took the remaining attendees downstairs to the Ward Room to keep the discussion alive. There, he reiterated that his deal with Mulvaney was that Zelenskyy's White House visit could only come after Ukraine announced the Burisma and 2016 Ukraine election interference investigations.

Vindman and Hill objected. They agreed that the ultimatum was a comingling of a "domestic political errand" with U.S. foreign policy. Hill pointed out that a White House meeting needed to be scheduled through proper channels — rather than through the secret negotiations they had used.

After she left, Hill told Bolton what had happened and he told her to tell the lawyers, because "I am not part of whatever drug deal Sondland and Mulvaney are cooking up on this." She did.

Zelenskyy did not get his meeting with Putin, but he actually was invited to speak with Trump in Washington in August. Hopes were not high for his inevitable request for help. "Donald Trump has made it abundantly clear he doesn't care about Ukraine — that he is either deeply skeptical or simply doesn't think it's an issue that should concern the United States," said Andrew Weiss, an analyst at the Carnegie Endowment for International Peace. "The most we can hope for is that Trump is changed from an intense Ukraine skeptic to someone who is grudgingly willing" to side with Congress and support U.S. aid to the country.

Weiss would be disappointed by what actually happened. On July 12, Trump's OMB placed a hold on all military support for Ukraine. On July 18, the OMB informed all relevant federal agencies that no military aid would be going to Ukraine, no matter what had been promised. They gave no reason for the hold, instead referring all inquiries directly to the White House. And they wouldn't talk.

It didn't go unnoticed in the corridors of power. NSC Senior Director for Europe and Russia Timothy Morrison was astounded by the move, as he considered Ukraine's military strength to be vital to U.S. interests. "The United States aids Ukraine and her people so that they can fight Russia over there, and we don't have to fight Russia here." Many officials investigated the legality of the hold. Their persistence led to two major resignations from the OMB, but the hold stood.

On the following day, Volker had a breakfast meeting with Giuliani and me at the BLT. Volker told Giuliani that Zelenskyy and Trump should definitely have a meeting. Giuliani told him, with great certainty, that Zelenskyy would not get a White House meeting until he announced the investigations.

Realizing there was no room for argument, he suggested a three-way conference call between him, Giuliani and Ukrainian Chief of Staff Andrii Yermak.

Giuliani agreed.

After he left the BLT, Volker texted Sondland and Taylor: "Most impt is for Zelensky to say that he will help investigation — and address any specific personnel issues — if there are any." It would later be revealed that the issue in question was Giuliani's visceral disagreement with Zelenskyy's desire to dismiss Lutsenko. Afterward, Sondland called Zelenskyy and advised him to play along when they spoke on the phone, to tell Trump that he "will leave no stone unturned" in the two investigations the President demanded. Then he emailed Trump's top people — including Pompeo, Mulvaney and Perry — telling them that Zelenskyy agreed to "assure" Trump that "he intends to run a fully transparent investigation and will turn over every stone."

Perry and Mulvaney both replied that Trump would agree that the call would happen soon. Sondland would later testify that Zelenskyy was not happy about what he was being forced to do because he "did not want to be used as a pawn in a U.S. reelection campaign." He was.

Even though the Ukrainians were well aware that Shokin's on-again off-again investigations really didn't have anything to do with the Bidens, they still had to deal with the fact that many people (especially those who supported the Trump administration) believed that it did.

So much so, that it became a primary part of the agenda for the beginning of Zelenskyy's presidency.

Very early in his term, he called a meeting with a number of his top advisers (including Chief of Staff Andrii Yermak) to discuss the national energy situation. But, according to at least three people with knowledge of the meeting who spoke with the Associated Press, "instead, the group spent most of the three-hour discussion talking about how to navigate the insistence from Trump and his personal lawyer Rudy Giuliani for a probe and how to avoid becoming entangled in the American election." It was evident that, whether Zelenskyy wanted to or not, he had to deal with Giuliani and his never-ending demands for an investigation.

Chapter 49
Terms and Conditions

As the heat from the American efforts was rising, the Zelenskyy administration couldn't help but feel it. Giuliani was determined to get me to keep the pressure on. But since we didn't know Zelenskyy personally, we dealt with other Ukrainian officials. When Giuliani canceled his Kyiv trip and met with the Ukrainian prosecutors in Paris, it was a compromise based on the fact that Giuliani didn't want to go to Kyiv and many of the Ukrainians were not allowed to travel to the U.S.

While the Ukrainians were falling over themselves trying to say what they believed Giuliani wanted to hear, they often contradicted each other. "They needed direct access to the U.S. president to convince him that they are the right group to represent Ukraine," an anonymous former prosecutor told The Washington Post. "They understood the best method to come closer to Trump is to bring something that contains information that is a real interest to U.S. politics."

It was July 22, 2019. Andriy Yermak, who held a job analogous to Zelenskyy's chief of staff, received a call from Giuliani. Their pragmatic cynicism meant that Giuliani, who held no office, was afforded the treatment of a head of state, as the Ukrainians knew that he spoke for Trump. According to Novikov, Giuliani began the call by praising Ukraine and Ukrainians — except for a few "really bad ones." He then offered to help Zelenskyy in his role "as the President's lawyer" (officially, there would be no help he could offer in that capacity). Without waiting for a response, he listed off his "areas of concern." They were:

1. Ukrainian officials provided "dirt" on Manafort and Trump for the Democrats
2. Shokin had been prevented from entering the U.S. and had been fired at the behest of Joe Biden
3. That Zelenskyy was surrounded by shady characters, including Kolomoisky
4. That Soros had influenced Ukrainian politics

Then he told Zelenskyy to "let these investigations go forward," which assumed "these investigations" were already underway. They weren't.

Giuliani tumbled on words a little bit, then said: "All we need from the President is to say: I'm gonna put an honest prosecutor in charge, he's gonna investigate about involvement in the 2016 election and then the Biden thing has to be run out." Then he suggested that Zelenskyy could "brag" about the investigation and that his legal experience led him to conclude that Biden's actions in Ukraine amounted to a bribe.

At best, it was a private U.S. citizen telling the leader of a sovereign nation what to do and say, but it was also a pseudo-official representative relaying what Trump expected and that there would be negative consequences if his requests were not fulfilled to his liking. To his credit, Giuliani skirted around any liability by saying that he didn't speak for the President, but as his friend. He then instructed Zelenskyy to "be careful," especially about who he surrounded himself with. Many would consider that a threat.

Giuliani pressed on, saying that he could forgive Zelenskyy and Ukraine for being "liberal" or having "supported Hillary," but he could not forgive people who said that Trump was "unstable" and that "he's gonna get impeached" — an obvious reference to Yovanovitch. More gangster stuff. Again, this is a private but connected U.S. citizen speaking to the government of a sovereign nation.

Yermak tried to buy time, telling him that the new government needed time to root out corruption before it could do much else.

Giuliani pointed out that he believed that Zelenskyy was dedicated to establishing an honest government, then complained that "the investigation" (about Biden) had been delayed so many times that it was hard to believe that Ukraine — a government that was inheriting a cesspool of corruption and an unofficial war with Russia — was taking it seriously.

Giuliani then made his veiled demand even more clear, saying: "I think it would be very helpful in clearing this up, if the President [Zelenskyy] at some point could say something publicly that he supports a full and complete investigation of these claims, to determine so that the truth comes out."

He then praised Zelenskyy in contrast to previous Ukrainian leaders, naming Yuschenko, and again asked him to "make a statement" about "the investigation." Then he added to his side of the deal, saying that he could talk to Trump and promote the two countries' relationship.

Yermak agreed to talk about it with Zelenskyy.

An aide to Giuliani then pointed out that Zelenskyy would be getting a call from Trump soon and it might be possible for Zelenskyy to mention the investigation then.

Yermak confirmed that Zelenskyy would.

Giuliani then told him, quite specifically, to say that he was not the driving force behind Zelenskyy's decision to undertake such an investigation, even though he clearly was.

Yermak agreed.

Giuliani then assured Yermak that what they discussed in the call would be the best plan of action, and ended the call.

Novikov thought that Giuliani was operating under the impression that the Ukrainian government was not only young, but naive. He also realized that following Giuliani's instructions would fall in line with Putin's plan to destabilize the governments of both Ukraine and the U.S. He found it amusing that Giuliani would warn Zelenskyy against surrounding himself with shady Ukrainians when he had been close with Derkach, who was a Yanukovych tough guy and widely believed to be a Russian spy, and Artemenko (who has since renamed himself Andy Victor Kuchma, gained Canadian citizenship and lives in D.C.), who had worked as a back channel to Putin.

It would be a bad idea, he believed, for Ukraine to do as requested (one could say ordered) unless there were compelling circumstances for them to do so. Those compelling circumstances came three days later.

Chapter 50
The 'Perfect Phone Call'

Less than a half hour before the call between Trump and Zelenskyy was to take place, Volker sent a text to Yermak, writing: "Heard from White House—assuming President Z convinces trump he will investigate / 'get to the bottom of what happened' in 2016, we will nail down date for visit to Washington. Good luck!"

The White House's National Security Council transcribed the 30-minute call, although they warned that it might not be precisely word for word (without saying why). Still, the messages were clear.

Although the official reason for the call was little more than a meet and greet, Trump got to his intentions right away. He expected Ukraine to open an investigation into the Bidens, particularly Hunter. "There's a lot of talk about Biden's son, that Biden stopped the prosecution and a lot of people want to find out about that so whatever you can do with the Attorney General would be great. Biden went around bragging that he stopped the prosecution so if you can look into it … It sounds horrible to me."

That talk, of course, came directly from the BLT Team. We knew there was nothing Trump wanted to hear more (other than undiluted praise, of course) than the potential weaknesses of his opponents, so Hunter Biden was a major topic of conversation with us.

Trump also held the promise of vital U.S. aid, which he had frozen, over Ukraine's head: "The United States has been very, very good to Ukraine. I wouldn't say that it's reciprocal, necessarily, because things are happening that are not good. But the United States has been very, very good to Ukraine." As always, he was talking like a gangster boss.

Zelenskyy appeared to give in, but — perhaps for his own amusement — asked Trump if the U.S. could provide something for Ukraine to investigate. "Since we have won the absolute majority in our Parliament, the next prosecutor general will be 100 percent my person; my candidate who will be approved by the parliament and will start as a new prosecutor in September.

He or she will look into the situation, specifically to the company that you mentioned in this issue. The issue of the investigation of the case is actually the issue of making sure to restore the honesty we will take care of that and will work on the investigation of the case. On top of that, I would kindly ask you if you have any additional information that you can provide to us, it would be very helpful for the investigation to make sure that we administer justice in our country."

Believing he had the Biden investigation in hand, Trump asked Zelenskyy about a belief of his that had never had any substantiation and had been investigated and found to be untrue, but was a favorite topic of the BLT Team — that the accusation that the Russians helped the Republicans in the 2016 election was simply a ruse to cover up the Ukrainians helping the Democrats. He mentioned Crowdstrike, a software company the DNC hired to investigate Russian hacks, who many Trumpians believe covered up Ukrainian dealings with the Democrats. Neither Trump nor Giuliani were aware that the conspiracy theory originated from 4Chan. "I would like you to do us a favor though because our country has been through a lot and Ukraine knows a lot about it. I would like you to find out what happened with this whole situation in Ukraine, they say Crowdstrike ... I guess you have one of your wealthy people ... The server, they say Ukraine has it. There are a lot of things that went on, the whole situation. I think you're surrounding yourself with some of the same people. I would like to have the Attorney General call you or your people and I would like you to get to the bottom of it. As you saw yesterday, that whole nonsense ended with a very poor performance by a man named Robert Mueller, an incompetent performance, but they say a lot of it started with Ukraine. Whatever you can do it's very important that you do it if that's possible."

As well as dissing Mueller, Trump took a moment to undermine the integrity of Ukraine's western neighbors. Trump had a history of casting aspersions on America's NATO allies (except Turkey and Hungary) — an action that wouldn't gain anything for anybody, aside from Putin and Erdoğan. "Germany does almost nothing for you. All they do is talk and I think it's something that you should really ask them about. When I was speaking to Angela Merkel, she talks Ukraine, but she doesn't do anything. A lot of European countries are the same way so I think it's something you want to look at but the United States has been very good to Ukraine."

Trump also took a moment to let Zelenskyy know that Giuliani spoke for him, and even put him on par with Barr in that department. "Mr. Giuliani is a highly respected man. He was the mayor of New York City, a great mayor, and I would like him to call you. I will ask him to call you along with the Attorney General. Rudy very much knows what's happening and he is a very capable guy. If you could speak to him that would be great."

And, finally, he decided it would be appropriate to take one last stab at Yovanovitch. "The former ambassador from the United... the woman... was bad news and the people she was dealing with in the Ukraine were bad news I just want to let you know that."

Zelenskyy, clearly an intelligent man, didn't need a magnifying glass to read between the lines. Trump's instructions were clear — announce an investigation into the Bidens if you want any aid and, if it helps your enemy, we don't care.

Trump would later call the conversation a "perfect phone call."

Chapter 51
Negotiations

I hadn't been back long when Giuliani called me in Vienna and asked me to go to Spain to help improve relations between the White House and Guaidó. We were headed to Madrid because Giuliani had arranged to meet with Venezuelan billionaire Alejandro Betancourt López and Guaidó's father.

I didn't really know why he picked Spain at first, but I really liked the idea. I thought it would be a great way to take Svetlana and the kids on a vacation, so I told him that we'd love to go. They deserved to get in on some of the benefits I was enjoying from being so far inside the Trump team. I knew I'd have to work, but I knew they'd have a great time in Madrid.

We arrived a day earlier than Giuliani, but he had told me that we were going to have a conference with Yermak before our big meeting with Betancourt.

I went to the airport to greet Giuliani and, almost as soon as they got off the plane, Giuliani's girlfriend, Maria Ryan, realized that she didn't have her luggage. She was distraught and told Giuliani that she had nothing to wear. He handed her his American Express card and told Igor to take her shopping.

While they were away, Giuliani and I went to meet Yermak. After Giuliani caught me up on the latest information, we sat down to draft exactly what we wanted Zelenskyy to say when he announced the investigations. Giuliani showed me a draft he had prepared that spelled out what he expected to hear word for word.

At the actual meeting, he introduced me to Yermak, but I didn't say much after that. As I often did, I just listened.

It went pretty much the way I predicted, Giuliani pressuring him to get Zelenskyy to make an announcement about the investigations and Yermak trying to buy more time. It was all "we'll take care of it, bear with us."

Giuliani was also putting pressure on Yermak to tell Zelenskyy not to fire or replace Vitali Klitschko. His job, analogous with the mayor of Kyiv was set to end soon by constitutional rules. He didn't want it to, so he visited Giuliani in New York looking for help. Not only was he a close friend of Giuliani's, but Klitschko was a hero to many Americans. If they thought he'd been mistreated by the Ukrainian government, its already low reputation would take a nose dive. Yermak promised that he'd do what he could. The Ukrainian government later fudged the rules and Klitschko kept his job, but with a new title.

After finishing with Yermak, we met back to Betancourt's huge mansion, one of his many residences. This one, however, was a sight to behold. High up in the Sierra de Gredos, separated by miles and miles of rugged slopes covered in scrubby woodland, Betancourt lived in an actual castle — Castillo de Alamin. A castle has stood on the same grounds since Spain was in Arab hands in 930. It's since been rebuilt several times and now features tennis courts, a pool and a full-sized soccer pitch. When I first saw it, it was surrounded by Betancourt's fleet of all-white luxury and exotic cars. I has seen some impressive places in my recent travels, but this one really took my breath away.

Castles don't come cheap, and Betancourt had his thumb in many pies. His primary company, Derwick, won several government contracts to build powerplants; although critics claimed they weren't qualified and suspected some-

The view from Betancourt's castle in Spain.

thing fishy in the awards process. He also runs an oil and gas exploration company in Canada, a bank in Senegal and a sunglasses company in Spain. He was one of the super rich while most of the people in his country were finding just getting by increasingly challenging.

At first he was a bit standoffish with me, because of my relationship with Sargeant, and his not being sure on which side I supported in the Venezuelan conflict. But when we realized my loyalty was to Giuliani, things got a lot easier between us.

Before our trip, the Venezuelan tycoon was accused of being part of a major money-laundering scheme. So far, he had only been named as an uncharged conspirator, but he knew that could change at any second. Giuliani came to Spain to take care of his case.

In a prearranged exchange, Giuliani would be able to show the White House that Betancourt supported Guaidó. He actually even invited some of

Guaidó's family over to Betancourt's house, and got Guaidó's father to record a video message for Trump, about how Guaidó wanted a better relationship between Venezuela and the U.S.

Giuliani kept his promise and met a few weeks later with the Department of Justice criminal and frauds teams. He let me in on the plan, but told me: "Keep your mouth shut."

Me, with Venezuelan billionaire Betancourt and his wife, Andreína Rojas, aboard their private jet.

He explained that I would be breaking attorney-client confidentiality if I said anything.

When he wasn't working, Giuliani was kind of embarrassing. He was drunk much of the time and made a big show of making out with Ryan in the pool. It seemed inappropriate to me at the time. There were kids around.

Two days after the "perfect phone call," Trump was aboard Air Force One. He was returning from a trip to Japan that many considered a diplomatic disaster. Returning to his decades-old fixation about how other countries are freeloading on America's military budget (the result of a system designed to ensure America's unchallenged global power), he railed about how traditional allies were taking advantage of the U.S. "We have a treaty with Japan," Trump told Fox News. "If Japan is attacked, we will fight World War III. We will go in and we will protect them and we will fight with our lives and with our treasure. We will fight at all costs, right? But if we're attacked, Japan doesn't have to help us at all. They can watch it on a Sony television, the attack." He had similar words for Germany.

He also villainized India for taking part in a trade war that he had started without provocation. He then took time to call the Duchess of Sussex, Meghan Markle, "nasty" (and denied it, even after a video of him saying it began to make the rounds) and the Mayor of London, Sadiq Khan, a "stone-cold loser."

Media less fawning than Fox News pointed out that he had nothing bad to say about Putin — although the two countries were engaged in a spy war and Russia had just jailed two Americans on what were widely believed to have been false charges — nor Crown Prince Mohammed bin Salman of Saudi Arabia — who the United Nations accused of having ordered the murder and dismemberment of Khashoggi, a Saudi journalist and U.S. resident, in Erdoğan's Turkey.

Also on the plane was Mick Mulvaney, the acting White House chief of staff. Over the Pacific, he sent an email to Assistant to the President and Senior Advisor to the Chief of Staff Robert B. Blair that read: "I'm just trying to tie up some loose ends. Did we ever find out about the money for Ukraine and whether we can hold it back?" He was talking about finding a legal way to accomplish the President's secret order to withhold $391 million worth of sniper rifles, missile launchers, night-vision goggles, medical aid and other military equipment to Ukraine, which was still desperately fighting a war against Russian-backed rebels and, as many correctly believed, Russia itself.

Blair told his boss that it might be possible, but that he should "expect Congress to become unhinged." After all, both the House and Senate had approved the expenditure. He also warned Mulvaney that the move could advance the narrative that Trump was pro-Russia. I'm not sure if either even knew if it was legal or not.

Mulvaney could claim ignorance. He had developed a habit of leaving any room in which Trump and Giuliani were talking, to help preserve their attorney-client privilege.

He wasn't the only one to realize something was very wrong. Vindman, who had listened to the call between Trump and Zelenskyy from a White House situation room, summed up the pressure tactics for The Atlantic:

> "In the week leading up to the call, I'd discerned a potentially dangerous wrinkle in the Ukraine situation. Actions by the president's personal attorney, Rudy Giuliani, suggested a hidden motive for the White House's sudden interest in Ukraine. Operating far outside normal policy circles, Giuliani had been on a mysterious errand that also seemed to involve the U.S. ambassador to the

European Union, Gordon Sondland, and the White House chief of staff, Mick Mulvaney. Just a few weeks earlier, I'd participated in a meeting at the White House at which Sondland made a suggestion to some visiting top Ukrainian officials: If President Zelensky pursued certain investigations, he might be rewarded with a visit to the White House. These proposed investigations would be of former Vice President and current Democratic candidate Joe Biden and his son Hunter. Sondland's proposal was clearly improper. Little could have been more valuable to the new, young, untested leader of Ukraine — the country most vulnerable to Russia — than a one-on-one meeting with the president of the United States. A bilateral visit would signal to Russia and the rest of the world a staunch U.S. commitment to having Ukraine's back as well as U.S. support for Zelenskyy's reform and anticorruption agenda, which was crucial to Ukraine's prosperity and to closer integration with the European Union. That's what all of us in the policy community wanted, of course. But making such a supremely valuable piece of U.S. diplomacy dependent on an ally's carrying out investigations into U.S. citizens—not to mention the president's political adversary—was unheard of. Before I'd fully picked up on what was going on, that meeting with the Ukrainians had been abruptly broken up by Bolton. But in a subsequent meeting among U.S. officials, at which Sondland reiterated the idea, I told him point-blank that I thought his proposition was wrong and that the NSC would not be party to such an enterprise."

Many just chalked it up to Trump being Trump.

That didn't bother us. Trump would make his way through it like he always did. Besides, we had work to do.

On August 9, Sondland texted Volker and Giuliani to tell them that they should have a conference call "to make sure I advise Z correctly as to what he should be saying." Z, of course, is Zelenskyy.

Our feeling was that it didn't matter what he said, just as long as he announced the investigations.

But the Ukrainians weren't entirely sold yet. They needed more. Yermak texted that their would be no announcements from then until he was given a concrete date for Zelenskyy's White House visit.

That sent Sondland to speak with his State Department contact, Ulrich Brechbuhl, a top advisor to Pompeo, to discuss what Zelenskyy was to say and to set a date for his White House visit. He also emailed Pompeo himself about the effort.

As we were still all texting and calling back and forth about what Zelenskyy was to say, Trump made things more difficult. At one of his sessions with the media outside the White House, a reporter brought up Ukraine and its new President:

22222222222

Reporter: Mr. President, do you plan invite your Ukrainian counterpart, Volodymyr Zelenskyy to the White House? And what would be your advice for him ...

Trump: Who are you talking about?

Reporter: The President of Ukraine, Volodymyr Zelenskyy.

Trump: Yeah.

Reporter: Do you plan to invite him to the White House? And what would be your advice for him on how to communicate with Vladimir Putin to stop the conflict in Eastern Ukraine?

Trump: I think he's going to make a deal with President Putin, and he will be invited to the White House. And we look forward to seeing him. He's already been invited to the White House, and he wants to come. And I think he will. He's a very reasonable guy. He wants to see peace in Ukraine. And I think he will be coming very soon, actually.

So, everyone knew that a visit from Zelenskyy was close to becoming a reality.

Later that day, Yermak texted Volker with a draft of what we wanted and expected Zelenskyy to say.

It was disappointing, Yermak said that, although he would announce investigations, he would not specifically name Burisma, Hunter Biden or Ukrainian meddling in the 2016 election.

Volker texted back exactly what he wanted Zelenskyy to say if the deal was to go through:

"Special attention should be paid to the problem of interference in the political processes of the United States, especially with the alleged involvement of some Ukrainian politicians. I want to declare that this is unacceptable. We intend to initiate and complete a transparent and unbiased investigation of all available facts and episodes, including those involving Burisma and the 2016 U.S. elections, which in turn will prevent the recurrence of this problem in the future."

Yermak balked. He said that the script made it sound like Zelenskyy was directly involved in U.S. politics. Volker said that he saw his point, so they shelved the discussion, at least for the time being.

Without any definite news, Sondland texted Volker and asked if Zelenskyy was going to "to give us an unequivocal draft with 2016 and Boresma?"

Volker sent back, "That's the clear message so far ... I'm hoping we can put something out there that causes him to respond with that."

Chapter 52
Withholding

D ebate about Trump's policies and behavior raged as he prepared for the G7 Summit to be held in Biarritz, France, at the end of August. He wasn't going into it with a position of strength. The Democrats had regained control of the House as Trump failed to connect with voters while the economy faltered.

Since the Republicans had been in control until recently, he decided to blame the problems on two favorite targets, China and the Federal Reserve Board. Hitting both at once, he tweeted: "My only question is, who is our bigger enemy, Jay Powel or Chairman Xi?" Trump misspelled Fed Chairman Jay Powell's name and blamed him for the sluggish economy despite the fact that he was a Trump appointee.

Trump's only statement of substance at the summit immediately made headlines all over the world. He proposed that Russia be allowed to rejoin the G7 after it had been kicked out in 2014 for invading Crimea (the U.S. had voted to expel Russia). When reporter Yamiche Alcindor asked why he was in favor of reinstating Russia, he said that it would be wiser to have Russia take part in discussions than to isolate them. Then he downplayed the importance of the Crimea invasion and blamed it on Obama, saying:

"It was sort of taken away from President Obama. Not taken away from President Trump; taken away from President Obama. President Obama was not happy that this happened because it was embarrassing to him. Right? It was very embarrassing to him. And he wanted Russia to be out of what was called the G8. And that was his determination. He was outsmarted by Putin. He was outsmarted. President Putin outsmarted President Obama."

Ignoring the fact that Crimea, as part of a sovereign nation, was not "taken away" from Obama or the U.S., it seemed to many to be a dismissive way to describe the military invasion of a territory the size of Massachusetts that happened to offer Russia hugely lucrative strategic gains. Praising Putin for such a brutal move was also mystifying to some.

Appealing to his base who did not want to see Trump go easy on Russia, he said: "Whether you like it or not — and it may not be politically correct — but we have a world to run."

Putin's response demonstrated his usual dull attempt at wit: "How can I come back into an organization that doesn't exist? It is called the G7 today."

As the dust was settling from the summit, the Trump White House announced that the $391 million aid package to Ukraine would go under review, which would withhold it for delivery indefinitely.

It was shocking to many. The package had been approved by both House and Senate and it was popular with both parties at the time. By then, Ukraine had lost about three times as many people in its undeclared war with Russia than the U.S. had in Afghanistan and both of its adventures in Iraq.

Not realizing that Trump had secretly ordered the aid frozen more than a month earlier, the media attributed it to the fact that a Trump proposal to cut $4 billion in foreign aid had failed, so he grasped at what little money he didn't have to give away. Since he had long, since the 1970s, complained about other countries "freeloading" off the U.S. and that he was known to petulantly lash out with retaliation when his ambitions were blunted, they just considered it Trump being Trump.

One commentator had a more accurate handle on the situation than most. Adam Schiff, the Democratic Chairman of the House Intelligence Committee and a vociferous Trump critic, tweeted: "Trump is withholding vital military aid to Ukraine, while his personal lawyer seeks help from the Ukraine government to investigate his political opponent. It doesn't take a stable genius to see the magnitude of this conflict. Or how destructive it is to our national security."

As the Ukraine controversy was pushed to the back of the news lineup, Trump switched back to his normal administrative duties, drawing attention away from anything of substance with stunts like calling Secretary of State Rex Tillerson "dumb as a rock" for criticizing his tweet about North Korea:

> "North Korea fired off some small weapons, which disturbed some of my people, and others, but not me. I have confidence that Chairman Kim will keep his promise to me, & also smiled when he called Swampman Joe Bidan a low IQ individual, & worse. Perhaps that's sending me a signal?"

Then he blamed Australia for kicking off the FBI investigation that led to the Mueller investigation, apparently insinuating that his activities should not be investigated by anyone. And that people from other countries should mind their own business.

But the freeze on aid to Ukraine stood. The President can delay the re-lease of funds in some instances, but there had to be evidence of a change in the situation. Trump said he was withholding the aid because he wanted to force our European allies to "do more" to help Ukraine. He expressly denied that the delay was tied to Ukraine making a deal to investigate the Bidens and the 2016 election. He was lying.

And that's essentially what The New York Times was saying when they reported on our meeting with Yermak in Spain.

Giuliani had to reply. He could never let that sort of thing go by unchallenged. So, he admitted to the meeting and why it happened. He just said that the reporting was faulty because it should have been about some-thing else. "Times completely turned a story about astounding allegations of serious crimes of state concerning Dems into a piece trying to suggest I did something nefarious except they can't say what it is," Giuliani told NBC News. "Typical spin against Trump or anyone close to him." Then he added that it was a team effort in that the State Department put Yermak "in contact with" him. "Not other way around, and I told him they should not be cowered ... fully investigating serious possible crimes like bribery, extortion, fraud, money laundering and illegal interference in 2016 election. That's it. Reported all to State."

As Ukraine became prominent in the news again, Bolton flew to Kyiv on August 28. He was the highest-ranking member of the Trump administration to visit the nation. After speaking with Zelenskyy, he said that they had discussed the two presidents meeting on Trump's planned trip to Poland.

Trump didn't actually go to Poland for the World War II memorial ser-vice. He blamed the weather. Instead, he sent Pence in his place. He spoke with Zelenskyy, who brought up the delay, but nothing was worked out.

While in Warsaw, Sondland spoke with Yermak and told him straight up that the aid would not be released until the investigations were announced.

That made its way to Taylor, who immediately recognized it as quid pro quo. He texted Sondland: "Are we now saying that security assistance and WH meeting are conditioned on investigations?"

Sondland texted back: "Call me."

In the ensuing discussion, Taylor managed to get Sondland to admit that the aid was indeed tied to the announcement, He said that trump told him he wanted to put Zelenskyy "in a public box" to pressure him into doing what he wanted him to.

At the end of the Poland trip, Pence held a joint media conference with Polish President Andrzej Duda. As it was wrapping up, Pence allowed one last question.

Associated Press reporter Jill Colvin jumped at the chance. She asked: "Number 1, did you discuss Joe Biden at all during that meeting yesterday with the Ukrainian President? And Number 2, can you assure Ukraine that the hold-up of has absolutely nothing to do with efforts, including by Rudy Giuliani, to try to dig up dirt on the Biden family?"

The first question was easy. Pence replied: "Well, on the first question, the answer is no." But then he stalled on the second, then deflected, talking a great deal, but saying little of any substance.

That the public was growing increasingly aware of our operation made us only more determined.

On September 4, Firtash's people told us that he had received an affidavit from Shokin that said: "I was forced out because I was leading a wide-ranging corruption probe into Burisma Holdings, a natural gas firm active in Ukraine and Joe Biden's son, Hunter Biden, was a member of the Board of Directors."

Although he tried to pull the old unrelated-sentences trick at the end, the first part is a fabrication. Still, good enough for us.

Zelenskyy was busy making moves of his own. With Lutsenko out, he persuaded his new prosecutor general to re-hire Vitaliy Kasko. Since Kasko had very publicly said that he quit the job because of his frustration over Shokin's corrupt practices, it showed that Zelenskyy was at least trying to put those days in the rear view mirror. It also tarnished Shokin's already-battered reputation even further.

He was hardly the only rich Ukrainian politician who raised suspicion. In September, I got a call from Artemenko, a friend of Igor's. He told me that he had some guys with real, hard evidence that would prove all of our theories once and for all. Naturally, I was intrigued. But once he told me that the guys were Derkach and Telizhenko, I told him that we were cool, I'd pass.

Later, Giuliani text me and asked: "Who's this Artemenko?" He had, of course, known Artemenko, but had an annoying habit of forgetting names, especially the Eastern European ones. Since he asked, I supposed that Arte-menko had reached out to him without me.

I told him not to deal with Artemenko, he was peddling Russian disinformation. In fact, I gave him other names of guys who were doing the same thing. Of course, I later learned that he was enthusiastically dealing with Artemenko, as well as Derkach and Telizhenko.

But with so much attention to the operation, we had some explaining of our own to do. Sondland spoke with Trump and called NSC Senior Director for European and Russian Affairs Tim Morrison to catch him up. In a masterpiece of Orwellian double-talk, Sondland said: "He told me … that there was no quid pro quo, but President Zelenskyy must announce the opening of the investigations and he should want to do it."

Shocked, Morrison told Bolton. He told Morrison to inform the NSC's lawyers. He didn't want to get taken down if it all blew up.

Chapter 53
It Hits the Fan

I t did blow up. On September 9, Inspector General for the Intelligence Community Michael Atkinson sent a letter to Schiff and Nunes describing a whistle blower complaint detailing our operation. It outed Igor and me as Giuliani's men on the ground pressuring Zelenskyy. Immediately, three House committees began investigations into whether our actions regarding the Ukrainian government was illegal. The chairmen of the three committees announced their plan by sending letters to the White House and State Department.

That was it for Bolton. He says he quit, Trump says he fired him.

And, on September 11, Trump lifted the hold on the aid to Ukraine just as easily as he launched it.

It didn't make a difference. If anything, it made the operation more obvious. It looked like the second he was caught doing something wrong, Trump stopped.

Talk of impeachment was rampant. There was just about nothing that would upset Trump more. He showed his anxiety on Twitter: "All Polls, and some brand new Polls, show very little support for impeachment. Such a waste of time, especially with sooo much good that could be done, including prescription drug price reduction, healthcare, infrastructure etc." And then: "....Knowing all of this, is anybody dumb enough to believe that I would say something inappropriate with a foreign leader while on such a potentially 'heavily populated' call. I would only do what is right anyway, and only do good for the USA!"

Trump sent Giuliani out for damage control. Instead, he did more damage. On September 20, he went on CNN hoping to incriminate the Bidens. It backfired. Chris Cuomo interviewed him, and this is how it went.

Giuliani: No. Actually, I didn't. I asked the Ukraine to investigate the allegations that there was interference in the election of 2016 by the Ukrainians, for the benefit of Hillary Clinton, for which there already is a court finding ...

Cuomo: You never asked anything about Hunter Biden? You never asked anything about Joe Biden ...

Giuliani: The only thing I asked about Joe Biden ...

Cuomo: ... and his role with the prosecutor?

Giuliani: ... is to get to the bottom of how it was that Lutsenko who was appointed ...

Cuomo: Right.

Giuliani: ... dismissed the case against AntAC.

Cuomo: So, you did ask Ukraine to look into Joe Biden?

Giuliani: Of course I did.

Cuomo: You just said you didn't.

It wasn't as widely seen, but on the same day, former U.S. Ambassador to Ukraine Steven Pifer told Ukrainian news outlet Hvylya writes that he gave Zelensky advice on how to deal with Trump. In summary: flatter Trump, try to find an option where no one loses, don't ignore Congress and beware of Giuliani.

The next day, Trump tweeted claims of his innocence nine times. As pressure mounted for him to release the transcript of the "perfect call," first he tweeted that he'd "rather not," then said that the whole thing was "a Democrat/Adam Schiff Scam!" Hours later, he announced via Twitter that he was going to release the admittedly rough transcript.

He did, but he did not provide Congress with the White House documents related to his call with Zelenskyy. On those grounds, Pelosi made an announcement. "The actions of the Trump presidency have revealed the dishonorable fact of the president's betrayal of his oath of office, betrayal of our national security and betrayal of the integrity of our elections," she said.. "Therefore, today, I am announcing the House of Representatives is moving forward with an official impeachment inquiry."

Chapter 54
I'm Famous

The media got it wrong. When I first became newsworthy, they all called me a fixer. I was never a fixer. Michael Cohen was Trump's fixer. At least he had been. Trump fired him in May and then, on August 21, Cohen surrendered to the FBI and confessed to eight criminal charges (five for tax evasion, one for making false statements to a financial institution, one for willfully causing an unlawful corporate contribution and, finally, one count of making an excessive campaign contribution at the request of a candidate for the "principal purpose of influencing election") against him. That's when Giuliani took over the role, among others.

I was no fixer. A fixer plays defense, I was all offense. To be specific about it, I was an operative. I was carrying out missions given to me by Giuliani and Trump. I was the man on the ground, not the guy behind a desk. I wasn't fixing problems. I was creating opportunities.

The media was throwing my name and what to call me around because of the impeachment investigation. Someone had sent a letter to Richard Burr, Chairman of the Senate Select Committee on Intelligence, and Adam Schiff, Chairman of the House Permanent Select Committee on Intelligence, that described Trump's "perfect phone call" to Zelenskyy for what it was — extortion. It also detailed how Giuliani had orchestrated Yovanovitch's dismissal, how we had recruited Lutsenko and other unsavory characters and how the whole thing was all about helping Trump win in 2020 by getting compromising information on the Bidens.

And the whistle blower — we found out later that it was a CIA agent — named names. Including mine. Suddenly, everywhere I looked I saw pictures of myself and Igor. We were news 24/7.

What I hated about the initial coverage — beside the fact that it existed at all — was they always called us "Soviet-born." It made us seem like Cold War-era spies. Okay, Igor I could see with his thick accent and business interests in Kyiv, but I had been in the U.S. since I was 3. I made my life here and knew no other. It was my culture, my country. I was no Soviet. In fact, the USSR appalled me.

Since the media seemed to be misguided about me, so I decided to go to them directly.

I honestly explained that I was working for Giuliani in Ukraine because I thought it was my patriotic duty to uncover any illegal or immoral activities by a Presidential candidate in Ukraine. I also mentioned that I believed running with the big dogs would help get Global Energy Producers off the ground. Besides, I told them, Giuliani was a close friend. They asked me about the evidence I had found. I told them that we weren't ready to release it yet. They knew about the Skype call between Giuliani and Shokin, so I owned up and admitted that I arranged it.

Then they asked if the whole thing was just an operation to help get Trump re-elected in 2020. Absolutely not, I told them. That time I lied.

As the news cycle kept rolling, I became less and less a part of the national consciousness. I'd get recognized every once in a while. They weren't throwing eggs at me, nor were they asking for my autograph. When my face did spur a memory, I was just that guy from the thing.

Far more important was the fact that the cat was out of the bag. Everybody knew what we were up to. The whole thing — Trump and Giuliani getting me to pressure Ukraine, the dismissal of Yovanovitch, the withholding of military aid — everybody knew.

Dowd was widely mocked for using Comic Sans in his official letter about Igor and me.

If you think that we might have given up on, or even just slowed the process in Ukraine, then you don't know Rudy. Despite having spent a career as a high-profile lawyer, he seemed to me to think of laws as trivial, things to get around when necessary, by any means at hand. He clearly didn't set out to break any laws, but if it happened, it happened and could be explained away.

Things were getting chaotic for all of us in early October 2019,

If anything, our activities intensified. Eager to present our evidence against the Bidens before Congress could set up any sort of roadblock for Trump, we in the BLT Team redoubled our efforts.

With the clock ticking, the finish line was in sight. I spent all of my time flying from D.C. to Vienna and back with only short respites in Boca Raton with Svetlana and the kids. It was my job to make it all happen and I did everything I could to do it right.

I was proud of myself. Using nothing but charm and chutzpah, I was making world-changing decisions with billionaires and heads of states. And all I had wanted was to make some connections for my business.

The preamble was over. It was time to act. So, when Rudy called a meeting for the entire BLT Team at the Trump International, I knew it was all going down.

I would fly to Vienna and seal the 2020 election for Trump.

Chapter 55
The Raid

I had asked Svetlana not to worry about me, but she did anyway. She was okay with me jetting all over the world, but she wasn't as happy with why. She later told me that seeing how far I had risen so quickly, how important my missions had become — it seemed dangerous, she said. And now that I was sort of famous, it just felt even more so.

Still, I went.

She was also a little more than concerned about the mania I had when it came to Trump. There was a picture of him in every room in the house. She said that I had been dazzled by him. Her? Not so much. She didn't really know him but had met him. She admitted that Trump could be charming and that his charisma filled a room as soon as he entered it — she said he was a "Republican version of a rock star." Still, there was something about him that seemed a little off to her.

On the evening of October 9, 2019, she was at home entertaining when she went out the front door. She was mildly surprised that there were no reporters or photographers out there. Finally, some peace. Our security guy had been sitting in his car in the driveway for hours, so she went to send him home. "Nothing to see here," she joked.

About 15 minutes later, at 9:15, she had just finished putting the baby to bed and was looking forward to some time to relax with her mom, who was visiting. But before she could, she went to go check on whatever the commotion out front was. The reporters and photographers who had been pestering the house for a while had been getting bolder, ruder and more intrusive all the time. She figured that they must have been hiding and then felt emboldened once the security guy had left. She went to go shoo them away, but stopped when she saw lots of people outside who clearly were not with the media. Some of them had their guns drawn.

They saw her, too, and a voice boomed from the other side of the door: "Open up, it's the FBI."

She had the presence of mind to ask if they had a warrant.

"We do," said the agent, and then added, almost sheepishly: "The physical part just isn't here yet."

Svetlana immediately called Correia, who usually knew where I was. No answer. She didn't know it, but his house was being raided too. Recalling how she had thought it was strange that I hadn't checked in, her mind raced.

Once she heard other agents breaching the back door, she knew she didn't have much choice but to let the FBI in the front. She watched as 14 agents filed into the house. The commotion had woken the baby, so she went in to go get him. She told the agents to be quiet because our 5-year-old son was sleeping in a nearby room.

The lead agent imperiously announced: "We have a warrant to take and search everything that has to do with Lev Parnas." Then he asked for any phones and computers. What he did not do was tell Svetlana why the house was being raided or that I had been arrested. "Where's your husband?" he asked (as if he didn't know).

"I don't know."

"What do you mean you don't know?"

"It's Lev, he could be anywhere."

"You'd better be honest with us."

"He was on his way to Vienna ..."

Another agent told her that "we have your husband" and said that she could talk to me over his phone. After we both made sure the other was okay, I told her not to worry, everything would be fine. I actually believed it.

As soon as she hung up, she called Giuliani. She asked him what was going on. He said he didn't know, but assured her that everything would be all right. Then she called Aaron, who was at school in D.C. Because she knew he had been with me at some Trump rallies, she thought that the FBI might think he was involved in whatever they arrested me for and wanted to make sure he was safe. He was, but terribly concerned.

The FBI sat all of them — Svetlana, her mom, the nanny and our sons Nathan and Andrew — in the living room while they ransacked the place. Hours after hours passed as they searched room by room, collecting personal electronics, photos, documents, anything that could remotely be considered evidence.

They asked why she had called Correia; if it was to warn him.

She told them it was exactly the opposite. She thought he might know what the hell was going on.

As they were questioning her, agents passed by with dozens of boxes that other agents had filled with old phones, laptops, my legal pads, her legal pads, whatever they could find. She overheard one of the agents on a phone asking about additional warrants, saying "what about the wife?" For the first time, Svetlana thought that she might get arrested, When the search warrant finally arrived, she noticed that it was signed at 9:15 p.m. and realized they must've been outside waiting for word to begin.

They asked for her phone. She gave it to them, but said that she needed it back as soon as possible, it was brand new. They assured her that it would be back in two days. It wasn't returned for three years.

The commotion had also woken up our 5-year-old son, and Svetlana went into the bedroom to turn on his white noise machine. An agent warned her that she had to turn it off, then silenced it and started threatening Svetlana until a female officer turned it back on again and scolded the other agent.

Finally, they hit what they thought was the jackpot — our safe. We bought one thinking we'd use it, but we never got around to it. We both forgot the combination right away and didn't really think about the safe afterward. It was just too much trouble to open, and we didn't have anything we really thought needed to be protected that way. They demanded Svetlana open it.

She tried twice, failing both times, and finally told them: "I forgot the combination."

That only made them even more sure they had found the mother lode. They called a locksmith, even though it was the middle of the night. He showed up, but they hadn't been clear, and he'd thought someone had been locked out of the house. He hadn't brought the tools for that kind of job, he told them.

Clearly frustrated, the agent snarled at Svetlana: "Open it right now or you will be responsible for anything we find inside."

She shrugged.

They took the safe into the backyard and blew it up. Literally blew it up. Inside was an old letter or envelope or something. The agent grabbed it and waved it in front of Svetlana's face. "We've got you now," he said, triumphant in his ignorance over his prize of nothing.

They finally left at 3 a.m. Svetlana spent the rest of the night bouncing on an exercise ball trying to get the baby back to sleep. I will always appreciate how strong, smart and quick-thinking Svetlana was that night.

The following day, she got back on the phone with Rudy. She asked a million questions, like what's going on? Why was Lev arrested? He said he still didn't know, but that everything would work out just fine, although he didn't give any details as to how.

The next day, Friday, she flew up to D.C. She got to the jail on Saturday morning, and they told her there were no visiting hours on the weekend. In fact, she flew between Boca and D.C. no fewer than six times trying to see me, with no success.

About a week after the arrest, I was finally allowed to call. I told her I was okay, but I had no idea what was going on. She told me that she didn't either. At home, my mugshot and Igor's were on every TV station constantly, but the information of why we were arrested was sketchy. Finally, she turned the TV off, hoping the kids wouldn't be bombarded by the fact that their dad was behind bars.

She kept calling Rudy. He would assure her that he'd take care of it, but he sounded less and less interested every time she spoke to him and offered no real action. After a while, he — and everyone else I knew in Washington — stopped taking her calls.

***

My oldest son, Aaron, was taking a break from studying at George Washington University Law School. He was enjoying a run on the National Mall when his phone rang. Since it was my personal assistant, van Rensburg, he picked up.

She told him that I had been detained at the airport and that the house in Boca Raton was being raided.

He said he'd get down to Florida as soon as he could.

She told him that it wouldn't a good idea, the place was crawling with FBI agents. She instructed him to go to the Trump International to meet Giuliani.

When he arrived, still in his running outfit, Aaron knew where to find Giuliani. He was sitting in his usual seat at our regular table at BLT Prime. He was alone except for a bodyguard.

Aaron was bursting with questions.

Giuliani didn't have any answers. He told Aaron that he had no idea why I had been arrested and had no other information about the incident. He assured my son that the best thing we could do was to talk to my attorneys to find out exactly what happened and what they could do about.

But hours on the phone resulted in nothing but frustration and the realization that I was going to spend the night, at least, in jail.

With nothing else to do and class the following morning (a Thursday), Aaron went home for the night.

The next morning, Igor and I were all over the news. Aaron told me that he felt numb at the news and it didn't really hit him for days. But still, he went to class, and then back to the Trump International.

While working the phones, Aaron overheard a conversation between Giuliani and Jay Sekulow. He told me that they were discussion whether Giuliani would be involved in the indictment and Sekulow asking if Giuliani wanted to stay attached to us or not.

The answer to that would soon become plainly clear.

***

I eventually managed to get Svetlana on the phone. I asked what Rudy was doing. Nothing. I asked what Trump was doing. Nothing.

And that's about the time Trump lied about knowing me.

Chapter 56
Back to Reality

The postcard from Giuliani had shocked me out of my trance. The illusion of the Cult of Trump had been shattered. It was all over for me. I finally saw Trump and Giuliani for what they were — two-bit hucksters who were using their gangster mentality to push around and shake down the whole country, even the world. And they were either too stupid or too deluded to see that Putin was playing them like a pair of marionettes. They had turned the U.S.A., the country I love dearly, into a laughingstock on the world stage and something of a Russian puppet in foreign policy.

Vengeful is too simple a word to express how I felt then. Sure, it would be great to see Trump and Giuliani pay for what they did to me, but there was far more to it than that. The thought of them selling out our country for a few bucks or satisfying the urges of a boy who wasn't hugged enough made me sick and scared at the same time.

They had millions of Americans believing the same hogwash I had believed. They had the whole U.S. government and at least some of the media on their side. And who was I? Just some operative who got caught and put in jail. I was already hearing the press drag my name through the mud.

But I had a secret weapon. The truth. Once I was out, I could reveal all of their double-dealing and underhanded tactics, the amoral way in which they applied grifting and extortion to their every move, as though it were the only way to operate. And if people didn't believe me, I'd make them believe me. I saw and heard everything, and I kept the receipts. I had texts, emails, phone records, photos, videos, financial paper trails. I wanted to bury those guys under a mountain of evidence.

Maybe it was the tension, maybe it was the withdrawal from my prescriptions, but my fevered brain at that moment knew one thing and one thing only. Save the postcard. It had turned me, so it could turn others. I wanted everyone to see the true face of who they had put in charge of their country.

As a guard approached, I had no other option but to stuff it down my pants. He was taking me out to be released. Shit, I thought to myself. I was in line for a strip search; or, at the very least, a pat down.

I did get frisked, but only just. He missed it. I literally thanked God for this guy's lousy work ethic.

Obviously, I needed a new lawyer after I fired Downing. I was disgusted by him. Now that I had escaped from the Cult of Trump, I realized that he, and his followers, thought of him not as a President, in service to the nation, but as a king, in service to himself. We have a word for guys like him — oligarchs. Downing was on Trump's side, not mine.

Luckily, I knew a fantastic defense lawyer, Bondy. He was a successful defender and his practice evolved into one primarily dedicated to working for people who he (along with me and millions of others) believed had been unfairly treated as a result of our country's schizophrenic laws regarding marijuana. He had a habit of "winning the sentencing" even when he lost cases, usually resulting in offenders being given greatly reduced sentences much lower than were historically handed down.

The last time I had spoken to him was in 2018. We had met for burgers on the beach with our families when he was vacationing in Florida. I told him about my political connections and some of the people I knew, and he was very interested. He had written a memo that outlined his positions on marijuana laws for me to share with my political connections in time for the midterm elections. I ran with it. I even brought it to the President. It formed a lot of the points I spoke about with people like DeSantis and Laxalt.

While I was behind bars, Bondy got in touch with my sister, who got in touch with me. I set up a time when I could use the Alexandria jail's "red phone" and called him. He was as I remembered him, and happy to help. He told me that he found it funny that Trump would furnish me with expensive lawyers, while at the same time claiming that he did not know me.

Bondy told me that after the news of my involvement with Giuliani came out that I might soon need his help. He said that he saw that Giuliani was "clearly overstepping his bounds" as the President's personal counsel, perhaps even into criminal territory. He told me he had "read the tea leaves" and had a feeling that I'd be calling him soon. Bondy joined my co-counsel Ed McMahon.

I was arraigned in late October. I pleaded not guilty. Of course I did. I had been told by both Giuliani and Dowd that I had executive privilege. I relayed that promise to McMahon and Bondy. "He did not work for the United States government," McMahon told the court. "He worked for Mr. Giuliani and Mr. Giuliani worked for the President."

The SDNY had predicted as much. "We're aware of those privilege issues," said their prosecutor, Rebekah Donalski. "We have a filter team in place and we've had a filter team in place."

Once we were outside of the courtroom, we were mobbed by the media. "Many false things have been said about me and my family. I look forward to defending myself vigorously in court and I am certain that in time truth will be revealed and I will be vindicated," I said. "I put my faith in God."

Bondy said it better: "We look forward to defending Mr. Parnas in court based upon the evidence and not a smear campaign that's been driven by self-serving and misleading leaks apparently from the highest levels of our government."

The prosecution talked tough. They said that their case against me was "overwhelming" and had "only become stronger since Parnas' arrest." They said I had much more money than I did and:

> "Given the weight of the evidence, the likelihood of forthcoming charges and the expected length of the potential sentence, any individual would be highly incentivized to flee; with Parnas' particularly strong ties abroad, that incentive is even greater."

I wasn't going anywhere, but they still wanted a million bucks for bail. Svetlana put up $200,000 as part of an agreement in which I would live under home confinement monitored 24/7 by an ankle bracelet.

Chapter 57
A Captive Audience

O nce back home, under all my conditions, I began to watch the political games play out on TV during the Impeachment Hearings. I was watching Giuliani spout off his hypotheses about what the Bidens did in Ukraine when I shocked to see that the guys who were with him were Derkach, Artemenko and Telizhenko.

Derkach, of course, had studied at the FSB academy in Moscow, Artemenko had masterminded Russia's lease of Crimea that led to the invasion and had told the New York Times that Putin himself had encouraged him to go after Poroshenko. Telizhenko had risen through the ranks to Putin's favor by accusing pretty well every pro-Western politician of something or other. They were, to be frank, nothing but Russian assets, puppets who were ferrying statements from Putin's mouth to Giuliani's ears. Even when I was at the peak of my pro-Trump brainwashing, I knew these guys were up to no good.

It hit me like a bucket of cold water. I knew that Giuliani was a pretty bad person from the way he ignored me and my family in our time of need, but I had still held out hope that he had the country's best interest at heart. He didn't. All he was doing was giving Russian disinformation a platform. In everything he did, Giuliani was working, knowingly or not, to destabilize and weaken the United States of America. He was sowing discord and animosity — and it was working. He was doing it for Trump and his own ego.

That shock made everything crystal clear to me. I hadn't been on a mission to help the President root out corruption, I hadn't just been on a cynical mission to get information that would help tip the scales in the 2020 election, I had been part of a team whose aim was to weaken the very foundation of the United States. They weren't patriots, they weren't even just cheats, they were traitors.

That's when I realized that it was my solemn duty to stop them, let people know the truth.

But nobody else knew that. I was being hounded night and day by a media that was obsessed by the fact that I was born in the Soviet Union and had been doing the White House's bidding, despite nobody in their realm ever having heard of me before. Everything to them about me was a mystery, except that they were all convinced I was a spy from another country feeding disinformation to Giuliani (even though, at the time, actual Russian assets were doing exactly that). It didn't help that every Republican, every single one of them, lied and said that they had no idea who I was.

The worst of them was Nunes. It was appalling to watch him parading around, saying that he would get to the bottom of all these mysterious Democrat lies, while he was completely aware of what was going on and that the Democrats had nothing to do with it. It wasn't collective amnesia, it was a conspiracy.

I, of course, wanted to shout all of my revelations and opinions from the rooftops. But Bondy advised me to stay off social media because I might say something that would affect my case.

Instead, he took over, and broke the news that I had switched sides in a gentler, more palatable way than I ever could.

To start, we went to Twitter, the same forum Trump and Giuliani used to make their announcements and air their opinions. Bondy began on January 13 with: "Earlier this morning, the Court granted our request for a second modification of the protective order. We have conveyed the contents of Lev Parnas' Samsung phone to HPSCI, and will be working to provide the other materials as soon as possible. #LetLevSpeak #LevRemembers." The hashtags were an awesome idea, and they would help us reach a larger audience. Then, he wrote, in more plain language:

> "After our trip to DC, we worked through the night providing a trove of Lev Parnas' WhatsApp messages, text messages & images — not under protective order — to #HPSCI, detailing interactions with a number of individuals relevant to the impeachment inquiry. #LetLevSpeak #LevRemembers."

With it, he attached a photo of a grinning me and Trump, smiling broadly and giving the old thumbs-up.

Before long, it was seen by millions of people. I had used Twitter, but had never seen such seemingly impossible numbers before. We would continue to use the hashtags for our announcements, always getting a colossal number of views.

While I considered that a success, I was really after a much bigger audience. I wanted every American to know what was really happening at the highest reaches of their government.

Chapter 58
As Seen on TV

G etting air time wouldn't be a problem. All of the major networks were after me for an interview, except Fox, of course, they didn't seem to be interested in the truth. Bondy handled it all and reduced it to two choices of who would get my first interview: It could be Anderson Cooper on CNN or Rachel Maddow on MSNBC.

At first, I was leaning toward CNN, because everybody watched it, but I decided on MSNBC for the simple reason that they were the ones the Trump people hated the most. Maddow was Public Enemy Number 1 in the White House. There was nobody that Trump hated more than Maddow. It was so bad that, when I was one of his people, I forbade her show to ever be watched in my house.

By appearing on Maddow's show, not only would I be relaying the truth to their sworn enemy, I would be forcing them to watch her show. Thinking about it for a moment, I realized why their hate for her was so intense. Maddow's job is to expose their lies, hypocrisies and misdeeds, and she did it better than anyone. She should take pride in their fear-based loathing.

Maddow was so overwhelmed by what I had to say, she broke what was to be a 15-minute interview into two entire shows on two nights. I brought Bondy with me. I knew I was making a lot of claims a lot of people wouldn't like, so I had him there to keep it all legal.

He told her about how I wanted to get my evidence to the Intelligence Committee before the transmission of the articles of impeachment.

She asked me why I wanted to testify, so I told her:

I want to get the truth out because I feel it's important for our country. I think it's important for me. I think it's important for the world to know exactly what transpired and what happened, because I think a lot — there's a lot of things that are being said that are not accurate. And I just want to make sure that they're accurate because things happened that need to get out, and I think the world needs to know.

She asked what the primary inaccuracy was, so I did what I had to do, I told her it was that many people believe that the President didn't know what was going on. Of course he did. Every order I got was from him or Giuliani. Not involved? He was the only person who would benefit and he's the only person he cares about. Of course he knew. I was accusing the President of illegal acts, but I wasn't scared because I knew he had done them. I had enough evidence behind me. It was all about the Bidens. He simply wanted accusations (genuine or otherwise) on them to come from Ukraine, so that he would have an advantage over him in the 2020 election. It's as simple as that. The ambassador getting dumped was just part of the cost of doing business. Both governments were deeply corrupt.

Maddow wanted to know why it was me. I pointed out that I was just an American businessman — of up-and-down success — who happened to get into the Trump crowd. They considered me their Ukraine expert because I was born there (of course, I have no memory of the place, we left when I was 3) and I spoke Russian, thanks to Brooklyn. I went from making real estate deals in Florida to trying to pressure world leaders to get what Trump wanted, through his sidekick, Giuliani. "I mean, they have no reason to speak to me. Why would President Zelenskyy's inner circle or Minister Avakov or all these people or President Poroshenko meet with me? Who am I?" I asked her, indicating that, without Trump and Giuliani to back me up, I would not have been a player. "They were told to meet with me. And that's the secret that they're trying to keep. I was on the ground doing their work."

After that, I told her about the nuts and bolts of the operation. About how Giuliani canceled his trip to Ukraine to intimidate them, how Pence was used as a bargaining chip, how Barr knew about the whole thing and did nothing about it. I even quoted Sondland, saying "everybody was in the loop." I told her, and the world, that Trump canceled his trip to Poland to meet Zelenskyy, not because of the lame excuse he gave (bad weather), but because he was angry at Zelenskyy for not having announced investigations into the Bidens. That's also why he withheld the desperately needed military aid to an ally that was at war. I gave her some of my evidence, like notes I took about the instructions I was given, all about using some lever to force them to announce the investigations.

We talked about Hyde, who was running for office as a Republican in Connecticut. I admitted that I thought he was a weirdo and that he appeared to be drunk all the time. I told her that I called Ahearn to ask about him and he told me that Hyde was dangerous, always believed someone was trying to kill him and was in business with Pence's brother.

Then I told her about the meeting in the BLT that resulted in my arrest. About how I was going to Vienna on behalf of the BLT Team to get help from Firtash and how we had to give him something to get something from him. Quid pro quo.

Of course, all the people involved were watching, hoping that I wouldn't mention their names. But I did.

My interviews on Maddow's show turned out to be her highest-ever ratings and she earned an Emmy nomination for one of them.

Then there was CNN — I figured that everybody watches it. I went on Anderson Cooper's 360 and told the people of the world what a segment of them really did not want to hear. Besides, It's Anderson Cooper. He is one of the most respected people in his field for his investigative skills and interviewing style.

Cooper asked me if I had loved Trump. As ashamed as I was to admit it, I did so in front of millions. I even told them Svetlana was embarrassed by my shrine of sorts in our house when it was raided by the cops. I told him that I had pictures all over. I mean, I idolized him. I mean, I thought he was the savior. He asked if we were friends. Here's what I told him:

> Absolutely. I mean, again, I went from being a top donor, from being at all the events where we would just socialize, to becoming a close friend of Rudy Giuliani's, to eventually becoming his ally and his asset on the ground in Ukraine.

He mentioned that the President said he doesn't know me, I told him that Trump was lying. I also found out that Pence denied having ever met me. He was lying.

Cooper then asked if Trump made any quid pro quo deals with Ukraine, which was one of the allegations in his impeachment. I told him that it had happened several times, with both Poroshenko and Zelenskyy. I explained that I had made it perfectly clear that, unless they made the announcements of investigations into the Bidens, there would be no relationship with the United States. He asked me if I had told them that weapons would be withheld. I replied to him that I had not, but I was sure that the words "no relationship" made that inference.

We then talked about the details of the operation until Cooper, clearly surprised by what I was saying, asked me how I had the authority to tell Zelenskyy's inner circle that Pence would not come to his inauguration. I said that it was what I was told to do. He asked by who. I answered that it was Giuliani.

Essentially I told him that Trump, Giuliani and their whole mob weren't working for the good of the country, but for the good of their boss. He asked me which individuals knew about the operation, rattling off a list of names. Giuliani, Bolton, Mulvaney were yeses. Pence was a maybe.

We discussed the Yovanovitch situation. He asked me if I had a problem with her. I told him I didn't know her personally, but since the Trump people hated her so virulently, I came to the opinion that she had to go. I told him about the time when I brought her name up over dinner, and Trump told Director of Presidential Personnel Johnny DeStefano: "Get rid of her, get rid of her now."

Cooper asked if "Giuliani and the President were in frequent communication?" I told him that it was beyond frequent — several times a day.

Then he asked me if I felt any pressure. I pointed out that Kolomoisky had threatened to kill Igor and me (I didn't tell him that it was on live TV).

We talked about the impeachment hearings and I told him I would have been the best witness because I alone saw everything. He asked me what I'd like to say to Trump, knowing what I know now, I told him:

> He needs to understand he's not a king. He needs to understand that there is a democracy. There's rules. You know, even if you don't like them, you know? Even if you don't agree with them. You know, it's all fine and dandy going to these rallies and standing up in the rally, I was there. I was front stage. I was the first one at the Trump rallies.

He closed by asking me if I would testify in the impeachment trial if asked. I told him I would.

I wouldn't get the chance. On January 31, 2020, the Senate voted not to call any witnesses. Not one. That effectively shut people like me and Bolton from providing our, I think very relevant, evidence.

The vote was close, though. All 51 yes votes were from Republicans, while 46 Democrats, one independent and two Republicans (Mitt Romney and Susan Collins) made up the other 49.

Once again, Trump slipped through a narrow legal crack.

Chapter 59
The Empire Strikes Back

Of course, my appearances sent shock waves through the establishment. Everywhere there were Republicans denying they knew who I was or that they had ever even met me. It might have worked out for them, but I kept all the receipts.

In some cases, I didn't even have to. Nunes had made a big deal about not knowing who I was.

On December 2, 2019 — in the heat of the Impeachment Hearings — House Intelligence Committee chair Adam Schiff charged that there was a conspiracy of communication between powerful Republicans, Solomon and me. He was right, Trump and Giuliani gave the orders, I did the legwork and Solomon was the mouthpiece. But, these days, being right isn't enough if the news is unpleasant. You have to have proof. And Schiff had it in the form of phone records between me, Giuliani, Nunes and Solomon, among others. He even cited one in which Nunes and I spoke for nearly nine minutes.

Congressman Eric Swalwell, a Democrat from California, called Nunes out on it. Swalwell pointed out that he had read media reports on what I had to say and that, if they were true, Nunes had coordinated with the Ukrainians and Harvey had helped him.

Making it more potent was the fact that Nunes had been accusing Schiff of doing exactly that, but on the Ukrainians' behalf. Swalwell said that Schiff had been "falsely accused throughout these proceedings by the ranking member [Nunes] as being a 'fact witness'" and added:

"Now, if this story is correct, the ranking member may have actually been projecting. And, in fact, he may be the fact witness if he's working with indicted individuals around our investigation."

Quickly, Nunes appeared on Hannity's show on Fox and said that his calls to Giuliani were just the pair of them laughing over how poorly Mueller had done his job.

It actually got worse. Even Hannity pretended that he didn't know me. "Did you ever talk to this guy Les Parnas or whatever his name is?" Hannity asked him, intentionally mispronouncing my name for the chef's kiss.

"You know, it's possible," Nunes told him. "I haven't gone through my phone records. I don't really recall that name."

Eventually, it got ridiculous, to the point at which Nunes could not deny knowing me anymore. Still, he appeared again on Fox and said:

"Yeah, and if you recall, that was brand new when that had come out when I came on your show. Because I just didn't know the name — this name Parnas So, you know, what I always like to remind people is, you know, we are dealing with people every day. We're an oversight committee. So we have incoming calls

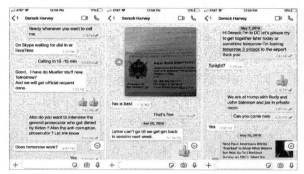

I saved all texts between me and Harvey, just in case.

that come to my office, to my cell phone, et cetera, et cetera. And then you know now that he had called my cell phone and I didn't know his name. I didn't remember the name. But I did remember going back, looking at where I was at the time. Because you know you can do that now. You actually know where you physically are. Checked it with my records and it was very clear. I remember that call, which was very odd, random. Talking about random things. And I said: Great, you know, just talk to my staff and boom, boom, boom. Which is normal, standard operating procedure."

Now, you'd expect anyone with any dignity, intelligence or morals to own up at that point. But that's not what Nunes did. He tried a number of excuses before settling on an alternate reality that I can't believe fooled anyone.

When Fox's Maria Bartiromo asked him about the call, Nunes came up with a bizarre rationalization:

"I got a call from a number that was Parnas's wife. I remember talking to someone, and I did what I always do which is that if you don't know who they are, you put them to staff, and you let staff work with that person."

Even if that had even the most infinitesimally tiny essence of truth (and it doesn't), it still doesn't explain why Svetlana, a Florida resident, would be calling a California congressman. It never happened.

The fact is that he and I did talk. Several times. Since he won't admit it, I'll tell you exactly what we spoke about on that one particular phone call.

Nunes and I had just found out that we were each running operations to get compromising material on the Bidens out of Ukraine. On the call, I suggested that we join forces to pool our talents and other resources. He agreed, and we decided that it would be a great idea for Nunes to go to Ukraine to interview prosecutors and other important people. At first he was all for it, but he reminded me that the Democrats were in charge of the House, so he would have to explain and justify any overseas trip to them. That's when I told him that he could just do the whole thing over Skype. It had worked for us already. I even told him that I'd set it up for him. He liked the idea and nominated his assistant, Harvey, to do the interviews.

Later, Nunes would sue me, Bondy and CNN for $435 million over what he called defamation. It would later be dismissed — the ruling contained the statement: "Plaintiff has not pleaded any facts from which the Court may reasonably infer that CNN entered into an agreement with Joseph Bondy, Lev Parnas, and others, in order to defame and injure Nunes" — but it was still sobering to be sued for that kind of money.

The White House went into damage-control mode, but it was hard for them to get a coherent message out when their leader just couldn't stop talking about things they'd rather he didn't. Trump would either whine or throw a tantrum at the tiniest of slights, so his reaction to what I was saying must have been outrageous. He was at a White House event to promote prayer in schools, when he said that the Ukraine scandal began because the Democrats "had done these fraudulent lies." As usual, everyone's a liar except him, no matter how much evidence they have. As for me, he kind of went a bit nuts, saying (in what seemed like one breath):

> "Well, I don't know him. I don't know Parnas, other than I guess I had pictures taken, which I do with thousands of people, including people today that I didn't meet. But — just met them. I don't know him at all. Don't know what he's about. Don't know where he comes from. Know nothing about him. ... It doesn't matter what he says. He's trying to probably make a deal for himself. I don't even know who this man is, other than I guess he attended fundraisers, so I take a picture with him. ... No, I don't know him. Perhaps he's a fine man; perhaps he's not. I know nothing about him. ... I don't know him. I don't believe I've ever spoken with him. I don't believe I've ever spoken to him. ... But I don't know him. I had never had a conversation that I remember with him."

Sure sounds like the truth. I was saddened, embarrassed and a little bit amazed that I ever believed in him.

Far more important was the fact that the cat was out of the bag. The American political world — including Trump, Giuliani and all their henchmen — knew that I had changed sides.

Of course, the rest of the media went wild. To the left, it looked like someone was finally telling the truth about what they already suspected about Trump. To the right, I was a life-long scammer, just looking to make a deal to shorten my sentence. Of course, they'd know I was never even offered a deal if they would just listen. But they never seem to.

It felt great to be taken so seriously by both Maddow and Cooper and to get my message out to so many people. I also believed that Trump and his gang had done everything they could do to me already, so I didn't have much to lose. I was still constantly referred to as "Soviet-born," but I don't think anyone believed I was a spy anymore.

I was so fortunate that I had Bondy on my side. On January 20, he faxed a letter to the office of Bill Barr, the Attorney General, that said: "Given the totality of the circumstances, we believe it is appropriate for you to recuse yourself from the ongoing investigation and pending prosecution of Mr. Parnas." It also pointed out that Trump had mentioned Barr in his "perfect" call to Zelenskyy as potentially taking part in any Biden investigation.

It caused quite a stir. I had mentioned on Maddow that Barr was aware of everything when it came to the Ukraine scandal, that he was on the team. Not to mention the fact that another whistle blower complaint (this one from a U.S. intelligence officer) prompted the Office of the Director of National Intelligence to be asked by the media if Barr was involved. Instead of the usual denials, they declined to comment.

When asked about my claim that Barr was in on it, Justice Department spokeswoman Kerri Kupec told the conservative Washington Examiner that it was "100 percent false." There's something about the Trump Administration that leads people to get hyperbolic in their claims and, especially, their denials.

Of course, he didn't recuse himself, which essentially meant that he was leading an investigation into his own actions, as well as those of the rest of Trump's allies. I'm not sure how that's fair, or even legal, but it seems par for the course in Trumpland.

On the same day that Bondy asked Barr to recuse himself, Giuliani went on the Ingraham Angle to deal with the major problem I had become. It did not go well. He admitted he was behind Yovanovitch's dismissal."I forced her out because she's corrupt," Giuliani said. "I came back [from Ukraine] with a document that will show unequivocally that she committed perjury when she said that she turned down the visa for Shokin because of corruption ... there's no question that she was acting corruptly in that position, and had to be removed. She should have been fired, if the State Department weren't part of the Deep State." Uh oh. "I believed that I needed Yovanovitch out of the way," he said, clearly forgetting that he was not actually part of the government. "She was going to make the investigations difficult for everybody." His big finish? He described the American-supported NGOs that work in Ukraine as: "Soros-like — they were left of left." All of it was delivered with more than his usual level of bluster and flailing.

We had given a copy of my video that contained Trump's soon-to-be-famous "get rid of her" line about Yovanovitch to the media. Schiff took the lead in explaining its importance, saying: "If the President at the urging of Giuliani, or Parnas or Fruman — if this is additional evidence of his involvement and that effort to smear her, it would certainly corroborate much of what we've heard." Then it went public, carried by just about every news organization in the world.

I knew I didn't have to change every mind in America. I just had to get the truth out there.

Chapter 60
Deal? No Deal

B y that time, of course, the many calls for me to participate in the Impeachment Hearings was growing louder. I was prepared, but I was never asked. Bondy given them them everything we had, even my phone, but they weren't at all interested. I decided to take the matter into my own hands. Since the process was an action of the federal government, the public could attend, but only if they could get tickets, which were in huge demand.

I was invited by New York's senior senator, Democrat Chuck Schumer, through Bondy. I couldn't wait to go, and was definitely prepared, but they caught me on a technicality. No electronic devices were allowed on the Senate floor, including my ankle bracelet. Bondy asked the judge on my case if it could be removed on my way into the building so I could attend and then have it reattached immediately afterward.

The request was turned down.

Trump had launched his defense on January 25. It was led by Alan Dershowitz, known for representing everyone from Mike Tyson to disgraced preacher Jim Bakker. He argued that while the President did engage in a quid pro quo deal — despite Trump's continued denials — since what he wanted wasn't illegal, then the whole thing wasn't illegal. That seemed specious, at best, to me.

A week later, the Senate voted against calling any more witnesses — again, silencing me and Bolton, who I'll bet had a lot to say.

I guess I knew Trump would be acquitted. It would take a two-thirds majority vote to convict him, and the ridiculously partisan Republicans would, of course, rally behind their increasingly unhinged leader. The votes on the two counts were 52-48 and 51-49. All of the no votes were Republicans, but two Republicans — Mitt Romney and Susan Collins — voted yes. "The grave question the Constitution tasks senators to answer is whether the president committed an act so extreme and egregious that it rises to the level of a high crime and misdemeanor," Romney said. Yes, he did. ... The president is guilty of an appalling abuse of public trust." I guess Romney found his backbone again after kowtowing to Trump earlier.

Many Republicans admitted that Trump had abused his office — "the president's behavior was shameful and wrong," said Alaska's Lisa Murkowski. But they essentially said they voted to acquit simply because it would help the Democrats if he wasn't. They were making a game out of the whole thing. An act, I think that if its not illegal, is at least contrary to their oaths.

Leader Mitch McConnell of Kentucky gloated about the win, saying that the process actually increased Trump's approval rating and then he taunted Pelosi.

Trump celebrated by firing Sondland, Vindman and Vindman's identical twin brother, who was also an army colonel.

Since then, I realized that, if the Republicans had the backbone and the conscience to remove Trump from office, we wouldn't have had the January 6 disaster (which, incidentally, is the day before Russian Christmas) or the divisiveness this country suffers from now.

Soon, my own trial was down to two, me and Kukushkin. Igor and Correia, fearing a longer sentence if they went to trial, took pleas deals. That kind of left me in a bind. Fruman was accused of the same crime as me for the same incident. If he admitted he was guilty — most people would think — how could I be innocent?

That crime, I heard in court, was "engaging in a scheme to funnel foreign money to candidates for federal and state office." The more serious charges, like espionage, had already been dropped. The DA charged that the money we donated — what little we actually did give away — was illegal because it had come from foreign sources and was funneled through a shell company.

It actually took me a while to figure that out. The company they called a shell was Global Energy Producers. That's ridiculous, because we genuinely tried to get it off the ground. I sincerely believed that it was my future, my way to get rich. And the foreign source? That meant Kukushkin's partner Muraviev.

Without my knowing, Igor had put the money we had gotten from Kukushkin into the same account as the money he had gotten from refinancing his real estate holdings that we used to give Laxalt to help get us a cannabis license in Nevada. To me, that didn't make me guilty of anything. Igor hadn't told me that he had done that, and so I thought we were dealing only with his money. In fact, Igor assured me he hadn't mixed the two sources of money.

The ironic part was that the federal government had created the situation that led people like Muraviev to people like Igor and me. Cannabis is legal for most Americans, making it a big business growing into a huge one. However, it's still federally illegal, which means that American banks won't invest a penny into it. So, attracted by the likelihood of huge revenues, the investors come from outside the U.S. And nobody has more money to invest than Russian oligarchs. All of those who haven't already been sanctioned are in the U.S. cannabis game. The idiotic reluctance of the federal government has given away an entire growth industry to foreign investors, some of them linked to the Russian mafia. The point of legalizing cannabis is to take the crime out of it and help the American economy, but the feds put the mafia back in and guaranteed that the revenues go overseas. It's stupid, but it's hardly the first time they've done it.

So, my crime was that I donated Igor's money to American political candidates, but some of the money might have come from a Russian without my knowledge.

I should also mention that all of my activities in Ukraine and Venezuela with Giuliani and the others was totally ignored in court. The third superseding indictment in our case contained only offenses related to campaign finance; specifically, if we were straw donors working on behalf of foreign contributors and if we had misrepresented the purpose of Fraud Guarantee to its investors.

Laxalt, of course, did the usual Republican song and dance about not knowing who I was and never having met me. But under cross-examination not much later, he admitted:

> "Every time — the few times that I met with Lev, he would have a couple of people with him. Lev was always the guy that spoke the most and the person that I obviously stayed in touch with as far as supporting my campaign."

It made me wonder why Republican officials seemed to be able to lie, even under oath, whenever it was convenient and not suffer any consequences.

All I had at that point was my family and my lawyers. Bondy was surprised by my stringent bail conditions. The judge even admitted it was harsh, saying: "I think the strict conditions that exist are appropriate."

Bail was set at $1 million with the conditions that I must remain at my home in Boca and that I be electronically monitored. I also had to give up my passport, be regularly tested for drugs and was not allowed contact with Igor, Correia or Kukushkin (I didn't want any).

What really surprised Bondy was that the SDNY wouldn't allow me to become a cooperating witness, which would have allowed them to catch much bigger fish. "I've seen them do much more for people who have much less to offer," he said. "You could have been very useful."

There did seem to be a lot of behind-the-scenes wheeling and dealing that did not include me. At first, they had a huge number of charges against me, but they began to drop — or as Bondy said "got streamlined out" — of their case. The first to go were charges related to my work to help dismiss Yovanovitch. "They just shaved them off," Bondy said. "And threw them away." They just weren't interested. At all. Like Bondy said, "we'll never know what happened behind closed doors" with the SDNY. I can't say for sure, but I have a feeling if they pressed all of the charges, lots of very important people would be in trouble. Essentially, the prosecution ignored everything I did in Ukraine and Venezuela for Giuliani and Trump and concentrated on what I had done for Laxalt, hardly an A-lister at anybody's party.

Then there was Fraud Guarantee. They said it was fraudulent because we had no clients, but that the company still gave Giuliani $500,000. They didn't say who it came from — Gucciardo's name wouldn't come out until later — but they did admit it was from a Republican donor.

They were painting a grotesque caricature of what actually happened. Fraud Guarantee was a real company, but we didn't have any clients yet because we needed an underwriter. The only way to get an underwriter, I believed, was to have a big name attached. That's where Giuliani came in. I gave him Gucciardo's money specifically to be the face of Fraud Guarantee. Gucciardo even said that it was his belief that Giuliani would be the company's spokesman. It was a business decision made on an investment.

Both Gucciardo and I know what really happened. Giuliani walked away with the money and did nothing at all for the company. I did not appreciate the irony of me being on trial for donating money that I didn't know might have touched Russian money while he was walking around Scot-free after stealing a half-million bucks.

The prosecution filed to revoke my bail. They said they believed I'd pull off a daring escape. "Parnas poses an extreme risk of flight, and that risk of flight is only compounded by his continued and troubling misrepresentations to the Pretrial Services office and the Government," the prosecution wrote. "Parnas's actions in the two months that he has been released, coupled with his substantial risk of flight, have shown that there is no set of conditions that will reasonably ensure his appearance and compliance with the terms of his release." Substantial risk of flight? Where am I going? Wait, you already know because I'm wearing an ankle bracelet.

They also said that I had "access to seemingly limitless sources of foreign funding." Not anymore, guys.

As the trial wore on, the SDNY brought out their secret weapon. Hundreds of photos of me with Trump, Giuliani, Pence and others who they said I used to gain interest in my cannabis venture.

Everyone could see that Laxalt and DeSantis had changed their minds to more lenience on cannabis once they received my donations, and DeSantis changed back after I was arrested, claimed that he'd never met me despite all of the pictures, videos and texts between us.

As always, Bondy put things in perspective, providing much-needed context. He described me as a businessman who was "over his head" in these dealings. I was dealing with Muraviev — perhaps not a billionaire, but definitely close enough. He'd earned his business stripes not just at American universities, but in the kill-or-be-killed Russian economy. I was dealing in the big-time when I just wasn't ready.

Yeah, I'll freely admit that I donated in a direct effort to get a cannabis license through legalization. Guess what. That's legal. It happens all the time. Pretty much with every single donation, something is expected in return. It's really easy to buy a plank in a politician's platform and surprisingly affordable.

And as far as where the money came from, Bondy pointed out that there was no evidence that the money I donated came from Muraviev. But Kukushkin, who was trying to pin everything on Igor and me, said that we had used the money to furnish ourselves with lavish lifestyles. Some of it did go to our expenses, because it had been intermingled with Igor's funds. Then he said that Igor was aggressively demanding money from Kukushkin and Muraviev, showing texts to back it up.

The SDNY's plan worked. They made the trial not about how I allegedly used money mixed up with Muraviev's to make my donations, but about how terrible it is that politicians sell their integrity. They figured I was to blame for that.

The jury came back with a verdict. I was found guilty on all six counts of federal election law violations by contributing money that had come from a Russian, making contributions in the names of others and lying to the Federal Elections Commission.

The normal sentencing guidelines for someone convicted of the same offenses as I was without pleas was 78 to 97 months. The prosecution said they wanted 72 months. But Bondy saved me, and I was sentenced to just 20 months.

Still, I was going to prison.

Chapter 61
Special Handling

When the day finally came, I tried to enjoy my last few moments of freedom. Then I flew to JFK. No private jet this time, I was paying for it myself. Once on the ground in Queens, I had some people to see. I was watching my money, but I was still the Lev who used to drive a Rolls-Royce. No Uber for this guy, I called for a limo.

The check-in was like what you see in movies. I was fingerprinted and photographed, stripped and searched.

What I did not know is that they would take me to the deepest belly of the beast. Plenty of people believe that I spent my incarcerated days in a Club Fed, a "prison" for white-collar criminals that was more like a country club than what many think a prison should be.

They are wrong.

It was still COVID time, so the check-in guard asked me if I'd had my vaccinations. I had taken the first one, but I had a severe allergic reaction, so I had put off getting the second. It wasn't a political thing. I told him that.

"Unvaccinated!" the guard shouted, so that another guard could record it. "You're gonna have to be quarantined," the guard told me.

Although I knew I didn't have a choice, I was cool with that. I understood their caution and wanted to make a good impression. You know, let them know that I wouldn't be any trouble.

It was clear to me that the guards didn't know what to do with me, so — after much discussion between them — they threw me in the SHU. The SHU (pronounced "shoe") is an acronym for Special Handling Unit. That's where they throw the worst of the worst. For the crime of donating the wrong money without knowing it, I was treated the same way that this country handles psychopathic murderers and rapists.

It was solitary confinement.

The only communication I had at all was with the guards, and that was almost entirely negative. They made fun of me for being Jewish. Many of the guards saw it all as a scam. The Jews, by eating kosher, were essentially guaranteed better food than the slop the other inmates had no choice but to eat. They thought that being Jewish was "playing the system" and having an easier time getting through our sentences. After my SHU experience, I beg to differ. And the food was still terrible.

They also mocked me for being "Giuliani's boy." They didn't strike me as a particularly politically savvy group, and they all believed that being in with Giuliani meant that I wouldn't have to serve my whole term, or that I would get some other form of special treatment. That Giuliani, a man of great power, would come and help his guy.

All that being "Giuliani's boy" had gotten me was a postcard.

Solitary lasted a week, and I sincerely thanked God when it was over.

When I was finally released into the general population, I was taken to the Otisville Camp, a satellite facility up the mountain from the main building. It kind of resembles a low-rent summer camp, with its temporary-looking chocolate-brown wooden buildings, except for a lack of windows and an overkill of security cameras. There are no actual fences. The camp is surrounded by dense forests, dotted with a few hamlets where the locals would recognize an escapee immediately. The nearest community of any size, Middletown, is a three-hour walk through mountains away.

It's a winding, tree-lined 1.2 miles up the hill from the prison to the camp, and Google says that it's supposed to take 22 minutes. It was more than that for me. After the sheer torture of solitary confinement, I savored every second of sunshine and every inhalation of fresh air. I was delighted to see a family of wild turkeys on the grounds. Later, I would encounter geese and even deer, the camp's only neighbors.

Once I was introduced into the camp's general population, I was surprised at how many of the guys I already knew. There were friends of friends, old acquaintances and guys I did business with. There were even some people from the old neighborhood — Jews, Italians and Russians. In fact, they had been watching the news and knew I was coming, so they put together a welcome-to-prison gift package to make my life a little easier. They bought me the things that they had found essential behind bars — toothpaste, slippers, a comfortable sweat suit and other useful items they had bought from the commissary.

I shared my first cell with a guy who was sentenced to 17 years. I don't remember much about him, even his name, because he was clearly in no mood to make friends. But the guys came to my rescue again, angling to get me a private cell with a bigger, better bed.

Boredom became my primary enemy. I spent a lot of time in the gym, working out, and in the synagogue. The perspective I had gained through all of my misadventures in Trumpland had drawn me much closer to religion. I also enrolled in several classes related to self improvement, and took them seriously. I really wanted to better myself.

Prison life in Otisville was no picnic, but I made the best of it while I was there.

And I had a social life, as much as one can in prison. Since many of the inmates were members of organized crime, a friendly poker tournament was inevitable.

They all thought they were pretty sharp until they ran into me. Trained in my high-stakes celebrity games in L.A., I didn't have much of a problem with these guys. I won the big pot twice, taking the much-desired bag of contributions from the commissary. It was great, because it had tuna — that was the best thing they had in the whole place. At least, legally.

If you were connected, you could get pretty much anything you wanted. There were many ways of smuggling (importing, if you prefer) contraband into the facility. The most successful was the old organized crime trick, later adopted by spies, called the dead drop. A visitor finds a place not covered by the security cams and leaves the contraband, usually hidden. When the inmate is allowed some outside time, he waits until he's not being watched, grabs the stuff and hides it in his clothes. Then it goes on the open market.

And, with hundreds of men brought together because they had broken the law or many laws, there were some disagreements. Fights were commonplace. The participants were left alone to duke it out, and many required ambulances after it was all said and done. I did my best to stay out of all that, but I couldn't help but ruffle a few feathers. It's prison. Everyone's tense.

***

When the day finally came for my release, I was over-the-moon excited. I really have to thank the Aleph Institute, an organization that helps Jews in prison and in the military. They were outstanding in their efforts both with my stay in prison and my release.

As soon as I found out the date of my release, I called everyone the facility would allow, including my cousin and an author who wanted to write a book with me.

My cousin would come pick me up and we would meet the writer at an out-of-the-way seafood restaurant in New Jersey.

As soon as we all got to the place, I ordered a big plate and savored my first decent meal in ages. We talked, but not about the book.

My cousin left and the writer drove me to Liberty airport in Newark. I was in a great mood, just to be free. My flight wasn't due for a while, so we sat in the food court and had coffee. He asked me about my luggage. This is all I've got, I told him.

"What is?" he asked.

This, I replied, while tugging at the neck of my prison-issue sweatshirt, was really all I had.

Free of the prison's restrictions, I started to call people, but received some bad news from home. I ran into a tremendous personal problem, but as upset as I was, I had to keep going, calling important people, including ones who could help solve the problem that suddenly showed up.

When I heard the announcement and went to the gate. I thought about how I used to drive a Rolls-Royce, how I helped shape America's role in Ukraine (which had since been invaded by Putin's Russia in an act of abject avarice and an illegal use of aggression under UN laws), how I helped get a President impeached, how I had $500,000 taken from me and continued to do business with the guy as though nothing had happened — was going home in my cheap, prison-issue sweatsuit and nothing else. I had no job, no money, few friends, problems in Florida and a reputation as a scammer, a criminal and a right-wing functionary. I had no choice but to keep on going.

Once I was free and put my personal problem behind me, everybody wanted a piece of me. Again. I was more than happy to give it to them. Along with this book, there will be a documentary about me (made by some of the world's premier documentarians, Billy Corben and Adam McKay) and

I am also planning a podcast. I appear on TV and other peoples' podcasts regularly, I have appeared in all of the major newspapers and TV networks (except Fox, of course), I tweet a lot and do X (formerly Twitter) spaces to huge response. Although the platform has taken a decidedly right turn recently (not to mention an ownership change, a new name and a major nose dive), my provocative tweets, lambasting and even taunting members of the Trumposphere, can draw millions of views. I've never backed down and my recounting of the facts has not changed in any way.

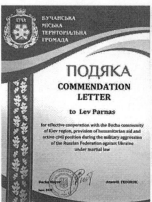

Since the Russian invasion, I have been working hard to help the Ukrainian people.

My media projects are all dedicated to the one subject that I will always care about. I've been through all they can do to me and I'm not scared at all. But it's not about revenge. I want to warn America, and the world about Trump, Giuliani and all the others. I want to make people aware of how often they and their allies disregard the law and take the U.S. government on their own, sometimes dangerous, paths that can cost thousands of innocent lives. I want to warn people about how close we came to having a ruling class that was untouchable and who answer to no one.

Trump already thinks of himself as a king, that's been clear for a long time. Empowering that view could make it closer to the truth. The problem is that Trump would not be a benign king. His open admiration, even desire to emulate, Putin — who imprisons critics, murders opponents, invades his neighbors and has spent his time getting richer as his people get poorer and more desperate — make it clear what he would do with more power and nothing to lose. It's the gangster mentality: I got mine, fuck everyone else.

His comeback would predicate a nightmare for America. If you want to know who Trump is, what drives him, you need look no further than Moscow. His admiration, almost infatuation, with the Russian leader appears to know no bounds. Perhaps most illustrative of that is the fact that he told a national audience that: "I mean this guy has done — whether you like him or don't like him — he's doing a great job."

Look, I've spent a lot of time in Russia, and not on all-expenses-paid, stage-managed tours. I can tell you that if Trump emulated his idol Putin and ruled like him, America would be poorer, more dangerous, angrier, more cynical, less free and more polluted. It would be Russia. But Trump would be richer and he would, like Putin, have the ability to live out his childish fantasies, like when Putin "scored eight goals" against a team of former NHL players who knew better than to actually try to stop him.

That's the thing with these megalomaniacs, whether it's Trump or Putin or Kim Jong Un or Erdoğan or just some lucky natural gas trader from Russia, they start to believe their own lies and fantasies. And that's dangerous for all of us. I know those places, America is a much better place to live. Let's make sure it stays that way. And not let Trump or anyone like him destroy this country that is already great.

Chapter 62
Epilogue

The legacy of the Trump Administration is easy to see. The country is divided and there's talk — though still in the fringes — of another civil war. The Republican Party is in chaos as the Trump-associated right wing of the party spends its time attacking other Republicans they believe aren't conservative enough or have been suspected of collaborating with the Democrats — look what happened to Kevin McCarthy. Freedoms for Americans that we took for granted are being whittled away with book bans, governments tearing away at the rights of women, the LGBT community and others, precedent-setting cases being decided by partisan judges and many Republican lawmakers making what appear to be arbitrary, even petulant decisions. The only thing keeping the party together is a unified desire to make life easier on the wealthy few (through lower taxes on them alone and eliminating, often quite important, regulations), no matter what the cost to everybody else.

The shock wave has been felt around the world. Republicans — copying Trump's rhetoric of "taking care of ourselves first" — have been desperately fighting to cut vital aid to Ukraine, which would essentially guarantee it being wiped off the map by Putin's Russia. Nations like China, Turkey and Iran have been emboldened by Russia's ability to attack a sovereign state with few significant consequences from the U.S. and have been flexing their muscles on their neighbors. Similarly, our real allies — who have a much harder time believing America is on their side after Trump's words and actions — have been making strategic plans without considering the now-less-trustworthy U.S. Meanwhile, many politicians around the world have gained popularity by using Trump's cynical game plan of promising disaffected voters anything they want, often reflecting their baser instincts, with no actual plan to deliver.

His followers even stormed the Capitol in an attempt to foment the first coup d'etat in American history — on the eve of Russian Christmas.

Trump himself is in what appears to be interminable trouble, making death threats, calling for violence and accusing everybody but himself of wrongdoing. As I write this, he's still by far the leader in the race for the Republican candidacy, even though he now faces prison.

The Parnases are a lot happier now that we aren't involved with Trump anymore.

As embarrassed as I am to say it, I had a big part in creating this monstrous situation. Not only did I work for the administration in Ukraine, but I actively campaigned for them and, as a member of the BLT Team, I helped set the agenda by telling Trump what I thought he wanted to hear and what I knew he would invariably act on. Keep in mind that nobody ever cast a single vote for me, but I played a much more significant part on the world stage than all but a very few people. And how did I get there? I promised the Republicans a million bucks that I never had.

Do you want to know the really scary part? When I was there, they handed me the keys. I didn't know what I was doing. I'm just a businessman that Trump and Giuliani happened to like. So, who'll have the keys next? It really could be just about anybody.

Even though I was one of them, I now find it ironic that people who are cynical about politics are the ones who are attracted to people like Trump and Giuliani. After I saw from the inside exactly how they work, I realized that they were politicians in the worst way — manipulating laws and rhetoric to enrich themselves, their families and their friends, often at the expense of the nation. If you're upset that so many jobs have left for China, realize that these are the kind of people who sent them there to make a few more bucks for themselves. They do their best to keep their dealings private — Trump banned the media from many events, often setting precedent — in an effort to prevent the public from knowing what they are up to. Everything about them is fake: Trump's wealth, Giuliani's leadership ability and DeSantis height (he wears elevator shoes). They might say the opposite, but they are the embodiment, even a caricature, of crooked politicians.

Since I was one of them, I know exactly what the Trump faithful are thinking about me now. They almost certainly believe that because I was loyal until the time I got arrested, that I have turned on Trump simply because I went to prison. While I will admit that prison was the wake-up call I needed to break the spell the administration had over me, it provided me time away from their cult to properly evaluate what I had done for them, what their goals were and how much damage they were doing.

You think you've got regrets? I unleashed Ron DeSantis on the American public. Far worse, I helped the administration destabilize the country of my birth, exactly when they were most vulnerable to attack from the east. Since then, tens of thousands of people have been killed, injured, made homeless and even been taken hostage.

Putin's excuses for the invasion are ridiculous. He's after the trillions of dollars of natural gas under the ground and waters of Ukraine and he wants to reunite the USSR and have Russia become a major global player again. If he succeeds, he'll get richer, but the people of Russia won't benefit at all and the people of Ukraine will suffer. That's what these guys do.

As soon as the invasion occurred, I have been involved in humanitarian efforts in Ukraine. I have been lucky enough to team with Michael Capponi, founder and president of Global Empowerment Mission, and my cousin, Oleksandr Bolbirer, to make large and important contributions to humanitarian causes. When the Ukrainian National Police in Kyiv released a video on May 4, 2022, thanking me specifically for my humanitarian contributions that they could distribute, many on social media were surprised. So many people still associated me with the other side that it was hard for them to believe I was actually on Ukraine's side. I'm doing all I can and hope I can encourage others to as well.

With my regret comes tremendous guilt. From the moment I got out of jail, I have been trying to tell everyone who would listen just how deceitful, underhanded and self-serving the administration and its individual members were (and probably would be again). That's why you have this book and why you see me on TV all the time.

I still have to do it. As this book goes into print, the Republicans are still trying to please Putin by cutting off much-needed supplies to Ukraine. And they have the audacity to try to impeach Biden. You know what they're using for evidence? The stuff I got them. And I can tell you, once and for all, that it's all fake. There is no evidence the Bidens did anything wrong. Shokin admitted it. Lutsenko admitted it. Even Volker admitted it. Nobody knows better than me, and I'm admitting it. It just didn't happen.

The fact that the leading Republicans are still fighting hard to bar me from providing evidence is a testament to how intimidated they are by what I know. And now you know. Do the right thing.